Apocalyptic Authoritarianism

JOURNALISM AND POLITICAL COMMUNICATION UNBOUND

Series editors: Daniel Kreiss, University of North Carolina at Chapel Hill, and Nik Usher, University of San Diego

Journalism and Political Communication Unbound seeks to be a high-profile book series that reaches far beyond the academy to an interested public of policymakers, journalists, public intellectuals, and citizens eager to make sense of contemporary politics and media. "Unbound" in the series title has multiple meanings: It refers to the unbinding of borders between the fields of communication, political communication, and journalism, as well as related disciplines such as political science, sociology, and science and technology studies; it highlights the ways traditional frameworks for scholarship have disintegrated in the wake of changing digital technologies and new social, political, economic, and cultural dynamics; and it reflects the unbinding of media in a hybrid world of flows across mediums.

Other books in the series:

Journalism Research That Matters
Valérie Bélair-Gagnon and Nik Usher

Voices for Transgender Equality: Making Change in the Networked Public Sphere
Thomas J. Billard

Reckoning: Journalism's Limits and Possibilities
Candis Callison and Mary Lynn Young

News After Trump: Journalism's Crisis of Relevance in a Changed Media Culture
Matt Carlson, Sue Robinson, and Seth C. Lewis

Press Freedom and the (Crooked) Path Towards Democracy: Lessons from Journalists in East Africa
Meghan Sobel Cohen and Karen McIntyre Hopkinson

Data-Driven Campaigning and Political Parties: Five Advanced Democracies Compared
Katharine Dommett, Glenn Kefford, and Simon Kruschinski

Borderland: Decolonizing the Words of War
Chrisanthi Giotis

Not Your Parents' Politics: Understanding Young People's Political Expression on Social Media
Neta Kligler-Vilenchik and Ioana Literat

The Politics of Force: Media and the Construction of Police Brutality
Regina G. Lawrence

Authoritarian Journalism: Controlling the News in Post-Conflict Rwanda
Ruth Moon

Apocalyptic Authoritarianism: Climate Crisis, Media, and Power
Hanna E. Morris

Imagined Audiences: How Journalists Perceive and Pursue the Public
Jacob L. Nelson

Pop Culture, Politics, and the News: Entertainment Journalism in the Polarized Media Landscape
Joel Penney

The Invented State: Policy Misperceptions in the American Public
Emily Thorson

Democracy Lives in Darkness: How and Why People Keep Their Politics a Secret
Emily Van Duyn

Building Theory in Political Communication: The Politics-Media-Politics Approach
Gadi Wolfsfeld, Tamir Sheafer, and Scott Althaus

Media and January 6th
Khadijah Costley White, Daniel Kreiss, Shannon C. McGregor, and Rebekah Tromble

Capturing News, Capturing Democracy: Trump and the Voice of America
Kate Wright, Martin Scott, and Mel Bunce

Apocalyptic Authoritarianism

Climate Crisis, Media, and Power

HANNA E. MORRIS

OXFORD
UNIVERSITY PRESS

Oxford University Press is a department of the University of Oxford.
It furthers the University's objective of excellence in research, scholarship,
and education by publishing worldwide. Oxford is a registered trade mark of
Oxford University Press in the UK and in certain other countries.

Published in the United States of America by Oxford University Press
198 Madison Avenue, New York, NY 10016, United States of America.

© Oxford University Press 2025

All rights reserved. No part of this publication may be reproduced, stored in a retrieval system, transmitted, used for text and data mining, or used for training artificial intelligence, in any form or by any means, without the prior permission in writing of Oxford University Press, or as expressly permitted by law, by license or under terms agreed with the appropriate reprographics rights organization. Inquiries concerning reproduction outside the scope of the above should be sent to the Rights Department, Oxford University Press, at the address above.

You must not circulate this work in any other form
and you must impose this same condition on any acquirer.

Library of Congress Cataloging-in-Publication Data
Names: Morris, Hanna E. author
Title: Apocalyptic authoritarianism : climate crisis, media,
and power / Hanna E. Morris.
Description: New York, NY : Oxford University Press, 2025. |
Series: Journalism and political communication unbound | Includes
bibliographical references and index.
Identifiers: LCCN 2024060235 (print) | LCCN 2024060236 (ebook) |
ISBN 9780197807675 paperback | ISBN 9780197807668 hardback |
ISBN 9780197807682 epub | ISBN 9780197807705
Subjects: LCSH: Climatic changes—Press coverage—United States |
Climatic policy—United States | Authoritarianism—United States
Classification: LCC PN4784.C624 M67 2025 (print) |
LCC PN4784.C624 (ebook) | DDC 070.4/493637—dc23/eng/20250326
LC record available at https://lccn.loc.gov/2024060235
LC ebook record available at https://lccn.loc.gov/2024060236

DOI: 10.1093/9780197807705.001.0001

Pod

Acknowledgments

The roots of this project began to grow nearly fifteen years ago when I moved to Berkeley to start my undergraduate studies and found myself a part of the burgeoning Occupy Movement. It was an exciting time. I met many passionate and thoughtful people committed to social change. The scholarly texts we read and the discussions we had were directly applicable to our projects on the ground. My professors were engaged and active and I saw the kind of work I wanted to do. Thanks to Paola Bacchetta who first introduced me to Foucault, Escobar, Shiva, Spivak, Said, and postcolonial theory. Thanks to Ignacio Chapela who bought each of us in his Environmental Biology class a copy of *Catastrophism: The Apocalyptic Politics of Collapse and Rebirth* (2012)—an influential text that first sparked my critical study of apocalyptic environmentalism. Thanks to Kate O'Neill who offered guidance, data analysis tips, and encouragement as the advisor for my first independent research project on climate change journalism—an honors thesis that would ultimately motivate my pursuit of graduate studies.

After Berkeley, I moved to the U.K. and lived in London during a daunting year of rising right-wing nationalism in Europe and the tumult of Brexit. While at the London School of Economics and Political Science (LSE), I first came across Stuart Hall's essays on representation and Othering—texts that have significantly shaped this book's approach. Thanks to Bart Cammaerts and Shani Orgad who introduced me to British Cultural Studies along with other critical theories of media, representation, hegemony, and power.

After London, my PhD career at the Annenberg School for Communication at the University of Pennsylvania began with a shocking presidential election in 2016 and ended with a devastating pandemic. The stakes felt high throughout my time as a PhD student. I spent my years at Annenberg trying to make sense of the tragic present by listening, working, and learning how to contribute thoughtful, grounded, and critical scholarship. My dissertation and this book are the product of this sensemaking.

Thanks to my brilliant advisor at Annenberg, Barbie Zelizer, for always pushing me to do better and challenging me to do more. I am incredibly grateful for all of your guidance while completing my PhD and in the years since. Thank you, John L. Jackson, Jr., for your constant encouragement—your confidence in my scholarship over the years has meant a great deal to me. I truly admire your leadership, advocacy for students, and commitment to critical and interdisciplinary research. Thank you, Guobin Yang, for your time and help with the development of my research during my studies at Penn—I learned so much from working with you through the Media Activism Research Collective (MARC), coursework, and our independent study on climate change and social theory. Thank you also for introducing me to Daniel Aldana Cohen and encouraging me to branch out into the field of environmental sociology. Daniel—thank you for all of the thought-provoking discussions about progressive climate politics and theories of social change. Your writings and public lectures are always a source of inspiration. Thanks also to my lovely cohort-mates and fellow grad student friends throughout my time at Penn—especially Jennifer Henrichsen and my dear "Annenberg Chicas": Celeste Wagner, Leeann Siegel, and Donna Lee.

I am profoundly fortunate to have landed at such a supportive institutional home as the School of the Environment at the University of Toronto following my postdoc and grad school at Annenberg. Thanks to all of my colleagues at the School of the Environment and especially to the School's Director Steve Easterbrook and my faculty mentor Kate Neville. Thank you, Kate, for your very generous feedback on my manuscript and your amazing support and help with organizing a book workshop for this project. A huge note of gratitude to Melissa Aronczyk, Matthew Tegelberg, and Lauren Richter who very generously offered their time, advice, and brilliant suggestions for improving my manuscript during this book workshop. Thanks also to Stella Kyriakakis for logistical support and Erica Leighton for note-taking during the workshop.

I am very lucky to have met and worked with many inspiring people from across the globe throughout my project's journey from dissertation to book. I am especially grateful for the encouragement I have received from my scholarly peers and friends who are part of the International Communication Association (ICA), the International Association for Media and Communication Research (IAMCR), and the International Environmental Communication Association (IECA). In particular, thanks to Kerrie Foxwell-Norton, Henrik Bødker, Pieter Maeseele, Libby Lester, Claire Konkes, James Painter, Candis Callison, Kristin Timm, Christine Gilbert, Franzisca Weder, Emma Frances Bloomfield, Jennifer Schneider, Silje Kristiansen, Robin Tschötschel, Emily Diamond, Kelly Perry, Brenda McNally, Kjell Vowles, Loredana Loy, Kathryn Thier, and Phaedra Pezzullo. Thanks also to Timmons Roberts and Robert Brulle from the Climate Social Science Network (CSSN) at Brown University for the opportunity to start a working group on Critical Studies of Climate Media, Discourse, and Power. This working group has been an important source of scholarly community for me. Thanks to all of the working group's members and to my amazing and always inspiring working group co-chair Rachel Wetts. I look forward to continuing to collaborate with such a dedicated group of scholars that inspire, motivate, and encourage me.

I am grateful for the generative conversations following several invited talks I gave related to various aspects of this book including at the Jan van Eyck Academie in Maastricht, Climate Action Beacon at Griffith University—Gold Coast, Division of Environmental Communication at the Swedish University of Agricultural Sciences, Climate Communication Interest Group at the Annenberg School for Communication at the University of Pennsylvania, and Networks and Opinions on Climate Action in the Public Sphere International Workshop in Buffalo, NY. It was also a great honor to be recognized by the 2021 IAMCR Stuart Hall Award and Top Paper Awards from the ICA and the Association for Environmental Studies and Sciences (AESS) for research that is now a part of this book's Chapter 1. Earlier versions of portions of Chapter 1 also appeared in the edited volumes *Climate Change and Journalism: Negotiating Rifts of Time* I co-edited with Henrik Bødker and the forthcoming *Intersectional Change-Makers in Environmental Activism* co-edited by Emma Frances Bloomfield and José Castro-Sotomayor. Sections of Chapter 4 contain revised text and ideas first published in the *Journal of Environmental Media* and sections of Chapter 3 contain revised text and ideas that first appeared in *Politique Américaine* and *Climate Change and Journalism: Negotiating Rifts of Time*.

I also want to thank the incredible editorial team at Oxford University Press including Angela Chnapko and Andrea Smith, the Press's copyediting and production teams, and the book series editors Nik Usher and Daniel Kreiss.

Above all, I am fortunate to have had the emotional support of my family over the course of this book project. From London to Philadelphia to

Toronto—thanks to my loving, kind, hilarious, and endlessly patient husband, George. We have been through quite a lot over the years, between long-distance and lockdowns with international moves and emergency room visits in between. Thank you for always being there for me through it all. You constantly keep me grounded and I am very lucky to have you as my partner.

Finally, I want to close this note of acknowledgments (a note that feels incomplete and inadequate in expressing my thanks to all of the many people who have helped me and inspired me over the course of this book project) with words of gratitude for my Mom and Dad. Thank you for supporting my various educational pursuits—ever since that dry erase board and teaching supplies you surprised me with many years ago to aid in my curriculum design and pedagogical commitment to teaching my stuffed animals about the plight of sea turtles.

Contents

List of Figures	xii
Introduction: Climate Journalism and Apocalyptic Authoritarianism in the United States	1
1. A New Marshall Plan for the Climate: Reclaiming National and Journalistic Authority Through the Myth of American Exceptionalism	31
2. American Earth: Planetary Optics of Control	57
3. Tyrant of a Trope: Visionary Sage Figure	88
4. Climate Death-World and Life-World	118
Conclusion: Alternative Climate and Journalism Futures	151
Notes	166
Bibliography	179
Index	197

List of Figures

1.1.	Cover of *The New Republic*. © [September 2016]	45
1.2.	Cover of *Mother Jones*. © [January/February 2020]	46
2.1.	Cover of *Whole Earth Catalog*. [Fall 1968]	59
2.2.	Cover of *Foreign Policy*. © [July 22, 2019]	64
2.3.	Cover of *Newsweek*. © [February 21, 2020]	67
2.4.	Cover of *TIME*. © [September 23, 2019]	76
2.5.	Cover of *Foreign Policy*. © [September 1, 2016]	79
2.6.	Cover of *Bloomberg Businessweek*. © [June 10, 2019]	84
2.7.	Cover of *The New Republic*. © [December 2015]	85
3.1.	Cover of *WIRED*. [April 2020]. Alvaro Dominguez/Wired; © Condé Nast.	93
3.2.	Cover of *National Review*. © [December 3, 2018]	96
3.3.	Cover of *The New York Times Magazine*. © [August 5, 2018]	99
3.4.	Cover of *TIME*. © [December 23, 2019]	102
3.5.	Cover of *The Nation*. © [September 11, 2017]	107
3.6.	Cover of *National Review*. © [March 11, 2019]	112
3.7.	Cover of *The New Republic*. © [June 2019]	115
4.1.	Cover of *Bloomberg Businessweek*. © [November 5, 2018]	122
4.2.	Cover of *Newsweek*. © [October 20, 2015]	131
4.3.	Cover of *The New York Times Magazine*. © [July 26, 2020]	136
4.4.	Cover of *The Nation*. © [October 5/12, 2020]	141
4.5.	Photo by Al Diaz/The Miami Herald via Getty Images, as appeared in *The Nation*, October 5/12, 2020 issue, with the caption: "Trapped and bereft: A Haitian woman stands on what remains of her home in the shantytown known as the Mudd, September 5, 2019."	142
4.6.	Cover of *New York Magazine*. © [November 8/21, 2021]	146

Introduction
Climate Journalism and Apocalyptic Authoritarianism in the United States

At the opening of the new decade in January 2020, renowned climate journalist Elizabeth Kolbert wrote in *The New Yorker*[1]: "In a Dantean sort of way, Australia's holiday-season infernos provided a fitting close to 2019, which has been called 'the year the world woke up to the climate crisis.'" She apprehensively added, "if 2019 was supposedly the year we 'woke up to the climate crisis,' the twenty-tens have been called the 'decade we finally woke up to climate change.' What will the twenty-twenties bring?" In short, Kolbert predicted an apocalyptic decade to come. This fire-and-brimstone image of what lies ahead is not anomalous in U.S. news media, and neither is it without consequence. Apocalyptic anxieties have melded together in very peculiar ways in American climate journalism to the detriment of more nuanced modes of reporting and more robustly democratic processes of decision-making. The question of how these peculiar representations of climate change have come to be and to what political end motivates this book.

As this foreboding quote by Kolbert signals, a collective sense of doom took hold of American newsrooms at a very distinct moment in historical time. For journalists working in the U.S. in the latter half of the 2010s, the immediate impacts of climate change were becoming increasingly apparent at the same time as the risks of antidemocratic politics were too, following the presidential election of Donald Trump in 2016. The destructive floods in the U.K., massive wildfires on the west coast of North America and in Australia, and deadly heatwaves across Europe were occurring in tandem with the highly visible violence of white supremacy, misogyny, and xenophobia under the likes of an authoritarian-aspiring Trump. These distinct threats to the Earth's climate and to the U.S.'s democracy were in many ways transposed upon each other and interpreted by wary journalists through a singular lens of "total crisis."

Apocalyptic Authoritarianism. Hanna E. Morris, Oxford University Press. © Oxford University Press (2025).
DOI: 10.1093/9780197807705.003.0001

This subsuming of climate change within an all-encompassing image and narrative of "total crisis" is troubling, as this book will show, because it ignites an intense longing among traditionally privileged groups for the return to supposedly less precarious and more stable times in the U.S. *before* the "total crisis" began. The violent exploitation of unpaid and slave labor, Indigenous people, and land is conveniently elided in these nostalgic tales of the nation's past.[2] This elision is deeply consequential because instead of a journalistic reckoning with the exploitative political-economic structures that propel both climate change and social injustices,[3] these structures are left largely unquestioned and unexamined in stories of apocalyptic disarray.

It is within these decontextualized conditions of "total crisis" where self-proclaimed heroes—who are typically well-resourced and historically privileged men—emerge and are celebrated as *visionary sages* in climate news stories. The visionary sage figure is a recurrent protagonist in U.S. climate journalism and is represented as a God-like genius in possession of an unmatched ability to bring *back* national and climatic stability through all-encompassing "fixes" of the sage's own design. Conversely, collectivities who demand more transformative change beyond a quick technological or market "fix" are denigrated as ignorant obstructionists preventing the return to a previous steady state. Young progressives who advocate for climate and social justice are especially singled out by journalists and cast as impediments to the sage's pivotal Earth-saving work. This vilification of young progressives is evident across the conservative *and* centrist press from *The Wall Street Journal* to *The New York Times* where the apocalyptic glare of "total crisis" transforms the dynamic positionalities of a diverse group of young progressives—deemed the "new" New Left by *The New York Times*[4]—into a singular category of unruly Others endangering the *former* greatness, order, stability, and perpetual progress of the nation.

This bipartisan Othering via strong appeals to American nationalism in climate reporting at some of the most prominent news publications of record in the U.S. may at first glance seem surprising but not when assessed via a historical vantage. The fear of the loss of the nation via the infiltration of Others is a persistent neurosis of the American psyche from the conservative right to the liberal center.[5] This neurosis runs deep in American culture and is intrinsically linked with the nation's foundational myth of Manifest Destiny.[6] First coined by the journalist John Louis O'Sullivan in 1845 to legitimize the nation's westward expansion as God-ordained and inevitable,[7] he wrote in *The New York Morning News*: "The right of our manifest destiny to overspread and to possess the whole of the continent which Providence has given us for the development of the great experiment of liberty and federated self-government entrusted to us."[8] According to this logic, those who sought to impede America's westward expansion—such as Native Americans whose land settlers violently seized—were marked in unholy terms as blockading the U.S.'s glorious mission as an exceptional nation chosen by God to spread the light of liberty across the continent and eventually, the whole world. The end of the nation's expansion was equated with the end of all that is good in the world. In other words, any hindrance to America's Manifest Destiny—and those professing it—would be apocalyptic.

It is through this myth of Manifest Destiny that the foreboding glow of apocalypse is refracted in a way that marks those who contest the visionary sage's *gospel* or *"god-spell"*—which literally means "good story" or "good news"[9]—as ungodly enemies of the nation. Within the post-2016 apocalyptic tale of "total crisis," young progressives of the "new" New Left who advocate for social and climate justice are repeatedly reduced to *bad* news and as little more than villainous impediments to the return of the U.S.'s rightful glory. This book illuminates how young progressive women of color, in particular, are frequently portrayed by U.S. news media as distinctly Other and as violent, uncivil, and menacing enemies of the nation. In turn, calls for the policing, detainment, and removal of "radicalized" young Indigenous, Black, and Brown women—such as climate justice advocate and progressive Congresswoman Alexandria Ocasio-Cortez (D-NY)—are normalized across centrist media and by establishment Democrats in addition to conservative media and the Make America Great Again (MAGA) right. The simultaneous disparagement of young women of color (a historically marginalized group in the U.S.) as threatening Others, and glorification of older white men (a historically advantaged group) as visionary sages, is consistent with wider patterns in U.S. climate reporting following the tumult of the 2016 presidential election of Trump and is definitive of what this book refers to as *apocalyptic authoritarianism*.

Fundamentally, apocalyptic authoritarianism describes the reactionary posturing and political alignment of historically privileged figures, transcendent of the partisan center and right, who are united through a common enemy of the "new" New Left and a shared appeal to apocalyptic fears of "total crisis." Fearmongering about a supposedly America-hating contingent of "woke" leftist radicals who are threatening the nation and impeding the Earth-saving work of visionary sages is precisely where apocalyptic authoritarianism in the U.S. hardens the line between "us" and "them." There is little room for imagining dynamic subjectivities, identities, and alternative futures beyond the one supposedly fated path that is discursively sedimented within a strict dualism of good and bad/right and wrong. The supreme authority of visionary sage figures is justified through their claimed singular capacity to shepherd the wayward American people back onto this one and only righteous path where "dissent must never lead to disorder," in the words of former President Joe Biden to condemn the spring 2024 antiwar student protests led by an intersectional coalition of young progressives.[10] According to this reactionary logic, it is the job of "traditional" authorities and "pro-American" saviors to bring *back* order by eliminating all unruly Others leading the nation astray.

This book sheds light on how U.S. climate journalism is bolstering apocalyptic authoritarianism as opposed to reckoning with the roots and ramifications of both climate change and reactionary politics. To be sure, comprehensive journalistic work is incredibly challenging and is only becoming more difficult with fewer jobs, less public support, and scant financial resources available for reporters.[11] Clearly, journalists have been navigating extremely turbulent waters for quite some time now, with an unprecedented drop in public trust amid a long-term failure to financially adapt to the shifting tides of digital platforms and social media.[12] Instead of changing course away from hyper-capitalistic business models[13] and an increasingly elite-oriented and inaccessible style of news,[14] however, advocates of "traditional journalism"—in the words of the publisher of *The New York Times* A. G. Sulzberger[15] to describe the type of reporting done by well-established news publications with professionally trained reporters in a hierarchy of staff and a national readership—are buckling down on the "old ways" with fervor. This book illuminates how these "old ways" fall short of what is required to contend with the unresolved grievances of the past and the societal and climatic shifts of the present. Traditional journalists are failing to grapple with the complexities of climate change and are deepening as opposed to investigating the false equivalencies, myths, and politics of enmity that propel apocalyptic authoritarianism at the expense of more robustly democratic alternatives.

Through a multimodal visual and critical discourse analysis of climate cover stories, special issues, and features published by an ideologically diverse selection of some of the most prominent U.S. news publications[16] that cater to a national audience between the years 2015 and 2023, this book elucidates the role of traditional journalism in legitimizing apocalyptic authoritarianism. It does so by revealing how visual and textual media representations of climate change are often characterized by four recurrent tropes that also lie at the crux of apocalyptic authoritarianism, including (1) *appeals to nationalism and discursive processes of Othering,* (2) *the celebration of planetary-scale "solutions,"* (3) *the admiration of visionary sage figures,* and (4) *necropolitical claims of the "inevitable" climate deaths of racialized Others.* This period of 2015–2023 is important because it not only comprises the crucial years leading up to and following the notable 2019 spike in climate news coverage that this Introduction will turn to next, but it also encompasses the pivotal years between Trump's first and second presidential campaigns. This book critically examines the reasons for this surge in climate media attention during these years of such pronounced political and social turmoil and illuminates the ultimate direction that the "climate beat" took because of it.

To this end, this book reveals how these four tropes hinder more deeply contextualized ways of making sense of and responding to the complexities of climate change. More dynamic forms of climate reporting require a fundamental "reckoning," in the words of critical journalism scholars Candis Callison and Mary Lynn Young,[17] with the structures of power that sustain traditionally privileged figures' authority—including the authority of traditional journalists themselves—above all Others. In place of this reckoning, many journalists in the U.S. are elevating historical centers of power and closing off deeper and more nuanced considerations of the fast and slow violences[18] of climate change.

Ultimately, this book shows how apocalyptic anxieties during the age of Trump have shaped and continue to shape journalistic and political interpretations of climate change in ways that severely limit how it has come to be known, imagined, and contended with both inside and outside of the newsroom. The chapters that follow illuminate how these anxieties and the reactionary responses to them are sculpting an exclusionary regime of climate journalism and politics. As a sort of Frankenstein's monster of reanimated national myths and memories, this book uncovers how the U.S. climate beat is becoming an amalgamation of categories and concepts that are not only outmoded but also dangerously myopic and narrow. Climate journalism does not *need* to be like this.[19] This book underscores the contingency of these patterns of reporting and points towards different, more robustly democratic—as opposed to apocalyptic authoritarian—paths forward.

2019: A Defining Year for the "Climate Beat"

The year 2019 was a critical juncture for American climate journalism. This was the year when climate change "trended" and a verifiable climate beat gained substantial traction. Editorial boards across the country committed to the Covering Climate Now initiative cofounded by the *Columbia Journalism Review* and *The Nation* in association with *The Guardian* and WNYC in 2019.[20] Covering Climate Now was in part a response to the unprecedented and sustained attack on both climate science and journalism from a Trump White House. Through this new initiative, major media outlets within the U.S. promised to dedicate the resources, personnel, time, and attention required to produce more climate change reporting amid worsening environmental and political conditions. Reflective of this commitment, the Media and Climate Change Observatory at the University of Colorado at Boulder found that newspaper coverage of climate change was up 73 percent in 2019 compared to 2018.[21]

Within this milieu of increased news coverage, there was also a parallel spike in climate themes across popular culture. Trending musicians such as Billie Eilish sang about wildfires in California while the writers of hit American shows like *Big Little Lies* developed plotlines around kids' climate anxieties.[22] Oxford Dictionaries even named "climate emergency" its 2019 word of the year and had an all-climate-related shortlist including "climate action," "climate denial," and "eco-anxiety."[23] Moreover, the majority of Americans in 2019 expressed that they were not only convinced that climate change was real (a question that quite notoriously lasted for far too long in the U.S.) but that they were also both concerned about the threats of climate change *and* wanted to do something about it.[24]

This was a striking moment of change. For so many years prior to 2019, climate communication and journalism scholars were largely preoccupied with how to accurately and effectively communicate and translate the science to raise widespread public concern and inspire "climate action" (very broadly—and perhaps *too* broadly—defined). But now people *were* concerned, and the attention *was* there. Public awareness, interest, and a motivated desire for action were all evident in the U.S. for the first time. Americans wanted radical change. And yet, the ultimate direction that climate journalism would take in the U.S. stifled, as opposed to bolstered, this incredible momentum.

The journalistic treatment of climate justice activists during this period of heightened climate concern is one illustrative example of how U.S. news media dampened these prodigious calls for change. Notably, many of the most popular visions for how to effectively respond to climate change came from youth-led (and, in particular, young women of color-led) climate justice groups and grassroots movements. These movements were formed prior to 2019, before the media took serious note of climate change. Progressive climate activist coalitions like the Sunrise Movement began in 2017 in the wake of an alarming Trump election and built upon decades of community organizing, as did the development of the widely popular Green New Deal (GND)—a dynamic climate policy proposal that centers historically marginalized groups such as young women, low-income communities of color, working class oil and gas laborers, and Indigenous people in the design and implementation of a "just transition" to green energy. Rep. Alexandria Ocasio-Cortez (D-NY), a young progressive woman of color, ran with the GND as a core policy commitment during the 2018 Congressional election—an election that she would go on to win, ousting a longstanding Democratic Party figure and ushering-in a more vibrant and hopeful vision for what American politics could look like amid a demoralizing Trump presidency. Eventually, Rep. Ocasio-Cortez filed the resolution for a GND with the U.S. Congress on February 7, 2019.[25] Although the resolution ultimately did not pass, it nonetheless marked a key turning point in contemporary American climate politics by illustrating what an alternative identity and more robustly democratic direction for the U.S. *could* look like. It cannot be underscored enough that the GND's commitment to a comprehensive and justice-oriented climate policy program was incredibly popular at the time.[26]

A reimagination of what U.S. politics *could* be—with climate justice and robustly democratic decision-making processes at the center—inspired and united a diverse coalition of people who envisioned a future entirely distinct from the vitriol and violence of a reactionary Trump America.[27] And yet, despite this movement-building and momentum, prominent national news outlets failed to take note of its popular appeal. And when the media eventually did take note in 2019, reporters severely shortchanged the movement by casting supporters of the GND as "extremist," "hysterical," and "uncivil" young radicals out of step with the desires and views of the "average American"[28]—which, according to extensive polling data, was not true.[29] Conversely, "moderate" visionary sages were positioned as the opposite of these youthful "extremists" and represented as stoic, far-seeing, and ingenious (as well as older and whiter) saviors capable of leading the U.S.—and the entire world—out of today's "total crisis."[30]

Accordingly, top-down technocratic and market mechanisms proposed by visionary sages were—and continue to be—centrally featured in climate news stories and positioned as the *only* way forward to "solve" climate change in a sensible manner.[31] These top-down designs starkly differ from the more comprehensive and radically bottom-up proposals put forward by, for instance, the GND—which, it is once again pivotal to note, had widespread public support across the political spectrum before it was picked up and disparaged by the U.S. press in 2019.[32] The national press from the center-left *New York Times* to the center-right *Wall Street Journal* reported on the GND as a threatening policy proposed by a demagogic young radical Rep. Ocasio-Cortez and her dangerously militant young followers.[33] The GND and its supporters were—and still are—demonized by national news media through the image of a menacing, young, and militant Other.

Considering this and in revision of Kolbert's opening quote, 2019 can more accurately be understood as the year when *journalists* "woke up to the climate crisis," not the world, but with just one eye open. Journalists writing for leading national news outlets fell back onto Cold War binaries of militants versus moderates[34] and failed to take note of shifting public desires, contexts, and identities. Instead of reporting with both eyes fully open, many journalists squinted with rose-colored glasses *back* towards an imagined, post-World War II (WWII) "golden age" that is collectively remembered as a time when both American journalism and the U.S. were at their pinnacle.[35] The desire for this reclamation of a rosy and gold-encrusted midcentury America continually orients journalistic interpretations of mass movement-building happening on the ground and in the present, including among a sizable coalition of young people organizing for large-scale change and a more robustly democratic U.S. that never was, but surely could be. Clinging to nostalgia for an imagined postwar American past, reporters who are part of a burgeoning climate beat denigrate, fearmonger, and delegitimize vibrant collectivities of young, diverse, and engaged people who are actively contending with the exclusionary structures of the U.S. nation-state and proposing alternative political, economic, and national visions. Young activists are painted as villainous enemies impeding the reclamation of American glory, stability, and security as opposed to dynamic subjects working towards building more just and democratic futures.

This book reveals how nostalgic memories of America's past are brought forward in climate news stories in ways that impede comprehensive engagements with these more robustly democratic visions and identities. Myths of American grandeur, exceptionalism, and dominion are repeatedly reactivated as opposed to being questioned and challenged within a nascent U.S. climate beat that took definitive root in 2019. There is a palpable desire for a "new American exceptionalism," in the words of former President Joe Biden's National Security Advisor Jake Sullivan, and a return to an imagined postwar past when the U.S. was supposedly more stable, secure, and unanimously respected by all.[36] It is not inconsequential that this romanticized period of an early postwar/midcentury America was before the Civil Rights movement and revolutionary politics of the late 1960s began and when historically privileged figures—including journalists writing for prominent national news outlets—were on more solid ground. This privilege is precisely what young social and climate justice activists are again questioning just like their progressive forebears and, in turn, precisely what traditional figures of power are desperately trying to cling to, protect, and fortify once more.

Through appeals to Manifest Destiny, historically privileged figures are vying to secure their centrality by positioning themselves as God-ordained beings on a holy path, overcoming evil to bring *back* order, civility, and goodness to a temporarily off-kilter nation and world. According to these tales of American exceptionalism that are manufactured[37] and amplified across U.S. news stories on climate change, there is just one moderate, moral, and U.S.-led way forward to "solve" the "total crisis" of societal and climate chaos as per the Earth-saving plans developed by just a few very smart men who are celebrated as visionary sages. This limited purview impedes a plurality of possible paths forward by casting all who get in the way of this one "right" way as unholy Others who must be purged from the national body for the sake of "us all." With the imagined specter of apocalypse ever-looming in the background of the U.S. climate beat, the suspension of democratic procedures and the ascendence of apocalyptic authoritarianism are legitimized as wholly necessary for the survival of the U.S. nation-state in a warming world.

Nation-Centric Climate Journalism

Journalism scholars point to the fact that the modern nation-state and news media emerged together, and that nation-centric reporting is a standard.[38]

According to Benedict Anderson's classic study on nationalism, journalism was key for the modern nation-state's project of unification and conformity.[39] Anderson argued that the daily act of reading the newspaper every morning served as a ritual that united a geographically dispersed population. Citizens, Anderson contended, grew to feel connected to each other through the imagining of fellow compatriots reading the very same news stories at the very same time. Journalism was central to the fortification—and legitimization—of an "imagined community" of citizens melded together into one national body.[40]

In this way, "traditional journalism"[41]—this book's object of study—can be understood as a vehicle for both national and social control. Elites of early (and present-day) nation-states feared disorder and sought to rein in the "unruly masses" who were believed to be violent and destructive if left to their own devices. Objective and rational news reporting and commentary could, according to its advocates, educate "the people" and stabilize the nation by "civilizing" them. Reading the newspaper as a daily ritual was, therefore, seen as essential for buttressing a modern and advanced nation-state as well as encouraging a sense of national belonging. And of course, the most sensible among the national body were understood to be the educated and erudite elites who were doing the reporting.

Journalists then and now view themselves as absolutely indispensable for the success of the nation. In turn, "the masses"—who are still met with a level of suspicion and apprehension—continue to be charged with the task of reading/watching/listening to the news and learning from the important work of journalists in order to become more civilized in the process. Since the twentieth century, according to journalism scholars Barbie Zelizer, Pablo J. Boczkowski, and C. W. Anderson, "the mantra repeated in newsrooms and codified in journalism textbooks around the world has been that reporters and editors at leading mainstream news organizations should cover the most newsworthy stories of the day, independently of how much audiences are interested in them."[42] In other words, journalists—as self-proclaimed conduits of civilized and sensible thought—know best and "the audience is there to read, watch, listen and, ultimately, learn and be enlightened."[43]

The localized interests of different groups of people that may differ from journalists' understanding of what is "newsworthy" are often viewed as ill-informed, wrong, and potentially perilous for national stability and unity. Journalism and political communication scholar Daniel Kreiss clarifies how "journalists, the foundations working to save journalism, and many scholars do see a public starved of quality information as a central issue in contemporary democracy."[44] Kreiss illuminates how "the people" are in part blamed for a presently failing democracy due to their supposed avoidance of "quality information" produced by quality (i.e., "traditional") journalists.[45] Journalists' own avoidance of the lived experiences of "the masses" is, however, largely left unquestioned. The traditional practice of journalism, according to this point of view, is not the problem. *The people* are the problem.

As opposed to viewing traditional news values such as objectivity, fairness, and balance as ideals developed during a particular moment in historical time to legitimize both the modern nation-state and the news media as a national institution, liberal democratic principles are repeatedly taken as givens and as central to the production of "quality information" required for *all* democratic societies irrespective of time or place. Zelizer, Boczkowski, and Anderson argue that "a major problem with contemporary journalism is that it takes certain aspects of its existence for granted, seeing cases and conditions as permanent states of affairs rather than contingent adaptations that can evolve if the situation demands it."[46] In particular, Zelizer, Boczkowski, and Anderson identify "one of the most prevalent aspects of journalism, as it evolved in the Global North and insofar as its rhetoric has penetrated the imagined conditions of journalism elsewhere" as the news media's "fundamental liberal democratic political orientation."[47] Political theorist Chantal Mouffe similarly warns that this liberal democratic orientation undergirds the modern nation-state and its institutions—including the news media—and actively excludes a diversity of people such as women, the working class, migrants, Indigenous people, and communities of color in the Global North.[48] These Others are relegated to the realm of the irrational and unenlightened that need to be civilized or controlled, policed, and suppressed for the sake of the nation.

Despite these exclusions, traditional journalism and the liberal democratic values it depends on continue to be revered as transcendent, universal, and self-evident.[49] Instead of seeing newswriting—and the nation—as fluid, contingent, and changeable, many journalists today are buckling down on the outmoded values of yore. This book argues that this buckling down is to the detriment of the practice of more robust modes of reporting capable of contending with the mounting threats of climate change and reactionary politics by centering a plurality of lived experiences as opposed to the values and sensibilities of a small number of privileged elites.

Interestingly, the widely noted failures of climate journalism over the past half-century have revealed the limitations of these values, and yet have not altered their power. For example, the claim that "fairness" and "balance" in reporting are key for a thriving democracy is made suspect when fossil fuel industry-backed climate deniers were for decades given equal access and attention in news reports along with climate scientists in the name of journalistic professionalism and objectivity.[50] *The New York Times* publisher A. G. Sulzberger even admits this failure and the limitations of traditional news values in past climate reporting by his publication.[51] Yet despite this noted failure, Sulzberger still passionately defends the importance of "traditional journalism" by making a strong appeal to U.S. nationalism and the role of the news as a vehicle for national stability, writing how journalism produced by publications like *The New York Times* "not only makes our society more informed, it makes our nation more secure, our economy stronger, our people healthier, our society more just."[52] Sulzberger goes on to paint a patriotic and romanticized portrait of national unity facilitated by traditional journalism reminiscent of Benedict Anderson's *Imagined Communities*[53] by musing how: "For decades, spreading a newspaper on the kitchen table or gathering to watch the nightly news was an essential part of being a good citizen. The rituals may have changed, but the need hasn't."[54] Clearly, Sulzberger is preoccupied with the myth and promise of an imagined community of enlightened citizens and the central role of journalism in this civilizing project of nation-building. As opposed to reckoning with and reimagining how journalism could be different and perhaps better than it has been,[55] defenders of traditional journalism are longing for an illusory golden age of both U.S. journalism and the U.S. nation-state while reanimating the myth of American exceptionalism in the process.

Here again, through the myth of American exceptionalism, Sulzberger blames "the people" as the problem, not himself or traditional journalists, whom he views as visionary sages trying to right the ship and return the nation back to its fated course of Manifest Destiny. The unruly and polarized masses, according to Sulzberger, have led the nation astray.[56] The U.S. *needs* traditional journalists and sages like him more than ever to ensure "the masses" remain civilized and orderly for the sake of the nation's stability. Sulzberger proclaims how traditional journalism is:

> the exact tonic the world needs most at a moment in which polarization and misinformation are shaking the foundations of liberal democracies

and undermining society's ability to meet the existential challenges of the era, from inequality to political dysfunction to the accelerating toll of climate change. [...] [H]istory shows that the better course is when journalists challenge and complicate consensus with smart questions and new information.[57]

This statement assumes the need for an elevated press independent of "the people" in order to guide and enlighten them and to show "the masses" the right way to think and behave with "smart questions" and "new" *quality* information. In contrast with Sulzberger's position, a core question that this book poses is whether journalism *should* be elevated above "the people"? Alternatively, what would an integrated—as opposed to elevated—form of journalism look like that emerges out of the everyday lives of a plurality of dynamic, complex, and irreducible subjects? This question is especially relevant considering the rise of reactionary and antidemocratic politics and the mounting impacts of climate change that traditional journalism has failed to adequately contend with.

Ultimately, this book argues that traditional journalism needs to let go of an imagined golden age during which both the U.S. news media and U.S. nation-state were understood as more relevant, powerful, and stable. Contrary to this necessity, and via the specter of apocalypse and the myth of Manifest Destiny, this book exposes how the U.S. climate beat is becoming a key locus where this backwards-looking quest for journalistic and American relevancy is converging in problematic ways.

Static Subjectivities, Rigid Authorities, and Clear Temporal Horizons in an Emergent Regime of Climate Journalism

The modern nation-state demands static subjectivities, rigid authorities, and clear temporal horizons. The embedded theory of change is: *There is no change*. The past and future are clear—so why bother shaking things up and imagining alternatives? The apocalypse can also be understood, in the words of religious studies scholar Jamel Velji, as a "disclosure of ultimate destiny concerning the end of history."[58] Velji adds: "There is often no space for interstitiality in the apocalypse."[59] Both apocalyptic predictions and myths of national destiny leave little space for interstitiality, in-betweenness, or liminality. Traditional journalism, as a project of modern nation-building, embodies and propagates this rigidity around identity, futurity, and belonging. Only one theory of change, one national identity, and one legitimate mode of speech are valid. A subject is either "in" or "out" of line with a rational and right perspective. A person is either civil or uncivil, American or anti-American, good or evil. There is no room for complexity, difference, hybridity,[60] or interstitiality.

These clear-cut divisions are incredibly restrictive. By claiming authority over how social change manifests and what the future will inevitably hold, traditional journalism as a "technology of power"[61] tightens the lid around acceptability into an airtight seal. In this way, the representational prism of climate change as apocalypse entrenches a unidimensional understanding of time. In other words, the apocalypse is a clear and total disaster, and the nation-state can provide a clear and total way out of this disaster and towards salvation for a demarcated citizenry whereby all Others must be sacrificed or purged in the process. The role of journalism—according to "traditional" definitions advanced by figures such as A. G. Sulzberger—is to provide an objective report of the "world as it is."[62] This assumes that there is one absolute truth and one way of knowing, just as there is one true nation and one Manifest Destiny. It is the job of the journalist, according to defenders of traditional journalism, to reveal this ultimate truth to "the people" and bring en*light*enment to the land.

Sulzberger's apprehension that journalists writing for prominent national news publications like *The New York Times* are being questioned by "the people" instead of being wholly revered is striking. He laments how "journalistic decisions are continually being criticized in public by leaders, activists, journalists, celebrities, and influencers speaking for themselves or, just as often, for a broader community."[63] According to Sulzberger, anyone and everyone except for *traditional* journalists are capable of "succumb[ing] to their own forms of groupthink" and thus cannot—and should not—be trusted.[64] Climate activists, for instance, are chastised as irrationally misguided, and "the dynamics of social media have enabled pushback to be quicker, louder, and better organized, as supporters and opponents become more entrenched in their narratives and more aggressive in assailing anything that runs counter to their views or objectives."[65] These "aggressive" and "loud" assailants are frequently represented as young progressive women of color across news media and blamed for imperiling U.S. stability. Chapter 1 of this book shows how this delegitimization of young progressive women of color is patterned across U.S. climate journalism and reveals how this delegitimization closes off deeper considerations of responses to climate change that lie outside of the techno-managerial and green capitalist "solutions" espoused by visionary sage figures.

Philosopher and historian Michel Foucault pointedly argued that traditional journalism, as it continues to be practiced today, is the embodiment of the nineteenth-century liberal democratic "gaze" and therefore operates as a form of surveillance meant to control and civilize "the people."[66] Foucault contended that: "Basically, it was journalism, that capital invention of the nineteenth century, which made evident all the utopian character of this politics of the gaze."[67] This book illuminates how through images and narratives of apocalypse on the one hand, and via the reactivation of the myth of Manifest Destiny on the other, an emergent climate beat operates as a "regime of representation"—in the words of cultural studies scholar Stuart Hall invoking Foucault[68]—that fortifies this "gaze" by entrenching claims of authority among the traditionally privileged. As opposed to reckoning with and reimagining how both U.S. journalism and politics could be more just and robustly democratic, historically marginalized groups are cast as Others that must be surveilled and suppressed for the sake of the nation *and* planet. Concerningly, this buckling down on the authority of a supposedly enlightened few entrenches, as opposed to contends with, the inequities of the actually-existing-U.S.-nation-state that propel both climate change and apocalyptic authoritarianism.

Media and Power

Across his corpus of influential texts, Stuart Hall showed how patterned modes of representation uphold hierarchies of power and privilege, often along racialized lines.[69] Hall importantly underscored how critical analyses of media can reveal the contingency of regimes of representation and thus open-up possible pathways for de-naturalizing and unsettling sedimented stereotypes and derogatory tropes that normalize inequality.[70] Through critical media analyses, the field of cultural studies—in which Hall was and remains a foundational scholar[71]—emphasizes that the historically privileged position of a white and wealthy man is neither inevitable nor preordained. Current conditions of oppression and inequitable relations of power that uphold exclusionary political structures can be upended and are always being challenged.

"Power" is defined differently by various scholars of culture, media, and politics. According to critical theorists like Theodor Adorno and Max Horkheimer of the Frankfurt School, power is best understood as an elite-driven, top-down force of domination.[72] Conversely, according to Hall and the broader field of cultural studies, power is all about meaning-making, and meaning is negotiated and contested via appropriation and reappropriation in an often unpredictable and circuitous pattern as opposed to an easily predictable, top-down motion.[73] In a similar stride with Hall, Foucault rejected a top-down understanding of power.[74] But unlike Hall, who built his theory of power via the complexity of meaning-making, Foucault focused on the "production of knowledge" and the discursive construction of "right" and "wrong."[75] According to Foucault, power does not operate via a simple top-down mechanism or circuit of meaning-making, but rather involves both discursive and nondiscursive "techniques and tactics" of control forged through notions of absolute "truth" and the production of objective knowledge.[76]

The Enlightenment's project of objectivity, absolutes, and universal truths, according to Foucault, served as pillars for the formation of the modern nation-state and the bureaucratic institutions that it depends on.[77] Foucault referred to these pillars as "technologies of power" with both discursive and material components that effectively entrench traditional centers of authority at the expense of more robustly democratic decision-making processes.[78] In this way, different ways of knowing outside of the hegemonic are suppressed by the structures and strictures of the modern nation-state and its elite-oriented liberal democratic values. Power, however, is not all-encompassing. Foucault, just like Hall, argued that wherever there is power, there is also resistance.[79] The radical potential for large-scale social change is always present.

This book puts both Hall and Foucault's understanding of power and resistance in conversation with decolonial and postcolonial scholars' emphasis on the consequential role of empire in forging the subject/object binary upon which modern forms of meaning-making and knowledge production rely.[80] This subject/object binary whereby an active, "enlightened" self is conceived of as singularly capable of uncovering and determining a stable, objective truth is critiqued by critical scholars of the subaltern as a core problem of "Western"/"Global North" nation-states and their imperial projects of discovery and domination. Critical anthropologist Arturo Escobar, for example, shows how "development discourse" operates via claims of absolute/universal truth and the persistent enforcement of a "right" way to act and behave and a "right" way to build and organize an "advanced" society (i.e., via capitalist projects of "modernization").[81] Escobar also underscores how the subject/object binary that lies at the crux of the modern, liberal-democratic nation-state enforces the idea of a "One-World World" whereby the possibility for different ways of knowing, being, and organizing societies are violently rejected.[82] Liminality, in other words, has no place in a clear-cut world of absolutes. In turn, the policing of a "right" way of being a citizen/enlightened subject is forcefully maintained while different ways of living are wholly rejected as Other or criminalized as deviant.

Traditional journalism's adamant commitment to the hard truths, rigid rationality, and positivistic traditions of the Enlightenment (as seen, for instance, through Sulzberger's strong defense of them) demands careful reflection. Climate change is given shape and color through news images and stories constructed and presented in particular ways. Certain ways of knowing and seeing become normalized and concretized through distinct modes of reporting on climate change. And it is through the designation of an us versus them and a right versus wrong that specific responses to climate change are (de)legitimized within and outside of the newsroom, with profound societal implications.

Tyranny of Moderateness: Enforcers of "Rational" Speech

It is clear that within the unresolved tumult of the 2016 U.S. presidential election of Trump, there was—and remains—a notable longing for balance, stability, and a renewed sense of self as a nation through a clear demarcation of an us versus them. The repeated fearmongering of militant Others across climate news stories, however, ultimately works in favor of a reactionary political project that once again propelled Trump to the pinnacle of U.S. politics in 2024. The image of civilizational collapse and a loss of American power ushered in by anti-American Others closes off more nuanced and transformative considerations of both the disparate impacts of and many possible responses to climate change. These considerations, arguably, could have sustained a stronger and more organized opposition to the MAGA right in the years following Trump's first electoral victory in 2016.

It is particularly striking that Rep. Ocasio-Cortez and young female climate justice activists of color who support the GND have been repeatedly singled out and represented as especially threatening to the U.S. across *both* conservative and centrist media alike in the years since Trump's 2016 election. The construction of a young progressive woman of color as a militant Other took off even more widely and visibly across climate journalism since further fuel was added to the perceived fire of "total crisis" when the COVID-19 pandemic began in 2020—a trend that is detailed in Chapter 1 of this book. Within the chaos of a devastating pandemic and at the heels of a tumultuous first Trump presidency, a regime of climate journalism solidified around a binary that clearly distinguished a "moderate" climate policymaker (who is reported on as capable of putting the U.S. and the globe back on a stable path) versus a "militant" climate justice activist (who is portrayed as impeding this return to normalcy that the American people supposedly desperately desire after so many years of disarray).

Centrist publications like *The New York Times* and Democratic politicians like Sean Patrick Maloney—who bitterly lost the 2022 midterm election and blames young progressives like Ocasio-Cortez for his loss[83]—repeat and amplify antidemocratic talking points typically characteristic of the Republican Party and right-wing media like *Fox News*. *The New York Times* and other centrist media have joined the right's fearmongering about the "new" New Left as a profound threat to the U.S.[84] This book reveals how since Trump's first election in 2016 and the pandemic years that followed, there has been a concerning concretization of the boundaries around who should and who should not be included in official decision-making processes. Young female climate justice activists of color are consistently Othered in U.S. news media and effectively delegitimized as viable speaking subjects who should *not* be included in any climate, party, or national deliberations.

It is important to underscore that this construction of a threatening, young, progressive, and militant climate justice activist as a dangerous Other is also evident in other places and in other national media contexts, not just in the U.S. This Othering is reflective of a global shift towards a reactionary mode of antidemocratic politics especially since the pandemic years[85] that can be seen, for example, with the outrage and stridently negative perspectives featured across national news media ranging from the U.K. to Canada to Australia following the Just Stop Oil tomato soup protest that took place in London, U.K. on October 14, 2022. During this protest, two young activists in the U.K. named Phoebe Plummer and Anna Holland threw the contents of a can of tomato soup on the glass-protected Vincent van Gogh painting *Sunflowers* in the National Gallery in London.[86] This act of protest was intended to inspire a shared civic reflection on public values and to urge peers to ponder why climate change is not of more immediate and widespread concern. The protest gained a lot of traction on social media among young progressives and inspired other similar speech acts across the globe from Vancouver to Amsterdam. Yet despite this popular and peaceful act of protest (the painting was in no way damaged, and destruction was never the intention), the two young activists, a part of Just Stop Oil, were widely demonized by pundits and commentators across mainstream media locally in the U.K. and elsewhere.

This particular demonization of the Just Stop Oil activists is illustrative of a more general discursive construction in contemporary news media that this book refers to as the *climate justice warrior* stereotype. Climate justice "warriors" are reported on as young and usually female or nonbinary and often Black, Brown, or Indigenous. This new media stereotype reactivates very old prejudices. The climate justice warrior stereotype draws upon misogynistic, ageist, and racist tropes to lump together and delegitimize a diverse group of young activists by casting them as irrational, unreasonable, and threatening to liberal democratic order and "civilized" procedures. This stereotype formation is demonstrated, for instance, by the climate scientist Michael Mann's patronizing reaction to the soup protests published in an article for *TIME*.[87] Mann writes:

> The youth protesters have their heart in the right place. But the organizations behind these protests need to do right by them by being smart about the design of any public interventions. That means, among other things, choosing sensible actions and appropriate targets. If we are to win the battle against polluters and their enablers, we will need public opinion on our side not theirs.[88]

Mann goes on to add: "I worry that events like this could harm the cause to which I (and so many) have devoted my life."[89] Mann—a prominent American climate scientist who considers himself to be a leading "climate communicator"[90]—essentially calls for the exclusion of these young activists from the public climate conversation if they fail to get in line. He calls for the "smart" and "sensible" adults in the room to put these "youth" in their place before they can cause any further damage to the work and legacy of very smart men like him.

Mouffe offers key insights to help explain Mann's strong reaction to the affective speech act of these young protesters by revealing "the link that was established between the democratic project and the rationalist perspective [during the Enlightenment]."[91] Mouffe elaborates on how anyone who critiqued the "limits of Enlightenment rationalism" and who emphasized the importance of affect and emotion "were perceived as defending a conservative position. They were accused of undermining the very basis of the democratic project."[92] Hence, passionate *pro-democracy* activists who propose transformative visions that push beyond the limitations of an elite-oriented nation-state are transmuted into uncivil, irrational, and wholly threatening Others by "moderate" and "rational" men such as Michael Mann and A. G. Sulzberger, who have unbending notions of what "appropriate" speech means and what "sensible" ways of responding to climate change entail. The role of traditional journalism is central to this boundary-formation around "rational" and "sensible" speech and dangerously limits the possibility for more *robustly* democratic and transformative responses to climate change that engage with as opposed to stifle the passions and lived experiences of "the masses" that may challenge the privilege and personal legacy of men like Mann.

Policing the Climate Crisis

The news media's transformation of young progressives into uncivil Others has happened before. Todd Gitlin in his important book titled *The Whole World is Watching: Mass Media in the Making and Unmaking of the New Left* discussed how both the Nixon administration and mainstream media tapped into lingering McCarthy-era red scare rhetoric to carve out a binary of the "moderate" versus "militant" activist in the late 1960s/1970s to fearmonger about young Civil Rights activists and Vietnam War protesters who were cast as dangerous Others infiltrating demonstrations and leftist political circles to the demise of the Democratic Party and the nation itself.[93] Gitlin explained how "the frame of moderation-as-alternative-to-militancy was now brought into play, and more deliberately so over time."[94] Gitlin underscored the role of news media here and how, by demarcating legitimate and illegitimate activists, journalists not only accepted President Nixon's talking points but also served to blame an entire segment of the U.S. population—that is, the original "New Left"—as a destabilizing force threatening the nation.⁹⁵ Young progressives were represented as "militant" and "anti-American" and criminalized as enemies of the nation-state. The state's suppression and prosecution of "militant Others" were, in turn, legitimized as appropriate and warranted.

Stuart Hall and his coauthors importantly highlighted in their groundbreaking book *Policing the Crisis: Mugging, the State and Law and Order* how media fearmongering and Othering were directly leveraged by the state to legitimize police violence against those deemed Other. In particular, Hall and his collaborators described how the U.K. media in the 1970s manufactured false narratives about a "mugging crisis" in U.K. cities that cast young Black men as violent criminals threatening the supposedly previously well-ordered British metro-areas.⁹⁶ This unsubstantiated and rampant claim of a mugging *crisis* across news media led to increased calls for and the ultimate implementation of more policing of young Black men in urban centers in the U.K.

It is disconcerting to see parallels between the late-1960s/1970s and today. At the same time as there is an evident concretization of a militant climate justice warrior stereotype across news media, there has also been a spike in police repression of young climate justice activists on the ground in the U.S., U.K., and other nations.⁹⁷ Through the passage of new "critical infrastructure" acts, for example, protesters who blockade the construction of oil and gas pipelines are specifically targeted and prosecuted as criminals in the U.S.⁹⁸ Moreover, young climate activists are being criminalized, arrested, and charged in Europe from France to Germany to Denmark and other nations.⁹⁹ The Just Stop Oil tomato soup activists, Plummer and Holland, were, for instance, sentenced to jail time.¹⁰⁰ Climate activists worldwide are being imprisoned with lengthy sentences and slapped with steep fines.¹⁰¹ The resuscitation of law and order narratives and strong policing in the 2020s is perhaps most vividly demonstrated with the political rise of former government prosecutors on both sides of the Atlantic, with Keir Starmer in the U.K. and Kamala Harris in the U.S.¹⁰²

Concerningly, through a mix of laws meant to prosecute organized crime and domestic terrorism as well as the critical infrastructure provisions put in place in 2017 in the U.S. following the #NoDAPL demonstrations at Standing Rock in North Dakota—a massive anti-pipeline protest movement led by Indigenous water defenders in opposition to the Dakota Access Pipeline (DAPL)¹⁰³—dozens of Cop City protesters were arrested and charged with acts of terrorism, among other crimes, in Atlanta, Georgia, in early 2023.¹⁰⁴

These arrests counter the public will. The Cop City protests in Atlanta were extremely popular and the majority of local residents expressed both support for the protesters and opposition to the proposed construction of a police training facility that local activists have dubbed "Cop City".[105] Despite this, city officials approved plans to build Cop City in the Weelaunee Forest—an important watershed surrounded by primarily Black residents. Plans for this police training facility include a mock cityscape to practice urban warfare against protesters a part of mass movements akin to the 2020 Black Lives Matter protests. Blueprints for Cop City show shooting ranges, a Black Hawk helicopter landing pad, and military-grade equipment.[106] Local Cop City activist Kwame Olufemi clarifies how "Cop City is not just a controversial training center. It is a war base where police will learn military-like maneuvers to kill Black people and control our bodies and movements."[107] He warns how the state and police forces "are practicing how to make sure poor and working class people stay in line."[108] Cop City protesters, up until a violent police raid in early 2023, had set-up an encampment in the forest to peacefully blockade its clear-cutting for construction. During this police raid, the forest defender Manuel Esteban Paez Terán, whose chosen name was Tortuguita, was shot and killed by police.[109]

Chilling Effects

This state and police violence against young activists of color is troubling for many reasons. Firstly, this state repression is clearly authoritarian, reflected by the fact that the majority of local residents in Atlanta opposed Cop City and expressed support for the protesters.[110] Despite this majority opposition to Cop City and widespread support for activists, the city still chose to approve the project and to jail and *kill* protesters. Moreover, unlike what "moderate" figures such as Michael Mann may say, protests like this and the soup demonstration led by the Just Stop Oil activists in London did not turn people away from or dampen support for the climate movement. In fact, a national survey found that a large majority of the U.K. public supports non-violent climate demonstrations such as the soup protests and opposes the passage of laws that give the police more power.[111] Likewise, in the U.S. in 2018, before the rampant media coverage disparaging the GND began in 2019, a majority of Americans across the political spectrum supported the policy proposal and other justice-oriented climate responses championed by progressives.[112] The circulation of news stories that represent young climate justice activists as militants who are threatening national stability is, arguably, the real problem—not the activists' democratic demands for more transformative and just decision-making processes. The repeated fearmongering and construction of a militant Other/climate justice warrior stereotype by traditional journalists, pundits, prosecutors, and politicians alike are legitimizing state and police violence against pro-democracy progressives.

If most people in the U.S. are in favor of a transition to renewable energy through transformative policies and justice-oriented responses to climate change,[113] then why do elected leaders keep implementing policies that counter what "the public" wants? Shouldn't "the people" be able to harness the power required to make the government implement their will? Isn't this what "democracy" means? While most people do support a "just transition" to renewable energy in nations such as the U.S. and U.K., polling also shows that this same majority of people do not think that others in their respective nations share their point of view.[114] Pessimism, in other words, abounds. Strong social ties are clearly broken. Collective action is kept at bay, and more robustly democratic modes of governance are kept out of reach when distrust of peers and neighbors proliferates. The discursive construction of a threatening, young, and militant climate justice warrior across news media is further fracturing these already broken social ties following years of neoliberal gutting of public institutions, law and order narratives, post-9/11 terrorist fearmongering, mass surveillance, and rampant trolling, hate speech, and misinformation circulating online, not to mention the years of isolation and anxiety during the COVID-19 pandemic. It serves an elite captured[115] state's best interests to keep collectivities broken, social ties shattered, fears high, and thus the formation of cross-partisan alliances and collective action at bay. Ultimately, this book's critical conceptualization of apocalyptic authoritarianism illuminates how when images and narratives of apocalypse are combined with appeals to nationalism and a singular vision for the future, more robustly democratic and transformative modes of politics are repeatedly thwarted.

Elite Panic

Indeed, at the crux of apocalyptic authoritarianism is the anxious (and elitist) claim that climate change will spell chaos *because* of a horde of ignorant

Others that will revert to incivility, violence, and barbarism. These Others are repeatedly represented as progressive, Black, Brown, and Indigenous young women. This fear of "the masses"—a term that is gendered, raced, and classed—prompts some techno-utopian ecomodernists, such as Michael Shellenberger, to critique "alarmist" modes of environmentalism for fear that a doomsday image of climate apocalypse will prompt panic and chaos among these imagined Others.[116] Shellenberger's critique of apocalyptic discourse is categorically different from this book's. Indeed, Shellenberger frequently mentions Rep. Ocasio-Cortez as a particularly threatening figure in his own hypocritical twist of logic that portends civilizational collapse if the "woke" left is not contained.[117] He describes her as the populist leader of a crowd of uneducated and irrational young women radicalized through her seductive appeal and alarmist rhetoric. Shellenberger fears that this climate alarmism is steering attention away from more "rational" and "pragmatic solutions" such as nuclear energy and green tech innovations proposed by very smart men like him.[118] In critiquing "alarmist" discourse, Shellenberger is the one who sounds alarmed.

Shellenberger's patronizing critique of both Ocasio-Cortez and a thriving climate justice movement that is largely led by young women of color can in part be explained by what sociologists Lee Clarke and Caron Chess call "elite panic," whereby elites assume that the "general public"—understood as uneducated, uncivil, and violent—will panic during a crisis and therefore they themselves panic about this predicted panic and install harsh policing practices and militarized oversight in the process.[119] The writer Rebecca Solnit[120] draws upon this concept of elite panic to argue how, in fact, the "general public" does not resort to violence during moments of catastrophe but rather consistently exhibits a profound sense of community, calm, and solidarity. Solnit writes how the momentary absence of formal, top-down procedures during disasters does not lead to "law of the jungle chaos"[121] as men like Shellenberger imagine and claim. Solnit describes how "what in fact takes place is another kind of anarchy, where the citizenry by and large organize and care for themselves."[122] Solnit adds that this coming together during moments of rupture reveals the otherwise obscured shortcomings of an elite-run state and offers an alternative vision for how to better organize society in a more robustly democratic manner. In other words, people tend to "build paradise in hell," not a dystopian doom-scape.[123] It is the heavy-handed policing and military personnel sent into communities that cause much more harm by obstructing the formation of organic and cohesive social ties that may have developed otherwise. Solnit suggests that this obstruction could be a purposeful, counterrevolutionary strategy.[124] That is to say, catastrophe does not inevitably spell barbarism, but the asymmetries of power and unequal access to resources that allow elite panic to enact brutal forms of militarized policing do.

Disdain for "the masses" allows blame to be placed squarely on Others as opposed to the ones in power. Elite panic and predictions of chaos advanced by visionary sage figures, often male and from the Global North, seemingly revel in the image of a Hobbesian "law of the jungle chaos"[125] because it opens-up a discursive paradigm through which they can reclaim their historical position of power currently under question by climate and social justice movements.

Elite Capture

Also at the heart of apocalyptic authoritarianism—and stemming out of elite panic—is the assertion of both omnipotence and transcendence among those who claim to possess the ultimate way out of the "total crisis." In other words, visionary sage figures can cast any and all opposition as obstructing the "right" response to climate change—as seen through representations of Rep. Ocasio-Cortez as a threatening and short-sighted Other by men like Shellenberger and across U.S. news media. Ocasio-Cortez may contribute to an apocalyptic discourse through her passionate warnings about the severity of climate change but, importantly, her alliance with campaigns for social and environmental justice centers the need for transformative political-economic change and a diversity of community-led responses. Apocalyptic authoritarianism, conversely, funnels apocalyptic anxieties through the lens of an overwhelming sense of hatred directed at young progressives of the "new" New Left. This hatred of young progressives is combined with claims of transcendence and only one way forward as delineated by visionary sage figures. In turn, justice-oriented and more economically transformative responses are either barred from consideration or deemed too "extreme." Predictions of climate chaos are thus ripe for co-optation by opportunists seeking power by closing off democratic procedures. Through images and narratives of apocalypse, traditional centers of power fervently advance their "innovative" visions as the ultimate "solution" and route back to the "good old days" of postwar America—which just so happens to be the romanticized period in time when their own positions of authority and privilege were more secure.

Notably, the specter of civilizational collapse is also advanced by some privileged intellectuals of the European academy's "old boys' club"—most vocally, Slavoj Žižek and the late Bruno Latour. Žižek is a proponent of the ideology (or perhaps more aptly: the self-declared prophecy) of accelerationism, which welcomes societal chaos as a means for ushering in the inevitable "end times" of the U.S. Žižek—as a prophet of accelerationism—went so far as to support a Trump victory over Hillary Clinton in the 2016 U.S. presidential election. The "total crisis" of Trump and climate chaos, according to Žižek, are two essential pillars of catastrophe capable of dethroning U.S. power.[126]

High-profile members of the French intelligentsia, such as Bruno Latour, echoed Žižek's gleeful welcoming of catastrophe and the predicted fall of the U.S. under Trump because of the possibility it presented for Europe—what Latour termed *"a second chance."*[127] Latour, in reference to the impending disasters of the new "Anthropocene" epoch—a term this book problematizes in Chapter 2—declared:

> How could one doubt that Europe may become one of the homelands of all those who are looking for ground? "A European is anyone who wants to be one." I would like to be proud of it, of this Europe, with all its wrinkles and seams; I would like to be able to call it my homeland—their refuge.[128]

Now replace every time Latour says "Europe" and "European" with "America" and "American." Clearly, the universal truth claims, moralizing, and necropolitical imaginaries of Europe as the default saved and saviors amid planetary chaos serve to reactivate the myth of *European* exceptionalism through the prism of "total crisis" in a similar manner as these discursive appeals embolden claims of *American* exceptionalism.

Prior to the devastating blows of the two world wars, the colonial powers of Western Europe considered themselves to be the hub and arbiter of Earthly knowledge and "culture."[129] This culture was represented through the image of goodness and light emanating from the European "center" across the dark "periphery" of the colonies, akin to the American myth of Manifest Destiny. Following WWII, the U.S. enthusiastically claimed this imagined position of centrality and saw itself as the new global purveyor of goodness in fulfillment of its glorious and God-ordained fate.[130] At the end of WWII, the U.S. dollar and culture of capitalism (or culture *as* capitalism) became the new guiding light through, for instance, Bretton Woods financial institutions like the World Bank and International Monetary Fund (IMF).[131] In this way, the U.S. embraced the hegemonic role formerly claimed by European colonial powers—but with the "enemy" mega-power of the U.S.S.R. as its foil during the Cold War. The U.S. vied to become the *only* purveyor of global affairs and framed its ambitions as a battle between good and evil. Stemming out of this discursive paradigm of national exceptionalism, U.S. leadership on climate change has been increasingly elevated by "moderates" since 2016 and positioned by centrist news media as an important route *back* to this imagined postwar position of U.S. global power understood as only *momentarily* "lost" with Trump's political ascendency (to the dismay of Latour and Žižek).

The rampant media fearmongering of a potential weakening or loss of American power, however, ultimately works in favor of the right's political project, and it is often a deliberate strategy. The threat of civilizational collapse is repeatedly leveraged by the right and its allied fossil fuel industry peers to obstruct systemic transformations of the economy and government, including a just transition to fossil-free energy.[132] Through "petro-nationalism," the fossil fuel industry and conservative advocates in the U.S. government repeatedly leverage apocalyptic images of civilizational demise to invoke fear and anxiety around the supposed further loss of "an American way of life" if the U.S. moves away from oil and gas and towards renewable energy too quickly.[133]

Critical analyses of the ideological roots of apocalyptic authoritarianism thus help make sense of the complexities, continuities, and contingencies of climate discourse by honing in on the discursive strategies of exclusion and Othering that are often naturalized and normalized in the journalistic and political practices of modern liberal democracies. Concerningly, through the guise of being "neutral," "non-partisan," and "apolitical," traditional journalism amplifies and entrenches these exclusions as opposed to fundamentally contesting the reactionary impulses of apocalyptic authoritarianism. This book argues that this move towards neutrality closes off a necessary reckoning with the "elite capture"[134] of the actually-existing-U.S.-nation-state that prioritizes a historically privileged few above all Others.

Ultimately, this book reveals how images and narratives of the nation, world order, and planet Earth on the brink are leveraged by a variety of privileged actors with a stake in maintaining the status quo, whether to bolster the authority of an old boys' club, the fossil fuel industry, Europeans' desire for a return to their imagined prewar position of global centrality, or Americans' dream for a return to their imagined postwar golden age. While this jockeying for power among historically privileged groups through the image of apocalypse is not necessarily unique to climate discourse, it is often definitive of it. And by either not recognizing or not taking elite panic and elite capture seriously (or by participating in it), climate journalism often falls short of illuminating—and may be contributing to—the reactionary thrust of apocalyptic authoritarianism as it manifests today.

Overview

It is important to note that an authoritarian future is not inevitable, and the present regime of climate journalism is not absolute. The oppressions and exclusions of the past and present are continually contested. Radically different futures are always possible. Critical projects that trace the roots of dominant modes of discourse and power can reveal both the continuities and contingencies of discursive formations and point towards alternatives— a collective task of intellectual labor that this book strives to contribute to. It is here where this book's critical conceptualization of apocalyptic authoritarianism and empirically grounded analysis of the discursive "techniques and tactics"[135] that propel it shed light on the role of traditional journalism in fomenting exclusionary responses to climate change. Each chapter that follows is structured around one of four tropes that lie at the crux of both apocalyptic authoritarianism and an emergent regime of U.S. climate journalism, including (1) *appeals to nationalism and Othering*, (2) *the celebration of planetary-scale "solutions,"* (3) *the admiration of visionary sage figures,* and (4) *necropolitical claims of the "inevitable" climate deaths of racialized Others.*

Chapter 1 of this book begins by identifying how allusions to well-known conflicts in U.S. history, including WWII and the Cold War, are used to orient—and limit—contemporary climate news stories. This chapter shows how these historical references amplify calls for the U.S. to reclaim its imagined post-WWII position of global centrality, understood as only momentarily lost in the age of Trump. This chapter ultimately illustrates how *appeals to nationalism* and a strong desire for national redemption limit the types of climate "solutions" featured in news stories by barring consideration of responses that lie outside of the liberal democratic norm and postwar global economic order. More economically transformative and robustly democratic responses to climate change are, in turn, delegitimized through *discursive modes of Othering* that draw upon racialized, gendered, and generational stereotypes that cast young progressive supporters of justice-oriented climate policies as anti-American and militant Others.

Chapter 2 uncovers the lingering Cold War tropes that steer U.S. journalists' *celebration of planetary-scale "solutions"* across the climate beat. Through an analysis of climate news stories and images that center all-encompassing technological and market "fixes," this chapter reveals how the planetary scale often renders the present abstract to such a degree that the on-the-ground impacts of climate change and the exploitative political-economic structures that drive it are either obscured or erased altogether. Climate change is depoliticized and decontextualized through this abstract rendering. It is here where green capitalists and geoengineers are repeatedly lauded as morally and intellectually superior geniuses who will "save the Earth" without rupturing the status quo. Collective action and systemic change, on the other hand, are cast as misguided and potentially dangerous. Through a critical analysis of the optics and logics of the planetary scale across the U.S. climate beat, Chapter 2 reveals how this way of seeing is combined with appeals to rugged individualism and American tropes of masculinity to legitimize the unabridged reach of planetary-scale "solutions" designed by just a few very smart men and advanced as a panacea for all crises regardless of context, time, or place.

Chapter 3 further illuminates how these appeals are constructed through *the admiration of visionary sage figures* across the U.S. climate beat. This chapter unpacks how this trope contributes to the formation of a persistent binary of hero versus villain in a universal tale of American strength and goodness, transcendent of the present, particular, and proximate. This chapter also shows how this binary of good versus evil is often leveraged by those with a stake in maintaining the status quo—including traditional journalists themselves. Ultimately, this chapter reveals how certain responses to climate change are deemed right and legitimate while others are deemed wrong and illegitimate through the central elevation of the visionary sage figure (who is often wealthy, white, and male) in climate news stories. To this end, this chapter lays bare how the discursive construction of the visionary sage figure obstructs meaningful engagements with the complexities and uneven impacts of climate change. Consideration of more transformative and equitable responses to climate change that inherently question the unabridged authority of visionary sages is either ignored or reported on by journalists as shortsighted, ill-informed, and dangerous.

Chapter 4 draws upon the decolonial and postcolonial concepts of worlding and dualisms to decipher how predominant news images and stories of climate migrants are constructed for an imagined American community. Through the integration of critical theories of biopower and necropower, this chapter ultimately shows how fearmongering, on the one hand, and deterministic portrayals of already "drowned" and "damned" populations of Other people, on the other hand, shape climate reporting and embolden political responses to climate change that favor military interventions abroad and higher walls and tighter borders at home. Through *necropolitical claims of the "inevitable" climate deaths of racialized Others*, the need for more cooperative, comprehensive, and justice-oriented climate responses developed by a plurality of people from diverse places is repeatedly portrayed as pointless in stories published by some of the most prominent national news publications in the U.S.

The Conclusion chapter details how anti-authoritarian climate media and movements are actively reimagining different and more equitable futures beyond an apocalyptic vision of planetary collapse and beyond an authoritarian desire for total control. In particular, the last chapter underscores how pluriversal visions and the desire for "a world where many worlds fit" (in the translated words of the Zapatistas) guide very different ideas for how to report on and respond to climate change that importantly diverge away from apocalyptic authoritarianism and U.S.-centric climate journalism. This chapter proposes and illustrates how instead of fearing an uncertain future and unruly Others—both a commonplace in U.S. climate reporting and politics—the radical embrace of difference and the unknowable offers more productive and transformative routes forward.

Ultimately, this book points towards concrete avenues for reimagining climate journalism after reckoning with its current restrictions, oversights, and exclusions. It is here where the terminological introduction of *apocalyptic authoritarianism* and this book's critical analysis of U.S. news media expose how chauvinistic national myths, stereotypes, and tropes are limiting U.S. climate journalism and climate politics and thus stalling this crucial reimaginative work.

1
A New Marshall Plan for the Climate: Reclaiming National and Journalistic Authority Through the Myth of American Exceptionalism

The year 2020 was marked by U.S. journalists as a catastrophic year of overwhelming disarray. Year-in-review features published in December 2020 described it as "unprecedented" and, according to *The New York Times*, "a year like no other."[1] Fire-and-brimstone hues of chaos and the darkness of an American democracy in peril painted the covers, screens, and pages of major national news outlets. This narrative of the year 2020 as one of extremes built upon four years of reporting on the calamity of the first Trump presidency that reached a crescendo when it converged with the COVID-19 pandemic, blazing wildfires in the West, and mass public outrage regarding systemic racism and police violence against Black Americans following the murder of George Floyd to intensify a "total crisis" of seemingly unparalleled proportions. It is within these contexts where news images and stories of "total crisis" subsumed a newly vitalized climate beat—now dubbed the "apocalypse beat" by *The New York Times* climate journalist Brad Plumer in his former Twitter bio.

Amid this perceived disorder and chaos, comparisons to the well-known conflicts of World War II (WWII) and the Cold War began to steer U.S. journalists' interpretations of climate change. References to these familiar historical events from the past carved out a sense of control for weary journalists wading through seemingly "unprecedented" conditions of "total crisis." Allusions to these specific conflicts, however, are culturally loaded and carry a lot of meaning. WWII and the Cold War are collectively remembered in the U.S. as glorious victories over wholly evil enemies in fulfillment of the nation's God-ordained Manifest Destiny to spread the light of liberty and goodness across the globe. Equating climate change with these specific

Apocalyptic Authoritarianism. Hanna E. Morris, Oxford University Press. © Oxford University Press (2025).
DOI: 10.1093/9780197807705.003.0002

conflicts, in turn, burns a clear path forward, but through a very narrow paradigm of American exceptionalism that propagates a severely limited view of how to best respond to climate change.

It is through this paradigm of American exceptionalism that assertions of Manifest Destiny are used to transform universal claims into moral judgments, deeming responses to climate change as either right or wrong according to a very rigid definition of national identity and fate. This limitation on what is deemed a right response to climate change—that is, one that will secure the supposedly glorious and preordained leadership position of the U.S. as *the* global superpower—is highly exclusionary. It also demonstrates traditional journalists' nostalgia and desire for a return to an imagined postwar golden age when their own prestige and power were under less public scrutiny and more stable and secure. This chapter illuminates the consequences of this longing and how the desire for a renewed sense of control and relevancy amid "total crisis" shapes—and limits—a nascent U.S. climate beat.

Universal Truth Claims

During moments of perceived societal crises—when shared beliefs and collective identities are vulnerable and apt for radical transformation—there is a risk of falling back onto established myths and familiar ways of knowing that entrench traditional centers of power and exclusionary modes of governance. The philosopher and historian Michel Foucault spoke of how universalized discourses tend to emerge during times of great uncertainty and upheaval, such as the year 2020 and also at the time of Foucault's writing during the Cold War following the devastation of WWII.[2] Grand tales of national heroes, origins, and fate—like the myth of Manifest Destiny in the U.S.—are reanimated in an attempt to regain a sense of equilibrium and reassert a stable "régime of truth" during unstable times.[3]

It is here where the pivotal role of myths becomes clear. The philosopher Roland Barthes defined myths as "the transformation of history into nature" and clarified how certain ways of knowing can become so entrenched as to appear natural, essential, and universal, whereby the particularities of place and historical context become so blurred to the point of erasure.[4] According to media scholar Vincent Mosco, "myths transform the messy complexities of history into the pristine gloss of nature."[5] Myths, according to Barthes and

Mosco, are therefore more powerful than norms because they underpin the very structures of logic and thought that norms emerge from. In other words, myths are universal truth claims that coalesce to build discursive paradigms that national, social, and political institutions depend on.

The notion of discursive formations takes on further relevance for discussions of climate change with the work of decolonial scholars, such as Eve Tuck and K. Wayne Yang, who show how grand narratives of the Eurocentric tradition tend to erase long histories of imperial oppression and trauma while upholding colonial institutions and extending exclusionary modes of governance.[6] Cultural studies scholar Heather Davis and anthropologist Zoe Todd argue that "a logic of the universal" is often "structured to sever the relations between mind, body, and land" and used to quell environmentalist, anti-capitalist, and anti-colonial resistance movements tied to particular places and specific grievances.[7] This means that experiences of environmental destruction, violence, and harm among Indigenous and historically marginalized peoples are discursively erased through the void of the "transhistorical," in which no cause is decipherable or even relevant.[8] Within the timescale of an open and abstract History, accountability is impossible. Universal tales of Humanity, therefore, are often used to validate the way things are or to endorse absolutist claims of how they should be. In turn, established modes of traditional journalism and traditional politics are cast as natural, inevitable, unquestionable, and therefore unchangeable—even as they perpetuate inequities and legitimize environmental devastation. For representations of climate change, this suggests that universal truth claims obscure its root causes and obstruct the possibility for accountability and structural transformations of the political-economic system.

America as Exceptionally Moderate

Universal claims of what is morally right and good, according to political theorist Chantal Mouffe, took on more weight with hegemonic interpretations of crises more generally following the Cold War and the advent of globalization.[9] Through all-encompassing claims of Humanity and History (with a capital "H"), a plurality of perspectives and experiences melded into one story of good versus evil told as a universal truth, gravely injuring radical politics and post/decolonial movements that centered specific, longstanding harms[10] and called for large-scale, systemic change notably at odds with U.S.-led projects of global economic development. Morality as determined by the U.S.—the now *lone* world superpower with the fall of the Berlin Wall in 1989 and crumbling of the Soviet Union—directed attention away from the unresolved and ongoing harms of imperial and capitalist systems of extraction and instead blamed immoral individuals and immoral behaviors or social deviancies as the source of all crises and conflicts in the world.

Following from this, certain political ideologies and even entire nations were—and continue to be—cast as either good or bad based on stereotypes that reduce complex histories into simple caricatures told within a universal tale of moral goodness. Within the context of the Cold War, the U.S. and capitalism were naturalized as the default "good" and the Soviet Union and communism as the default "bad" in messages circulated by politicians, pundits, and journalists. Postcolonial liberation movements that espoused socialist ideals during the postwar time period were therefore also cast in the latter category. The American historian Eric Foner explains how "Cold War intellectuals provided historical justification, differentiating 'good' from 'bad' revolutions."[11] The American Revolution was applauded as good because it was led by "educated elites," which differed from the bad "class-based violence" of France, Russia, and the postcolonial revolutions in the "Third World."[12] Foner critiques this dismissal of revolutionary politics by American intellectuals during the Cold War and expresses his agreement with the historian Herbert Bolton, who lamented that "by treating the American past in isolation from the rest of the world, historians were helping to raise up 'a nation of chauvinists.'"[13]

In other words, the reactivation of the myth of American exceptionalism by academic, media, political, and business elites during the Cold War flattened multifaceted independence and liberation movements in the Global South through absolutist claims and morally charged binary formations. Significantly, this flattening led to the quelling of different ways of governing through, in many cases, the forceful implementation of "models of democracy" and "models of development" that treated "nation-building" as a one-size-fits-all product that the U.S. could export to "unstable" nations.[14] Foner clarifies that "the exceptionalist paradigm [...] homogenizes the rest of the world as having a single history" that is different and lesser than the U.S. and laments that this is "the deepest problem of American exceptionalism—the conviction that Americans have nothing to learn from the rest of the world."[15]

This hubris, along with the notion of a uniquely stable society, upholds and entrenches the myth of American exceptionalism. Significantly, during the Cold War, the U.S.'s unparalleled goodness was understood as in no small part due to its supposed moderateness that distinguished it from other volatile and violent places. The U.S. was exceptional and good because of its claimed immunity from extremism and large-scale social upheaval. This championing of American moderation drew upon claims circulating since the Russian Revolution that the U.S. was unique in the fact that it wasn't susceptible to Marxist ideology or socialist revolt because of its unparalleled economic (i.e., capitalist) and political (i.e., liberal democratic) institutions that ensured its moderateness, morality, and stability.[16]

Sociologist and media scholar Todd Gitlin showed how this reverence for moderateness during the Cold War was turned inwards and manipulated as a political strategy used by President Richard Nixon and later as a discursive strategy by journalists to delineate good from bad protesters in coverage of the anti-Vietnam War and Civil Rights demonstrations.[17] The antiwar protests and radical politics within the U.S. during the 1960s/1970s threatened to dampen the shining image of a moderate and stable nation that was used to justify U.S. interference and centrality in global economic and political affairs. Nixon, according to Gitlin, therefore tried to extinguish these progressive movements by demarcating "militants" from "moderates" and criminalizing the former.[18] In other words, Nixon drew upon the myth of American exceptionalism to conjure the image of unholy, anti-American, and militant Others infiltrating demonstrations and leftist political circles to the detriment of the nation itself.[19] These militant *Others* were demonized as unpatriotic extremists in contrast with the supposedly patriotic and moderate *Americans* who were celebrated as good, rational, and right.

Gitlin made the critical observation that this "official narrative" coming from the Oval Office soon began to shape media accounts of the protests—despite what was actually happening on the ground.[20] Gitlin explained how the framing of "moderation" as patriotic and good and "militancy" as unpatriotic and bad was deliberate and strategic.[21] Gitlin further discussed how "by accenting the difference between legitimate and illegitimate movements, by elevating the former and disparaging and/or withdrawing attention from the latter, [the media] could work to restabilize American politics" around a new "moderate" consensus.[22] To this end, Gitlin noted that through this construction of the binary of militant versus moderate, "the subtleties of situations and processes [went] under" in news reports.[23]

Moreover, with the institutionalization of the McCarthy-era House Un-American Activities Committee (renamed the House Committee on Internal Security in 1969), this Othering had very real, material consequences for individuals who were cast as militant and therefore socialist and thus un/anti-American, morally bad, and criminal. It is through this paradigm that Black activists were especially disparaged both then and now. Gitlin observed how "the moderate-militant split became a standard component of reporting about the black movement [in the 1960s/70s], especially after the assassination of Martin Luther King and the riots [that followed]."[24] Racist undercurrents repeatedly steer media representations of Black demonstrators—from the Civil Rights movement in the twentieth century to the Black Lives Matter movement in the twenty-first—and cast protesters who are Black as militant and violent and therefore outside of the limits of American moderation and morality.[25] Black people are repeatedly cast as the default militant Other within this binary and subjected to invasive surveillance[26] and harsh policing tactics because of it.[27]

Constructing and Fearing Climate Justice "Warriors"

News coverage of the Indigenous-led #NoDAPL protests at Standing Rock in 2016 similarly echoed this militant/moderate binary forged along racial lines. During the Standing Rock demonstrations that were in opposition to the construction of the Dakota Access Pipeline (DAPL), journalists writing for prominent national news outlets across the ideological spectrum operationalized the stereotype of the "violent Indian" in North Dakota as distinct from the "peaceful" (and white) climate protesters who were part of more "moderate" climate demonstrations elsewhere in the U.S.[28] Cast as criminal and militant across media coverage, a large number of protesters at Standing Rock—many of whom were young Indigenous women—were subjected to violent policing and arrested in large numbers.[29] Moreover, many of those who were arrested were dehumanized through humiliating strip searches and charged with acts of terrorism.[30]

Stemming out of longstanding racist stereotypes, the journalistic transformation of social and climate justice *activists* into social and climate justice *warriors* is pronounced in news coverage of protests and indicative of the predominance of white journalists in American newsrooms.[31] The stereotype of a young, violent, climate justice warrior of color is noticeably leveraged by journalists writing for the national press in patterned ways via the central image of a militant Other who is infiltrating a more moderate (i.e., whiter and older) climate movement and nation writ large. These media representations repeatedly draw upon gendered and generational modes of Othering in addition to racist tropes to paint a portrait of a menacing and threatening enemy. Young women of color who are active in the climate movement are especially singled out and described in threatening terms across news reports. This Othering can be seen in the extensive negative press coverage of Rep. Alexandria Ocasio-Cortez (D-NY), for instance, across both centrist and conservative media ranging from *The New York Times* to *The Wall Street Journal*, among other major national news outlets.[32]

Notably, Ocasio-Cortez cites her participation in the #NoDAPL movement at Standing Rock as a primary inspiration that propelled her to run for office.[33] It also motivated her championing of the Green New Deal (GND).[34] At Standing Rock, Ocasio-Cortez witnessed first-hand how intrinsically linked colonial and capitalist systems of extraction are and how both lie at the crux of climate change.[35] Moreover, she saw how alternatives to these systems are not only required to address the interconnected harms of climate change and social injustices but are also desired by many young people.[36]

Tellingly, in a reactionary-show-of-force against the popular #NoDAPL movement and the young progressives who were a part of it, like the soon-to-be Congresswoman Ocasio-Cortez, one of the first moves Trump made after officially taking office in January 2017 was to sign an executive order approving the construction of the Dakota Access Pipeline.[37] According to Trump, this executive order was necessary for national stability and progress by putting the "radical leftists" and "anti-American" militants at Standing Rock in their place, behind bars and out of politics. Following the #NoDAPL protests, nonviolent demonstrators continue to be criminalized and charged through the brutal enforcement of anti-terrorism, critical infrastructure, and other laws that protect pipelines and economic profit over people.[38] The #NoDAPL movement and its harsh suppression, however, ignited immense solidarity and support across a growing contingent of progressive young Americans.[39] As opposed to dissipating, this intersectional coalition rallied around a very different vision for what the U.S. *could* be that starkly contrasted with Trump's America. It is here where the GND became a key locus for progressive organizing during Trump's first presidency and after.[40]

The GND is animated by the idea of a "just transition" away from fossil fuels and an exclusionary system of politics towards renewable energy and more robustly democratic decision-making processes.[41] Crucially, what makes this transition "just" is the explicit centering of typically marginalized groups such as working class oil and gas laborers, Indigenous people, and low-income communities of color in the development, design, and implementation of the GND from the very start. This concept of a just transition had an overwhelming level of public support in 2018, but then a quick and surprising drop among both conservatives and centrists following extensive negative media coverage of the GND beginning in early 2019, soon after Ocasio-Cortez took office.[42] Across the legacy press, the GND was reported on as "the most preposterous thing" (in Trump's words) and an out-of-step "green dream" (in former Speaker of the House Nancy Pelosi's words) proposed by a threatening cohort of "Millennial Others" first radicalized at Occupy Wall Street in 2011, Black Lives Matter in 2014, Standing Rock in 2016, and now by the so-called young, "socialist extremist" Ocasio-Cortez in 2019.[43]

Generational Othering has become a cornerstone of climate news and commentary in mainstream U.S. media.[44] Millennials are, for instance, referred to by *The Wall Street Journal* as a "band of ignorant brats" in an article titled "On Climate, the Kids are All Wrong."[45] Dumb, spoiled, and militant Millennial "brats" are described as blindly following their equally dumb, spoiled, and militant leader Ocasio-Cortez, who is called a "pied piper" by both the center-left *New York Times*[46] and the center-right *Wall Street Journal*.[47] This generation-bashing spans the ideological spectrum from centrists to conservatives and demonstrates the intense anxiety felt by older Americans at the prospect of losing their relevance amid progressive movements and shifting national identities. There is a clearly gendered element to these anxieties as well. Through misogynistic and ageist portrayals of emotional crowds of young *women* galvanized during the #MeToo movement in years prior, Ocasio-Cortez is represented as an alluring and dangerous siren further radicalizing "woke" leftist women in a continued crusade against all white men that is described as nothing short of national ruin.

Fear and loathing are repeatedly directed at young women who are reported on as being led astray by the "pied piper"/siren/populist demagogue, Ocasio-Cortez. *New York Magazine*—a center-left publication, for example, highlights Ocasio-Cortez's age, gender, and "emotional" supporters when describing her as "the 30-year-old freshman member of Congress from Queens and the Bronx" who is "the youngest woman elected to the House of Representatives in the body's 230-year history" with a passionate following of "fans" who leave "an explosion of affirmation cribbed onto thousands of Post-it notes, a neon-green-and-pastel-pink flower bursting outward" for their idol in Congress.[48] The author of the *New York Magazine* article specifically describes these "fans" as fan*girls* by adding: "Go there at the right time, Hill aides say, and you can see groups of people, usually women, often young, weeping at the sight of [the Post-it note shrine]."[49] This emotional following of young women is underscored again in the *New York Magazine* piece when the journalist details how at Ocasio-Cortez's town halls:

> fans, who line up for hours for selfies, often present her with shrines they've made to her: paintings of her, T-shirts, family keepsakes. At the one in December, when they finally reached the front of the selfie line, some of her fans just started cheering: 'Yea! Yea! *Yeaaaaa!*'[50]

This culturally familiar and misogynistic trope of an irrational crowd of crazed young women is leveraged by journalists to denigrate supporters of Ocasio-Cortez and the GND.[51] Reference to the strong emotions and supposed irrationality of young women plays a consistent role in the representation of progressives more generally across prominent national news outlets in the U.S., especially since 2016 and even more so since 2020 and the pandemic years. These representations are often paired with a palpable sense of unease, wariness, and fear specifically directed at young women.

Notably, this fearmongering in centrist media often encompasses the comparison of Ocasio-Cortez and Trump, with both tarred as "populists" and "extremists" threatening a moderate, morally good, and stable U.S.[52] A columnist for *The New York Times*, for example, remarks in an article entitled "In Defense of the Gerontocracy":

> Sure, Alexandria Ocasio-Cortez's youth (she's 29) is crucial to the passion in her voice, the ambition of her ideas and her ability to rouse a contingent of young voters who too often go missing from politics. But it probably also contributes to her heedlessness—to how cavalier she can be with facts. (Not that we don't have a 72-year-old president who surpasses her in this regard).[53]

This frequent false equivalency drawn between the pro-democracy Ocasio-Cortez and the authoritarian-aspiring Trump in prominent centrist publications like *The New York Times* is striking, the consequences of which include the delegitimization of an entire generation of young progressives looking to build a more robustly democratic alternative to Trump's America. Ocasio-Cortez and her peers of different genders and backgrounds are in favor of a more just nation, whereas Trump and his constituents want higher walls and tighter borders. The categorization of "extremists" via an all-encompassing label that lumps together Trump and the Proud Boys with Ocasio-Cortez and the Sunrise Movement is not only incredibly misleading and inaccurate, but it also legitimizes the exclusion and suppression of young women—a historically marginalized group—from U.S. politics. Clearly, the liberal democratic barometer of "rationality"[54] has grave limitations if pro-democracy progressives are equated with white nationalists in the same category as irrational extremists.

Without more precision and nuance in reporting, young women's perspectives—and even their very presence in politics—are positioned as potentially catastrophic for an already rattled nation. In conservative media, this enemy formation is made explicit and frequently draws upon racist appeals to cast young women *of color* who support the GND as a particularly lethal threat.[55] In particular, the four young progressive Congresswomen of color known as "The Squad" in 2019, including Rep. Ocasio-Cortez, Rep. Rashida Tlaib (D-Mich.), Rep. Ilhan Omar (D-Minn.), and Rep. Ayanna Pressley (D-Mass.), were and continue to be recurrently cast as violent enemies in conservative news media. Below the large and bolded main headline of a feature article in the right-wing news magazine *The New American* entitled "The **SQUAD**," for instance, there is a subheadline that labels the "Four freshman representatives in Congress [...] led by Alexandria Ocasio-Cortez" as being "liberal to the point of being pro-communist and dangerous."[56] Next to this subheadline is a large photograph of the four Congresswomen with the caption: "'The Squad' is made up of four women of color who can find sexism or racism in anything, even in conversations about the environment."[57] Notably, the Congresswomen are cast as threatening (i.e., "dangerous") and anti-American (i.e., "pro-communist") in part due to their support for the GND.[58] The headline photo vividly depicts this image of threat. Each of the Congresswomen is shown devilishly grinning, with Ocasio-Cortez standing at the center of the group and speaking behind a podium in the Halls of Congress—almost as if she fiendishly took it over as an outside enemy rather than as a lawfully elected official.[59] A distinct hue is laid over the photo to make the cast unnaturally red and glowing as if there is a fire in the foreground. This manipulation of the image conjures a fire-and-brimstone atmosphere of apocalypse.

This representational prism of apocalypse in *The New American* is especially significant because images of civilizational collapse are often leveraged by the right to blame a designated group of "foreign Others" for this collapse.[60] Xenophobic and racist tropes are consistently brought to the fore in conservative tales of apocalypse.[61] Racialized Others feature centrally within apocalyptic narratives spun by the right, with Black and Brown people portrayed as conduits of evil and as unholy "outsiders" intent on destroying the U.S. and "Western civilization."[62]

Across conservative news media, unidimensional characters of doom are forged through sexist, racist, and ageist tropes where Ocasio-Cortez, Tlaib, Omar, Pressley, and their young female supporters are reduced to hysterical and militant Others ushering in chaos and, in turn, threatening the stability of the U.S.[63] This fearmongering reduces each Congresswoman to nothing more than a harbinger of apocalypse—or, in the words of Trump reprinted by *The New American*: "the Four Horsewomen of the Apocalypse."[64] Indeed, these young women's very presence in politics is portrayed as evidence of an impending civilizational collapse—quite literally in the right-wing press. Ocasio-Cortez, Tlaib, Omar, and Pressley are transformed from dynamic, multifaceted, and full-speaking subjects into unidimensional and villainous *apocalyptic subjects*.[65] They are represented as wholly bad and evil and as signaling the end times as foretold in biblical tales that are familiar to the strong evangelical base of the Republican Party. "The Squad's" very being, in other words, is inseparable from the apocalypse and the destruction of the nation.[66]

The profound risk here is that this form of Othering can lead to the violent suppression of those deemed outside of, and a threat to, the national body. Fascism looms on the horizon of sexist and racist stereotypes that repeatedly demarcate young progressive women of color as evil and dangerous enemies. Chillingly, *The New American* article closes with a foreboding call to action, stating: "we should all play a role in defeating these anti-American representatives"[67], evidently encouraging the forceful suppression of lawfully elected officials and their supporters. This call takes on added weight when Ocasio-Cortez and "The Squad" were named targets during the *actually* violent and threatening January 6, 2021 insurrection at the Capitol.

While not as hateful as coverage across right-wing news media, more centrist publications also report on Ocasio-Cortez, Tlaib, Omar, and Pressley, as well as their progressive supporters, as threatening and menacing.[68] In particular, this image of threat hinges on the prospect that these young women's presence in politics will damage the Democratic Party's electoral prospects and thus prolong the Trump-era and "total crisis"—a central claim across centrist news media during both the 2020 and 2024 election cycles.[69] Ahead of the 2020 election, for example, a columnist from the center-right *Wall Street Journal* stated that "the Democratic cause will suffer in 2020 if their party's radical approach to just about everything is exposed by Republicans making an effective case."[70] Another columnist, also writing for *The Wall Street Journal*, stated in an article titled "The Socialist That Could; Meet Alexandria Ocasio-Cortez, the secret Republican weapon for 2020," how Ocasio-Cortez is like "a freight train gaining speed by the day—and helping Republicans with every passing minute."[71] Writing for *The New York Times*, a different columnist warns how Ocasio-Cortez's "rise has stirred a backlash among some congressional Democrats, who are seeking to constrain her anti-establishment streak and fear her more radical ideas could tar the party as socialist" and thus will cost the Democrats victories in upcoming elections.[72] The overarching message is: *These young women must either fall in line with the right way of doing politics, or they must be suppressed and purged from the national body for the sake of our continued existence and the stability of the nation.*

The War on Warming

The political consequence of this widespread Othering of young progressives in U.S. news media is the delegitimization and, in some cases, criminalization of those deemed a threat to "our" national community. This criminalization of young progressives is not new and was common following WWII when the Cold War saw a spike in U.S. surveillance, red-scare fearmongering, and state violence against Civil Rights activists, student organizers, and antiwar protesters.[73] This policing of "subversives"[74] melded together into a mass of intersecting discursive and material "technologies of power"[75] that are now extremely difficult to break apart. The brutal police force used against Black activists and young progressives, who were blamed by the White House, corporate heads, and national news media for causing social and economic strife during the Cold War, ushered in an ongoing period of state violence against members of the "New Left" who were criminalized for their politics.[76] This criminalization continues today against the "new" New Left and social and climate justice "warriors."

It is not inconsequential that the post-WWII era was also the time period when journalists began to view the news media as an essential tool for securing a precarious postwar world on behalf of Western liberal democracies.[77] So-called militants at home were reported on negatively because they threatened an image of U.S. stability, moderateness, and perfection that Washington, U.S. capitalists, and by extension the U.S. press wished to showcase to the world as a model society. If not disparaged, then entire social movements were either erased from coverage altogether or activists' perspectives were excluded from reports because their speech acts were deemed "too extreme" and an affront to the airbrushed image of the nation that the media wished to foster and portray across borders.[78] The press during the postwar period, therefore, played an extremely consequential role in demarcating what and who were in the "best interest" of the nation and, conversely, what and who were not. In the eyes of traditional journalists in the U.S., this "quality information"[79] was absolutely critical for safeguarding both national and global prosperity, security, and stability.

Today, U.S. journalists are seeking to reestablish their authority and relevance on par with this imagined postwar "golden age."[80] Markedly, climate reporting has become a key locus where this quest for relevance is occurring. Traditional journalists—especially since the "total crisis" that is understood to have begun in 2016 with Trump's election and intensified in 2020 with the pandemic—are flexing their moralizing muscles in distinct ways. For instance, through the militant/moderate binary, reporters are clearly demarcating a national self as distinct from a threatening Other/enemy in coverage of climate politics. Notably, this demarcation is done through both enemy formation and fearmongering, as well as through the discursive transformation of climate change into a "total war" amid a more totalizing crisis.

This discursive transformation of climate change into an all-out war is distinct and draws a clear boundary between an "us" versus "them." Notably, romanticized tales of U.S.-led WWII and Cold War victories are specifically drawn upon by journalists reporting on climate change. In conservative media, the battle of good versus evil is made explicit through biblical references, patriotic appeals, and anti-communist Cold War allusions, leading to an ultimate message of climate denial. Centrist news media also often leverage the militant Other stereotype and the myth of American exceptionalism via references to the Cold War and WWII, but to advance planetary-scale "green capitalist" economic schemes and "innovative" technologies developed by historically privileged figures as the "solution" to climate change. It is here where the transformation of climate change into a "total war" amid "total crisis" is used to advance calls for the U.S. to reclaim its imagined twentieth-century global leadership position to rescue the nation and world from an otherwise apocalyptic demise via "tried and true" methods from the U.S.'s "glorious" past.

It is especially significant that climate change is represented as not just *any* war but as analogous to WWII specifically. According to collective memories shared by traditional journalists in the U.S., the WWII/early postwar period is remembered as the heyday for both U.S. journalism and the nation itself.[81] If climate change is equivalent to WWII, so the logic goes, then this "total war" unequivocally calls for U.S. leadership to once again usher in a new age of global stability to "save" Western civilization and the entire world. This call for U.S. leadership likewise bolsters traditional journalists' own claims of relevancy. If climate change is an all-encompassing and all-out war, then reporters are once again needed to witness and report from the frontlines back to an imagined national community. Journalistic authority is sedimented during wartime. To this end, reporting on climate change as a "total war" akin to WWII demands a greater degree of conformity and patriotism than "normal." The discursive transformation of climate change into a "total war" analogous to WWII thus carves out space for both the U.S. and U.S. news media to reestablish their central positions as an uncontested arbiter of what is good, true, and right during an "unprecedented" time of chaos, conflict, and disarray.

It is here where a palpable longing for an "imagined community"[82] of Americans united as "one nation under God" is evident in more centrist and center-left U.S. climate reporting. Images of Rosie the Riveter, for instance, are paired with headlines calling to "MOBILIZE TO DEFEAT CLIMATE CHANGE" and to **"WIN THE WAR ON WARMING"**[83] in the left-leaning magazine *The New Republic* in fall 2016 (see Figure 1.1). The January/February 2020 cover of the center-left *Mother Jones* similarly extends this WWII reference through an image of what appears to be a crumpled piece of paper with the declaration: **"WARMING IS OVER!"** alluding to the flyers announcing that the "WAR IS OVER!" strewn across American cities following the end of WWII (see Figure 1.2). Underneath this main headline on the cover of *Mother Jones* is written in smaller text: "**IF WE PAY FOR IT**" and "**Only massive climate R&D can save us now.**"[84]

Figure 1.1 Cover of *The New Republic*. © [September 2016].
Courtesy of The New Republic. All rights reserved. Used under license. https://newrepublic.com/

These historical references reactivate visions of past American glory and reflect a longing for a time when U.S. centrality and global leadership were understood as more solid and more celebrated at home and abroad.

These patriotic tropes hearken back to a period when the national community was imagined as much more united and stable. With the corruption, polarization, and incivility of the Trump presidency, the idea of

Figure 1.2 Cover of *Mother Jones*. © [January/February 2020].
Courtesy of Mother Jones.

an exceptional U.S. was shaken to the core. It is within this fray of a rattled sense of self that post-2016 media accounts at more center-left and centrist (i.e., liberal) news outlets reflect a desperate search for American identity—and journalistic relevancy—through the nostalgic reactivation of collective memories of when the U.S. was more widely recognized and respected as an exceptional nation capable of leading the world out of darkness and into a "new world" of freedom, prosperity, and progress through America's exceptional liberal democratic political system, capitalist economic strategies, and advanced technological developments (i.e., "massive R&D").

Notably, this call back to an imagined American golden age in climate reporting at centrist and center-left publications reveals a deep desire for the recentering of liberal institutions—including the news media—under attack by Trump and his supporters. These institutions and the liberal democratic norms they perpetuate are presumed essential not only for U.S. stability but also for global and climate stability. Former president Joe Biden's appointed National Security Advisor Jake Sullivan, for example, demonstrates this commitment to the resurrection of embattled liberal democratic institutions in a special issue of *The Atlantic* through nostalgic references to postwar American glory days, claiming how "for centuries, European states waged war with grim regularity. The fact that the major powers have not returned to war with one another since 1945 is a remarkable achievement of American statecraft."[85] Significantly, this "achievement" of world stabilization is brought forward by Sullivan to specifically stoke rallying cries for what he calls "a new American exceptionalism" on par with the patriotism and prowess of WWII-era America.[86] Sullivan contends that this *new* American exceptionalism is absolutely essential to successfully combat the lethal threats of illiberalism and climate change.

The election of President Biden and the defeat of Trump in 2020 came to be represented by many journalists across the centrist national press and moderates of the Democratic Party as a profound opportunity for the reclamation and fortification of national pride and power akin to 1945. Sullivan states how:

> reclaiming America's place in the world will be an extraordinary challenge. For decades, the country neglected needed updates to the international system. Now Donald Trump is blowing that system up. The saying goes that when a natural disaster hits, "build back better." The same applies to foreign policy. Not since 1945 has the U.S. had the chance to go back to basics and decide which parts to keep, which to scrap, and, above all, which to reinvent. After Trump, it can do just that.[87]

This reclamation/reinvention requires the U.S. to once again demonstrate that it is "an unusual power"[88] through an "update[ed] purpose in a changing world."[89] And it is here where American leadership on climate change is positioned by both traditional journalists and political moderates like Sullivan as *the* area where this necessary "update" could occur but through very old methods.

This desire for a reclaimed position of U.S. global centrality through a "new" American exceptionalism forged via American climate leadership is imagined by moderates and interpreted by journalists writing for the centrist national press through the very same exclusionary confines of morality, moderateness, and modernization that problematically guided American wartime and postwar economic recovery schemes eight decades ago. It is significant to note that this perceived "opportunity" to reassert the singularity and centrality of the U.S. via a new—or perhaps more aptly, *re*newed—American exceptionalism is also described by liberal moderates and traditional journalists as fragile and at great risk of slipping away if the "wrong" responses to climate change are enacted. Responses to climate change are therefore marked as either right or wrong in national news stories that appear in centrist publications based on whether or not they are determined to be in or out of line with liberal democratic norms and an "exceptional" American way of life, represented as only momentarily upended by Trump.

The November 16, 2020, "New Economy" issue of *Bloomberg Businessweek* with the headline "**LET'S NOT BLOW THIS**: An opportunity to address the world's biggest challenges" bolded on the cover, for instance, portrays climate change as an opportunity through which the U.S. can both save face and save capitalism following years of disarray through the level-headed management of global economic institutions and trade agreements.[90] Using the language of competition, the May/June 2017 special climate change issue of *Foreign Policy* also urges economic leaders in the U.S. to "lean in to climate change" in order "to maintain an edge against China."[91] Similarly, a feature article in the special climate issue of *Foreign Affairs* published in May/June 2020 makes "The Strategic Case for U.S. Climate Leadership" and details "How Americans Can Win With a Pro-Market Solution."[92] Capitalism is here equated with an American way of life and as *the* solution to "win" on climate change by "beating" both China and Russia. *The New York Times Magazine* makes a similar case in its December 20, 2020 cover story by lamenting that both China and Russia currently have the edge and are "winning" on climate change, thereby threatening a U.S.-led, market-based response that is assumed by the reporters to be absolutely and unquestionably essential.[93]

Across these and other prominent centrist publications in the U.S., climate change is presented as a battle for power between enemy nation-states in a war of capitalism versus communism. This reactivation of Cold War memories, along with references to WWII, presents a hodgepodge of historical allusions and demonstrates the inconsistency of collective memory work in journalism. This inconsistency reveals how images and icons from the past are reactivated by journalists in certain ways for specific purposes and particular ends. Journalism scholar Barbie Zelizer clarifies how "collective-memory studies presume multiple, often conflicting accounts of the past" and therefore dissipate "the notion that one memory at one place and one time retains authority over all the others."[94] More important than determining the most prominent historical allusion or memory that is reactivated to describe the present, the question of *why* "one construction has more staying power than its rivals" is pivotal for analysis.[95] And it is through the cracks and fissures of these allusions that the reactivation of the myth of American exceptionalism appears as the keystone for climate journalism today.

By marking out clear and familiar (i.e., communist/tyrannical) enemies, references to the physical and ideological struggles during and following WWII reaffirm the promise of Manifest Destiny and the exceptionalism of American values and morality. Via claims of what is good or bad for the nation, hyper-capitalistic solutions are positioned by journalists as the *only* way to win the war on warming, while all other proposals for change are denigrated as anti-American, morally wrong, and a threat to national, global, and planetary stability.

The Ghost of Bretton Woods

These WWII and Cold War allusions and subsequent framing of a post-Trump era as a moment of great—but fragile—opportunity where the U.S. can "win the war on warming" were leveraged by the International Monetary Fund's (IMF) Managing Director, Kristalina Georgieva, in the year 2020 to describe the present as a "new Bretton Woods 'moment.'"[96] This reference to Bretton Woods bolstered the call for a return to U.S. hegemony via U.S.-led global financial institutions equivalent to the ones established during and immediately following WWII. This reference to the need for a new Bretton Woods System at the end of Trump's first presidency was widespread in centrist outlets from *The New York Times* to *TIME Magazine* to *Foreign Affairs* to *Bloomberg Businessweek* and more. For instance, in the Summer

2019 special issue on climate change, *Foreign Policy* claims that "central banks" and more responsible "global finance" could "save the planet."[97] Furthermore, in the previously referenced November 16, 2020, "New Economy" issue of *Bloomberg Businessweek*, Michael Bloomberg in an Opinion piece eagerly writes:

> A global standard for climate [financial] reporting is critical, but it will not happen without U.S. leadership. Just as Franklin Roosevelt gathered financial representatives from the allied powers at Bretton Woods, New Hampshire, to agree upon a set of monetary principles which have been the foundation for unprecedented global growth, we need a President Biden to convene a similar group for the purpose of adopting a set of climate-disclosure standards. If Biden seizes the opportunity, it may prove to be one of the most important turning points in the global fight against climate change.[98]

Likewise, *TIME* reports how "a surprising momentum has emerged" among world leaders for "a wholesale reform of the Bretton Woods institutions—the World Bank and IMF—with climate change in mind."[99] In this reactivation of the promise of a "reformed" Bretton Woods, there is a palpable nostalgia and longing for a time when the U.S. was celebrated as the great stabilizer/moderator of global affairs. This nostalgia once more demonstrates a yearning for an imagined "golden age" when the U.S. was understood as the provider and purveyor of superior economic policies and financial schemes, as well as when national journalists were regarded as reliable sources of "quality information"[100] and celebrated as essential in the fight for global stability, security, and truth.

This reanimation of WWII/postwar narratives and a celebration of U.S.-led global financial institutions and trade regimes across climate news stories in some of the most widely read national news magazines and newspapers that claim to be independent[101] and apolitical is highly problematic. The Bretton Woods System was by no means flawless and has been heavily critiqued by political economists and critical scholars as an exploitative scheme that weakened democracies and, notably, propelled climate change.[102] Along with the Marshall Plan, the Bretton Woods System was designed with the goal of safeguarding investments and global trade by fostering a secure and open flow of capital into anti-communist enterprise and the recovery/redevelopment of war-torn infrastructure abroad.[103] These trade and currency schemes were, of course, in line with U.S. economic interests. The IMF and General Agreement on Tariffs and Trade set stipulations and controls on exchange and trade that in name were meant to safeguard against risky investments, but in actuality were used to isolate communist nations and discourage postwar Europe and postcolonial Global South nations from joining the Soviet bloc after WWII amid growing Cold War tensions.[104] In what the historian Charles S. Maier termed the "politics of productivity," American private investors and bankers "sought to isolate Communist parties and labor unions as adversaries of their priorities of production [...] and to transform political issues into problems of output, to adjourn class conflict for a consensus on growth" through global economic institutions and a highly regulated sense of moderateness and morality—as determined by "American values."[105] The historian Greg Grandin further explains how in "the years after World War II, the 'frontier' became a central metaphor to capture a vision of a new kind of world order."[106] Via the myth of Manifest Destiny and the image of perpetual westward expansion, the U.S. "made a credible claim to be a different sort of global power, presiding over a world economy premised on endless growth."[107] In other words, the U.S. hoped to sustain an economic edge in the postwar market via the "force and fabulation"[108] of capitalist enterprise and the idea of endless economic growth as a panacea for war, crises, and conflicts of all kinds. This came, however, at the expense of *actual* democratic politics and the climate—ironically ushering in a destabilizing force of great consequence.

What is so insidious about calls for a "new"—or *r*enewed—American exceptionalism and the nostalgic desire for the nation's post-WWII global economic centrality is the fact that these politics of productivity caused so much suffering and strife, including the rapid proliferation of climate change. Yet despite this, a new Bretton Woods System for the climate is celebrated as the "right" way forward today. Because of the lack of specificity and context in climate journalism, via universalizing and moralizing narratives and a hodgepodge of historical allusions, simple binaries of good and bad have taken root and bar accountability for particular harms and specific grievances that remain unresolved. It is within this paradigm that only certain responses to climate change are elevated as right, and all others are demonized as wrong based on a tenuous calculation of whether or not certain climate actions are deemed a threat or opportunity for regaining the U.S.'s global standing akin to its romanticized twentieth-century position. Reforming and revitalizing the Bretton Woods System—a familiar scheme with familiar mechanisms—is thus portrayed as a safe route back to less extreme and more orderly times when the U.S. was imagined as the moderate and moral example for the world. This reanimation of Bretton Woods is done, however, without a critical reckoning with what this global economic system ultimately led to. Within a simplistic binary of right and wrong, there is little room for context and nuance.

Enemies of the Nation-State

Climate justice activists who push for a critical reckoning with U.S.-centric and market-based responses to climate change are, for instance, reported on by traditional journalists as misguided, wrong, and a threat to the nation, world order, and planet. This can be seen with the markedly different news coverage of the Inflation Reduction Act (IRA) versus the GND by the centrist press. In divergence from the GND's bottom-up and economically transformative approach, the IRA is a top-down and investment-based industrial policy. The IRA promises federal money to help incentivize green energy and green infrastructure projects and has been heralded by Democratic Party members and centrist media outlets as the most important climate bill to date. *The New York Times*[109] and *Washington Post*[110], for example, consistently preface the IRA as a "historic" bill and report on it as the ultimate achievement following decades of climate activism. The IRA is celebrated as *the* definitive solution to address both climate change and the social unease of the 2010s. Tellingly, the IRA is reported on as a superior policy that can guide the U.S. and other allied nations out of the dark present and into a bright and prosperous tomorrow. Described as part of "a new Washington Consensus," Sullivan imagines the IRA as a U.S.-developed economic model that can restabilize the domestic market and protect U.S. industry by setting the terms and conditions for a global green energy transition.[111] Elsewhere, centrist media amplify these talking points and positively report on the IRA as a part of a new "Clean Energy Marshall Plan" with a special feature in *Foreign Affairs*, for example, asserting "How the Fight Against Climate Change Can Renew American Leadership."[112] The IRA, in other words, is presented as *the* superior model for how other nations' economies *should* transition to green energy in the "right" way as determined by the U.S. Notably, this "right" way also happens to advantage U.S. trade while fortifying American centrality in the global market system as it weakens "enemy-nations" like China.

In sharp contrast with news coverage of the GND as a "green dream" conjured by militant Millennial Others[113], the IRA is reported on as a practical climate policy developed by older, more moderate, and enlightened politicians. When the IRA was passed in August 2022, for example, *The New York Times* ran two opposing headlines in their August 13, 2022, issue that entrenched this militant versus moderate binary. The first headline states: "For Biden, a Legislative Triumph and a Bet on America's Future."[114] Below this headline is a photo of older, suit-clad men and women—the majority of whom are white—standing around a gray-haired Biden on the White House's front lawn signing the IRA into force. This headline and image cast the IRA as a triumphant policy for a bright American future developed by older, more established, and moderate policy-makers. In contrast, the second headline reads: "Climate Bill Just a Start, Wary Youth Activists Say."[115] Below this headline are three photos that picture young women of color with climate justice protest signs, a young woman of color speaking at a protest demonstration, and a young man speaking at a rally. The overall message from this headline and these photos is that young militants—who are primarily young women of color—are impeding this clear path to a brighter American future. *The New York Times* makes this moderate versus militant binary explicit by declaring: "As Historic Climate Bill Heads to Biden's Desk, Young Activists Demand More."[116] Overly demanding and radicalized young climate justice activists are here—as elsewhere—portrayed as out of step and out of line. Young activists, according to *The New York Times*, are obstructing the "historic" IRA from becoming the national and global "triumph" it is otherwise destined to be.

Evident in this reporting on the IRA is the advancement of Sullivan's vision of a new Washington Consensus and a new Bretton Woods System. U.S.-led global financial institutions, trade regimes, and economic policies on par with those of the WWII and postwar time period are elevated as the "right" way forward to "win the war on warming" and to reclaim the nation's central position in the world. The IRA—a top-down and investment-based industrial policy—is reported on as the golden ticket that will stabilize the planet, the nation, and the international arena. In this way, the U.S. is cast as the much-needed source of light for a world in darkness. In stark contrast, the GND and young climate justice activists who are critical of the IRA for not going far enough are repeatedly reported on as fools, misguided, and threatening to this "historic" victory that, according to its proponents, promises a surefire route *back* to national, global, and planetary stability.

Communication scholars often refer to journalism as an "interpretive community"[117] through which journalists collectively interpret current affairs through a shared set of historical references and criteria that are drawn upon to determine what is or is not an "appropriate" or "correct" way of reporting on (i.e., interpreting) unfolding events. In the case of the passage of the IRA, there were clear boundaries drawn around "correct" media interpretations that were and still are, evidently, strictly policed and maintained. As an illustrative example, the popular climate justice newsletter and podcast titled *Hot Take*, produced by two women of color, Mary Annaïse Heglar and Amy Westervelt, were—they allege—canceled by their producers because they dared to cross this line set around an "appropriate" and "correct" interpretation of the IRA. In Heglar and Westervelt's words:

> We acknowledged that [the IRA] was the largest climate bill ever passed, but also that it came with some serious problems: it doubled down on the idea of "sacrifice zones"—areas that are allowed to be polluted because people who are less valued live there—for a start, and it carved out so many loopholes for the fossil fuel industry that it was hard to see how it would actually deliver on the best-case scenario that boosters of the bill were promising. We didn't pan it entirely, but we were real about it. A few days later, the network's heads took to their own shows to declare that anyone who was being critical of the bill was an idiot who didn't know what they were talking about and should be ignored. Shots fired?[118]

Here and elsewhere, climate justice perspectives and critiques of the IRA have been interpreted as threatening and have been met with fervent opposition by "moderates." In turn, there is the explicit call, among media producers and politicians alike, to exclude young progressives from official climate decision-making processes. Again, what is so striking here is that this exclusion is evident in centrist media like *The New York Times* and *The Washington Post*, and not just in overtly right-wing media like *Fox News*.

Elite perspectives and powerful and well-resourced figures are privileged in news reports produced by centrist national newspapers like *The New York Times*—a trend seen in general across this eminent newspaper's recent reporting history.[119] The impact of this is the Othering and delegitimization of critical perspectives held by progressives that question the IRA. As an interpretive community, journalists writing for well-regarded national publications of record like *The New York Times* and *The Washington Post* clearly report on the IRA as unquestionably good and right. In turn, the GND and climate justice activists who argue that the IRA overlooks the pressing concerns of Indigenous people and historically marginalized groups, who will bear the brunt of increased mining and extraction for EVs and batteries[120], are either totally excluded from coverage or cast as bad and wrong. Climate justice activists who critique the IRA are ultimately painted as uncivil obstructionists impeding the "right" response to climate change that would otherwise stabilize the nation, global commons, and planet via exceptional and "sensible" economic policies designed by just a few visionary sages from an exceptional nation.

The myth of American exceptionalism thus spans across centrist and conservative news media, as does the desire for an imagined postwar golden age when the nation was believed to have been at its peak. The problem with this nostalgic reference back to this pre-Civil Rights era is that it naturalizes the centrality of an educated, white, male subject position as the default "good" citizen. "The masses"—understood in gendered, aged, and racialized terms—in turn, are met with wary caution at best and outright animosity at worst. Reporters and commentators from *The New York Times* to *The Wall Street Journal* express fear that a "band of ignorant brats"[121] could be led astray by charismatic militants like Rep. Ocasio-Cortez to the nation's peril. Rational, mature, and enlightened *male, white*, and *moderate* visionary sages, therefore, are required to manage and eliminate this grave threat to an exceptional America. It is no coincidence that the postwar time period is romanticized by figures like Jake Sullivan. This was an era when both the nation and moderate men like him retained a greater degree of unquestioned power. It is also no coincidence that climate change is directly equated with WWII by moderate men too. If climate change is likened to total war, then the suppression of dissenting opinion among the "new" New Left is legitimized as required for the sake of the nation, global commons, and planet. Wartime demands a level of conformity. Within this paradigm of "the war on warming", moderate figures are empowered to condemn and police progressive climate justice activists who disrupt this conformity.

This condemnation, however, takes on dangerous implications when used by white nationalists who seek to literally purge young progressives from the nation through violence and force. Among the MAGA right, this fearmongering of social and climate justice warriors moves from the criminalization to the dehumanization of those deemed Other, and centrist media are fanning as opposed to fighting these antidemocratic flames. Through the specter of apocalypse and the narrative prism of a nation on the brink of collapse, news media from the center to the right are contributing to the discursive transformation of young female climate justice activists of color into climate justice "warriors" who need to be policed, suppressed, and purged from the national body. In this way, prominent publications of record from *The New York Times* to *The Wall Street Journal* are fortifying the "techniques and tactics"[122] of apocalyptic authoritarianism as opposed to contending with and combating the threats of both climate change and a reactionary mode of antidemocratic politics.

Conclusion

Despite the visibility and influence of climate justice activists and progressive movements such as the campaign for a GND, as well as the proximity and pace of environmental threats wrought by a changing climate, traditional journalists are obscuring, distancing, and even erasing the different consequences, localized experiences, grassroots movements, and popular alternative visions for how to justly respond to climate change. This disconnect between journalistic coverage and a clearly visible and popular climate justice movement is striking. Even more striking is the state and police force used against young progressive climate justice activists, who are cast as militants and enemies of the nation-state.

Nationalism is a rigid conceptual container and extremely difficult to break—especially during moments of perceived social change. As discussed in this chapter, the desire for a *re*newed American exceptionalism limits the ways in which climate change is represented and interpreted by U.S. journalists through, in part, strong appeals to American morality and moderateness via the myth of American exceptionalism. Analysis of this rigidity and the discursive construction of clear-cut binaries reveals a distinct pattern in reporting, with responses to climate change represented by traditional journalists as either in or out of line with the "inevitable" Manifest Destiny of the U.S. In turn, climate change is decontextualized through grand narratives of History and Humanity, while exclusionary and exploitative systems of economy and governance are expanded and reactionary movements gain deeper traction. The next chapter delineates how these antidemocratic systems are not only left uninvestigated and naturalized in climate reporting but are also extended via the totalizing lens of the planetary scale.

2
American Earth: Planetary Optics of Control

"Within our rich history, we can find the wisdom and the spirit we need to disenthrall ourselves and fulfill what is perhaps our ultimate manifest destiny: to save our earth."[1] These are the musings of the former U.S. vice president and climate change icon Al Gore in the book *American Earth* edited by the renowned American climate journalist Bill McKibben.[2] This book was published two years after the film release of Gore's blockbuster documentary *An Inconvenient Truth* (2006), which ignited the mainstream climate movement. This film is often said to be the source of common tropes that now characterize climate communication more generally: the stranded polar bear on a lonely iceberg, melting glaciers, global climate models (GCMs), graphs depicting rising levels of global greenhouse gases, and embers of fire in an apocalyptic landscape of destruction. Less often attended to, however, are the cultural roots of these tropes that, for instance, position Al Gore as both a spokesperson for the (neo)liberal climate movement and "green finance" as well as an early champion of Silicon Valley and its libertarian embrace of "green tech." This chapter excavates these roots and exposes how the myth of Manifest Destiny is leveraged to legitimize both hyper-capitalistic (neo)liberal and techno-utopian libertarian visions for how to "save the Earth."

Used initially to profess the "goodness" of westward expansion during the nineteenth century and then to justify capitalist and military expansion on a global scale during and after the Cold War,[3] America's Manifest Destiny is today advanced to justify planetary-scale market and tech "fixes" as "God's will." The myth of Manifest Destiny adopts and transforms God's command to "be fruitful and multiply and fill the earth and subdue it and have dominion over the fish of the sea and over the birds of the heavens and over every living thing that moves on the earth."[4] Since the early years of the nation, this myth has been leveraged to equate the will of privileged American men with the will of God. Indeed, the notion of an *American* Earth nominally and materially claims ownership of the planet by a nation of self-proclaimed masters. This chapter historically traces the logics and optics of Earthly containment from the *Whole Earth Catalog* to Google Earth to geoengineering to flesh out the dynamics of power advanced by this planetary point of view.

Ultimately, this chapter shows how the planetary scale renders the present abstract to such a degree that it obscures the on-the-ground realities and structural causes of climate change in U.S. news stories. This obfuscation is buttressed by the imperial imaginary of Manifest Destiny and the combined fantasies of perpetual progress via endless economic growth and patriarchal dominion that together advance a singular vision of an American Earth managed by just a few very smart men. This planetary perspective comes at the expense of more robustly democratic, transnationally cooperative, and justice-oriented alternatives.

From the Whole Earth to Google Earth

The Blue Marble photographic image of Earth taken on December 7, 1972 from a distance of approximately 45,000 kilometers above the planet's surface by the Apollo 17 spacecraft was the first photograph of the whole Earth taken by a person (as opposed to a composite from satellite images) and seen by the U.S. public.[5] The image of a lone sphere floating in a vast expanse of darkness showcased the vulnerability and precarity of the planet. At the height of nuclear anxieties and Cold War tensions, prevailing existential fears primed a U.S. audience to interpret *The Blue Marble* image through the lens of global risk.[6] Calls to "save the Earth" soon followed.[7] This image is one of the most reproduced images to date and remains an enduring icon of the global environmental movement.[8] It is within this context that two resonant discourse strands—one negative and one positive—emerged and remain cornerstones of mainstream environmentalism and mainstream climate journalism in the U.S.: (1) Humans are capable of mass destruction on a planetary scale and (2) humans are capable of saving the Earth on a planetary scale.

Tellingly, the "Bible"[9] of the back-to-the-land movement of the 1960s/1970s known as the *Whole Earth Catalog* (see Figure 2.1) placed the image of the whole Earth on its cover[10] along with the following statement of purpose written on the first page by its publisher and founder, Stewart Brand: "We <u>are</u> as gods and might as well get used to it." *The Blue Marble* image—which

Figure 2.1 Cover of *Whole Earth Catalog*. [Fall 1968].
Courtesy of Stewart Brand.

Brand himself claims he initiated via letters he sent to Congress and buttons asking "why haven't we seen a photograph of the whole Earth yet?" that he sold at local Bay Area universities—was here leveraged to assert the "godly" powers of *men* and to carve out a position of authority for Brand and his mostly male readership.[11] After comparing himself to a god, Brand's statement of purpose for the *Whole Earth Catalog* continues: "a realm of intimate, personal power is developing—power of the individual to conduct his own education, find his own inspiration, shape his own environment, and share his adventure with whoever is interested." Clearly inspired by the figure of the American pioneer-man on the western frontier and the masculine trope of rugged individualism,[12] Brand's interpretation of his twentieth-century present was reflective of and also influential in entrenching the two aforementioned discourse strands but with a slight tweak: (1) *Very smart American men* are capable of mass destruction on a planetary scale and (2) *very smart American men* are capable of saving the Earth on a planetary scale. This centering of rugged individualism in a budding environmentalist and countercultural space in the U.S. had profound implications for how climate change came to be known and, in turn, for what responses came to be championed as "right" by "very smart American men."

Subtitled "access to tools," the *Whole Earth Catalog* was modeled after the L. L. Bean outdoorsman catalog as the ultimate guide for what to buy, read, do, and think as a liberated man of the New Age.[13] Imagined as a tastemaker and rugged western pioneer-man himself, Brand and the extensive middle-class male readership of his *Whole Earth Catalog* found a sense of power through the libertarian impulses of believing one simply needed "tools" and freedom from all of the tyrannical restrictions of modern society to use them in order to reach a higher level of human consciousness.[14] With the image of the whole Earth and the mantra of "access to tools," Brand essentially created a catalog of items that mostly white middle-class American men could peruse, acquire, and possess to reach his full potential and be a "god" like him, thus enjoying dominion over *his* whole Earth. The communication scholar Fred Turner describes the readership of the *Whole Earth Catalog* as "cowboy nomads" who possessed very specific characteristics: "masculine, entrepreneurial, well-educated, and white."[15] Moreover, Brand—according to Turner—marketed his *Catalog* to this particular readership as the "new elite" that "would celebrate systems theory and the power of technology to foster social change."[16] Consequentially, the "new elite"—through its embrace of technology over the complexities of politics—"would turn away from questions of gender, race and class, and toward a rhetoric of individual and small-group empowerment."[17]

It is perhaps no surprise then that Brand, a Stanford University grad and longtime resident of the South Bay, claims to have been primarily responsible for bridging the California counterculture of the 1960s/1970s with the tech start-up culture that followed.[18] While Brand's claims of influence may be overstated, the *Whole Earth Catalog's* libertarian and utopian slant did resonate with a burgeoning Silicon Valley. During his commencement address delivered to Stanford's graduating class of 2005, the cofounder of Apple Steve Jobs, for example, stated how the *Whole Earth Catalog* "was one of the Bibles of my generation."[19] He added that it "was sort of like Google in paperback form, 35 years before Google came along: It was idealistic, and overflowing with neat tools and great notions."[20] Google's inventory of digitized information accessible via its curated search engine is compared by Jobs here with the *Whole Earth Catalog's* self-presentation as a comprehensive reference guide with its dense catalog of "tools." As with the *Whole Earth Catalog*, the goal for Google was and remains open *access* to vast amounts of information. This accessibility is imagined as the key for unlocking the potential of industrious young American men (understood by the likes of Brand and Jobs as thwarted by the emasculating forces of modernity and the state's "over-regulation") who are on the frontiers of technology. This unfettered potential is understood as essential for "saving the Earth" from the irrationality and tyranny of the modern world as well as saving the nation itself à la Frederick Jackson Turner's "Frontier Thesis," which conveyed the need for the American frontier to energize the pioneer spirit that supposedly makes the U.S. and American *men* so exceptional.[21]

Critical scholar Betsy Hartmann describes this rugged individualism and reactivation of the pioneer-man figure in the counterculture movement of the 1960s/1970s and later in the start-up culture of the 1980s/1990s as a reaction to the loss of control felt by historically privileged and educated white men during an era of not just nuclear anxieties but also of women's liberation and Civil Rights.[22] Similarly, Anna Wiener, author of the exposé on the toxic masculinity of Silicon Valley's tech-bro culture of the 2010s, *Uncanny Valley*, points out how the *Whole Earth Catalog's* "pioneer rhetoric" and "disdain for government and social institutions" have clear lines running through today's Silicon Valley's techno-libertarianism.[23] This "disdain" for any constraints put on the "pioneering" work of men in tech is vividly demonstrated by the billionaire Elon Musk's outrage over federal and state regulations and any oversight of his companies. It also explains Musk's intense hatred of young progressives who question his anti-union stance, largely unchecked amassment of wealth, and dream of colonizing Mars. Musk bemoans the supposed tyranny of what he calls the "woke" left overrun by radical feminists and social and climate justice warriors. This hatred has pushed Musk to align with reactionary figures on the right like Trump who also blame progressives (and especially young progressive women) as the root of all social ills and the downfall of the nation.[24]

Visual studies scholar T. J. Demos underscores how Musk's and other tech-bros' particular techno-libertarian strain of toxic masculinity is fueled by the fetishization of global dominion encouraged by a whole Earth way of seeing.[25] The feverish consumption of *The Blue Marble* image on buttons, books, t-shirts, and posters in the twentieth century offered a sense of pleasure and power through the containment and consumption of the whole Earth in a photographic image. The *Whole Earth Catalog* extended this pleasure through a compiled book of "tools" that American men could read and attain to master *their* planet "as gods." Derived from the visual mastery of the whole Earth, the desire for total control was taken to a further extreme decades later with Google Earth's extensive compilation and containment of satellite images of the entire globe. Every corner of the globe is presumed capturable by Google Earth, according to its engineers, with everywhere on Earth freely *accessible* to men like them who desire to look. Nowhere and no one can escape the free and liberated gaze of the engineers of Google Earth and other planetary technologies. "Every living thing that moves on the earth"[26] is reduced to a mere object to be observed, contained, and managed by very smart American men "as gods."

Control of Earth and Containment of Earthlings

It is important to highlight that the visual "tools" of satellite technologies were developed in partnership with the U.S. government and military—as were the first computer and the internet, despite the rugged individualism/independent "start-up" fantasy that Silicon Valley's very smart men present to the world.[27] These global imaging technologies—originally developed to monitor and track military threats, including the nuclear arsenal of the U.S.S.R. during the Cold War—are also now used to survey, map, and monitor the threats of Earth's changing climate.[28] And despite Stewart Brand's claims that his letters to Congress and sale of buttons at Bay Area university campuses were responsible, *The Blue Marble* image taken by the Apollo 17 spacecraft is a military artifact of the Cold War "Space Race." The militarized gaze in addition to the masculinized gaze are pertinent for understanding climate journalism and politics today because both shape how climate change has come to be imagined and known in the U.S.

The militarized optics of planetary containment and control characterize the imaging technologies still used by climate scientists to produce GCMs.[29] Environmental humanities scholars Allison Carruth and Robert P. Marzec detail how global satellite images collected by the Central Intelligence Agency (CIA) during the Cold War were declassified in 1996 but "were made available only to a select group of 'patriotic' environmental scientists working on the then nascent issue of climate change."[30] The images produced by these Cold War satellite technologies shaped the development of GCMs and, in turn, shaped the way climate change was originally conceptualized. Climate change came to be seen by "patriotic" scientists as akin to the threat of an atomic bomb. Climate change, however, is categorically different from nuclear warfare, which was only ever a possibility, not a present reality. Moreover, the causes of climate change are rooted in the high-energy and hyper-capitalistic modern nation-state, of which the U.S. military has a very strong stake in maintaining. Through the erasure of on-the-ground experiences, historical contexts, and inequities of power, the gaze of abstract global models offers a sense of control over Earth, but at the expense of *actually* seeing and understanding the intricacies and complexities of climate change that are in fact distinct from nuclear warfare.[31]

In the attempt to "see all" as omnipresent and omnipotent "gods," GCMs obscure the material differences and political realities of climate change on the ground and impede more transformative responses capable of actually addressing the roots and ramifications of climate change. The responses to climate change that emerge from this abstract view of the world evacuate the subjectivities of those placed on the other side of the modeler's gaze. Diverse subjects are transformed into passive objects and are reduced to either threats to be contained or victims to be saved. It is no small irony that the rugged individualists of the *Whole Earth Catalog* and Google Earth reserve the position of a full/rational/enlightened subject for themselves (white, educated, American men), while all others are relegated to the status of objects that can and *should* be manipulated, managed, and controlled for the sake of the planet's salvation. The reduction of people to 1's and 0's and climate change to GCMs decontextualizes the problems of the present while elevating a small minority of self-declared "geniuses" to the echelon of visionary sages and Earth's keepers.

The July 22, 2019 special climate issue of *Foreign Policy* reflects the two previously outlined resonant discourse strands of: (1) *Very smart American men* are capable of mass destruction on a planetary scale and (2) *very smart American men* are capable of saving the Earth on a planetary scale.

Figure 2.2 Cover of *Foreign Policy*. © [July 22, 2019].
Courtesy of Party of One Studio.

It also reveals the deeply embedded anxieties that propel these discourse strands. Written in a shadowy and tilted font over a dry, dead, and destroyed ground that is brown and broken, the cover of *Foreign Policy* (see Figure 2.2) asks "**WHO WILL SAVE THE PLANET?**"[32] Almost like an "SOS" call for help, this headline expresses deep uncertainty and fear. A desperate search for Earth's "saviors"—as the subheadline states—follows from this fear. The charred and cracked Earth of a barren landscape renders the planet as "lost" if not "saved" by a select few visionary sages who can "fix" and "solve" Earth's decline. These select few are positioned as the Godsent answer to an all-encompassing planetary threat. Following from this logic, there is no alternative route to secure a flourishing planet without visionary sages as "saviors of the Earth's climate crisis"—in the words of the *Foreign Policy* feature story printed inside the magazine's pages. These sages are required to keep the global commons tilled, hydrated, and alive.

Totalizing visions of the whole Earth provide a clear, negative classification of the problem *and* a clear, positive solution. The Earth will be uninhabitable for humans if the Earth's "saviors" are impeded—as depicted through the broken and parched landscape on the July 22, 2019 cover image of *Foreign Policy*. On an inside page of this special issue, there is a picture of a brown and dead whole Earth along with the identification of five "saviors of Earth's climate crisis" who are specifically named as masters of finance, tech, space research, youthful innovation, and green capitalism.[33] Accordingly, it is presumed that without these "saviors" and their technological and market innovations, Earth will be totally uninhabitable like the brown, burnt, and dead globe printed along with the magazine's feature story.

Sidestepping political complexities, projects of technological innovation, green capitalism, and consumer-oriented eco-friendly lifestyles are promoted as *the* solution to climate change. Under the neoliberal edict of unfettered freedom and "access" to all, the currents of globalization during and following the Cold War naturalized the virtue of "act local, think global" through the purchase of "green" products and adoption of individual "green" lifestyles like the ones promoted by the *Whole Earth Catalog*. It is here where the call to "save the Earth" through individual innovation and ingenuity can be read as part of the neoliberal depoliticization of climate change.

The historian Finis Dunaway critiques an attendant appeal to what he calls a "mythical 'we'" that often accompanies neoliberal stories of global warming.[34] Dunaway underscores how this "we" and the blaming of a generalized "humanity" as the cause of global warming "obscure[s] the geographies of risk and responsibility."[35] This obfuscation deflects attention away from the root causes of climate change while promoting "ecological individualism" and "green capitalism" as *the* solution by "merg[ing] the personal with the planetary."[36] The comfortable simplicity and sense of control achieved by disciplining one's own personal consumer choices are welcomed by historically privileged figures in response to the overwhelming anxieties provoked through renderings of planetary catastrophe because this disciplining doesn't rupture the status quo. Communication scholar Norie Ross Singer points out that this reverence for green capitalism "illustrates the re-emergence of myth to explain chaotic times and uphold America's exceptional character" including the "exceptional character" of the nation's rugged individualists.[37] This helps explain why during the chaotic times of "total crisis" in the age of Trump, market-based responses have been repeatedly elevated as natural, right, and inevitable by traditional journalists writing for the national press while alternative political-economic proposals for change—like the Green New Deal—have been positioned as an existential threat to both the nation and the whole Earth.

The looming image of a charred, brown, and dead Earth is leveraged across prominent national news publications in the U.S. as the foil to a flourishing, green, and thriving Earth "saved" by industrious, innovative, and rugged individuals. On the cover of the February 21, 2020 issue[38] of the centrist national news magazine *Newsweek*, green arrows moving upwards into infinity, for example, visually portray the headline's edict of "**GROWTH** CAN BE GREEN" (see Figure 2.3). A man in business attire with a watering can is pictured standing on one of these green profit margin arrows—hydrating the flourishing economy as if it were an organic and natural being. In contrast with the dry and cracked whole Earth that is "lost" in the *Foreign Policy* cover image (see Figure 2.2), unfettered economic growth here promises a green, good, and healthy planet—it is the natural as well as the most desirable solution. The November 16, 2015 cover of the center-left news magazine *The Nation* similarly asserts this vision of perpetual progress via unabridged economic growth with the headline: "Think we can't stabilize the climate while fostering growth?"[39] Below this headline, a 100-dollar bill is pictured but transformed into a solar panel—literally equating green energy with green cash/green profit margins. In contrast with a brown and burnt planet, these green renderings of a sustainable and thriving future offer a more compelling vision of a life without limits and without death—a welcomed image and edict for navigating climate change that elides systemic transformation or any personal discomfort for the historically privileged.

Figure 2.3 Cover of *Newsweek*. © [February 21, 2020].
Courtesy of *Newsweek*. All rights reserved. Used under license.

Anti-Politics of the Apocalypse and Anthropocene

A big problem, as the geographer Kathryn Yusoff indicates in her analysis of the limited purview of GCMs despite the modelers' claims of "total sight," is that the individual consumer choices of the neoliberal, green capitalist variety can pale in comparison to the scale of the problem.[40] In comparison with the totalizing, planetary images of climate change that are presented via GCMs and reproduced by the media, individual consumer actions can be understood as not enough to combat the severity and extent of a warming world. Concerningly, a vociferous response to these feelings of disempowerment among a faction of rugged individualists who maintain a whole Earth worldview but question the "emasculating" forces of a modern industrial and global economy is one of apocalyptic environmentalism as opposed to climate justice.

Apocalyptic environmentalism leverages Cold War imaginaries of nuclear fallout/doomsday dystopia to prophesize a planetary catastrophe wrought by runaway industrialization.[41] Over-industrialization and the destruction of nature are critiqued by apocalyptic environmentalists, but not the fundaments of the myth of Manifest Destiny, rugged individualism, or the desire for unfettered freedom among white American men. Gaining some traction during the early years of the Iraq War and then again following the financial recession of 2008 through the peak oil movement, apocalyptic environmentalism was generally considered to exist only on the fringes of the environmental movement until the mid-2010s.[42] The peak oil movement—adherents of which predict an imminent collapse of industrial civilization due to the exhaustion of world oil supplies and subsequent spike in price per barrel, thus wreaking havoc on the global economy—consists of predominantly (~89%) white, American, middle-aged, college educated, self-described "liberal" men.[43] Interestingly, spikes in "peakism" parallel with moments of profound political and economic disruption in the U.S. such as the Iraq War, the 2008 recession, and the 2016 election of President Trump. In his study of the peak oil movement, American studies scholar Matthew Schneider-Mayerson interviewed and surveyed a wide array of peakists who reported feeling a palpable sense of anxiety, depression, personal irrelevancy, lack of control, and powerlessness before learning of peak oil.[44] To this end, peakists spoke of a sense of satisfaction, control, and overall improved mental health after "enlightenment" and knowledge of the imminent global catastrophe that "the masses" were ignorant about.

It is perhaps no surprise, then, that Silicon Valley is a hotbed of "preppers" who are preparing for—and also profiting from—the supposedly imminent collapse of contemporary civilization. Described by *The New York Times* as "a long time Silicon Valley entrepreneur," one prominent prepper who started the blog *The Prepared*, John Ramey, "was involved in the creation of the Defense Innovation Unit Experimental, a Pentagon project to improve ties between the Department of Defense and the technology industry—a formerly tight relationship Mr. Ramey felt had grown cold."[45] Self-described as liberal and shown sporting a buzzcut and military-style vest in a photo of him accompanying *The New York Times* article, Ramey epitomizes the rugged individualism that links patriarchal military and techno-utopian logics together through the shared desire to be on the "frontier" of a "new world"—even and especially if this entails the devastation and destruction of the old one. Preppers in Silicon Valley, for example, were among the first to begin stockpiling and leaving the Bay Area for less populated rural areas in response to early reports of a new virus overseas in early 2020. As the pandemic spread and lockdowns followed in the U.S. and elsewhere, preppers celebrated their foresight in a morbid embrace of tragedy. The death and suffering of Other people are viewed as inevitable by preppers and therefore "ungrievable."[46] Preppers and peakists understand themselves as above and separate from the faceless, nameless, and "inevitably" lost lives of Others—eliding any ethical responsibility or political obligation to prevent the passing of people outside of their privileged group through, for example, the development of strong collectives and robust public services.

The rise of the academic discipline of Collapsologie in France and the intellectual and artistic projects of the Anthropocene elsewhere in Europe and the Anglosphere closely parallel with these demographic and ideological features of the U.S. peak oil and prepper movements. In stride with the expressed sense of satisfaction felt by peakists and preppers following their "enlightenment," adherents of Collapsologie and the "new epoch" of the Anthropocene are similarly energized and filled with a sense of personal purpose from possessing knowledge of global catastrophe, deriving from it a sense of control, power, and superiority above the "unenlightened." Schneider-Mayerson importantly underscores how peakists and preppers like John Ramey are largely apolitical and do not engage in collective action—they instead pursue personal preparations for survival as rugged individuals/pioneer-men akin to the back-to-the-land movement of the 1960s/1970s.[47] Indeed Schneider-Mayerson highlights how peakists are rather fatalistic and regard the climate as already lost, so therefore contend that little can be done about it.[48] A third dominant discourse strand here emerges from a whole Earth way of seeing: *Very smart American men are fully capable of saving* themselves *on a planetary scale.*

Collective action and robust democracies are perceived as idealistic at best and ignorant at worst, among the "climate change edgelords" of the peak oil movement and Collapsologie.[49] The writer Mike Pearl describes climate change edgelords as active internet users who identify themselves as liberals—*not* progressives.[50] Pearl writes how "if you express a modicum of can-do spirit, or tweet about taking action to 'stop' climate change, an edgelord will see it as their job to throw cold water on your enthusiasm."[51] Schneider-Mayerson also reports that peakists tend to invest heavily in the fossil fuel industry because of the presumed profit they will apparently earn on the stock market in the years preceding total climate breakdown and the collapse of industrial civilization—thus actively contributing to the worsening of the problem.[52] Leading thinkers of Collapsologie and the Anthropocene view themselves "as gods," in similar stride with Stewart Brand and the tech-bros of Silicon Valley, and passionately advance a singular vision for the future: an inevitable dystopia that they will be able to navigate through their superior skills, preparation, and rugged individualism while all Others will not. This apocalyptic fantasy of edgelords essentially fetishizes planetary destruction through the visual pleasure of mastery and control and the elimination of everyone but themselves.

Taken to further extremes, in Brand's *A CoEvolution Book* spinoff of the *Whole Earth Catalog*, he features an entire magazine's worth of self-designed plans and procedures for literally colonizing the universe. When Earth inevitably dies, as predicted by edgelords and men such as Brand, Ramey, and Musk, these very same visionary sages presume that they will inevitably profit as the engineers and architects of a literal new world (hence, Musk's heavy investment in technologies to colonize Mars). The political-economic causes of climate change are therefore irrelevant for these men. The development of transformative responses through robustly democratic procedures to comprehensively address the complexities of climate change *on Earth* is thus also deemed irrelevant by edgelords. Sci-fi fantasies of planetary collapse and the subsequent colonization of Mars obscure the on-the-ground realities of climate change that *can* be prevented on Earth. At the same time, these men "as gods" dismiss justice-oriented responses that *are* possible but that will involve a rupture in their own historical privilege and power.

Eyes from Above: Climate Change as a Weapon of Mass Destruction

The militarized and masculinized gaze of a whole Earth way of seeing guides visions of prepper bunker societies, space colonies, and GCMs. Traditional journalists at major national news outlets in the U.S. notably adopt and amplify these planetary optics of containment and control when reporting on the impacts of climate change–intensified storms. The September 25, 2017 cover image of the centrist magazine *TIME*, for instance, pictures the now common satellite imagery of massive storm systems—here, of Hurricane Irma. The eye of the storm appears as a blood red center within a yellow bruise-colored spiral looming over the Gulf Coast of the U.S. in a satellite image that looks almost like a bullet wound. The headline ominously states: "The storms keep getting stronger," but in a bigger and bolded font and as a rhetorical show of force following this statement, the subheadline proclaims: "**And so do we.**" The unspecified "we" is imagined as capable of combating the moribund spiral depicted on the cover—but the "we" does not necessarily refer to the reader or the people impacted by the storm. The cover story penned by the journalist Jeffrey Kluger states how:

> A hurricane is a monster with two orders of magnitude. It is a weapon of mass destruction–an atmospheric daisy cutter that descends on a region and claws away whole cities at a time. And it's a precision-targeted weapon too—a disturbance that begins in the sky, travels across an ocean and, when it arrives, picks off its victims one at a time: the child swept under by the onrushing flood, the first responder who saves a life and perishes in the process.[53]

A monster and a weapon of mass destruction (WMD)—two terrors that require, according to this representation of the storm, a military response to contain the threat. The "we," then, is the U.S. military and technological innovations supported by well-funded programs of research and development —not the different people and communities living in the places impacted by the storm.

Notably, the hurricane is described by Kluger as a "precision-targeted weapon" and as "a disturbance that begins in the sky, travels across an ocean and, when it arrives, picks off its victims one at a time."[54] This description places Hurricane Irma within a national security discourse but just as much through what is left out as through what is actually said. According to Kluger's description, the storm formed "in the sky"—seemingly out of nowhere and with absolutely no indication of its cause or how climate change contributed to the formation and force of the storm. Moreover, the specific storm itself—Hurricane Irma—is obscured through the generalized category of "monstrous" hurricanes as an all-encompassing totality. The event is swept into a transcendent discourse of other storms in other times. The people impacted by Hurricane Irma are evacuated of specificity and agency—referred to as "victims" being "pick[ed] off [...] one at a time" along with children being "swept under by the onrushing flood." The specific causes and specific impacts of Hurricane Irma are erased and subsumed within the spectacle of a horror story that requires a heroic savior to rescue the vulnerable Others who are in desperate need of saving.

This representation of Hurricane Irma parallels with other stories of climate-intensified storms. The anthropologist Joseph Masco clarifies how this pattern of coverage began with Hurricane Katrina in 2005—the first majorly catastrophic climate-intensified storm that was extensively reported on by the U.S. news media.[55] Masco points out how coverage of Hurricane Katrina largely failed to identify or link the causes of the storm with climate change and instead directly positioned the hurricane within a nuclear warfare discourse.[56] The spectacle of disaster from Katrina, including thousands of displaced people and deaths, was appropriated "to linguistically transform Hurricane Katrina into an atomic explosion [...] in part to evoke mass destruction in its ultimate form, but [...] also [as] a way of capturing the event on terms historically useful to the national security state."[57] The highly visible images of death and destruction from the powerful and temporally immediate hurricane were easily transformed into an image of atomic war.[58] Moreover, the timing of Hurricane Katrina at the start of the Iraq War is critical for understanding why this particular storm gained so much media traction compared with other earlier storms. To this end, Masco argues that subsuming Katrina—and subsequent storms such as Hurricanes Sandy and Harvey—within a national security purview was/is strategically valuable to bolster support for the Pentagon and to legitimize military-led climate responses and technological developments.[59]

A national security discourse matters to both green capitalists and an elite-captured state because it elevates military-industrial responses to climate superstorms—what the writer Naomi Klein famously terms "disaster capitalism"[60]—as opposed to systemic political-economic change. Hurricane Katrina disproportionately impacted the Black population of New Orleans—with the trauma of death and displacement still reverberating today. This disparity of impact and harm was brushed aside by many media and governmental accounts.[61] The news media and White House–led public conversation following Hurricane Katrina was about how to prepare for future catastrophe through a stronger and quicker storm response akin to preparing for a military battle. This battle-oriented outlook overpowered the specific development of more robustly democratic responses capable of addressing the root causes of climate change and disparities of risk.[62] In the *TIME* cover story featuring Hurricane Irma, racial, gender, and economic inequities are sidestepped in analysis, and climate change itself is only mentioned once at the very end of the article through a denialist quote by the Trump-appointed former head of the Environmental Protection Agency: Scott Pruitt.[63] Through references to WMDs and comparing the hurricane to "D-Day" while describing its effects as "carpet-bombing" islands, the *TIME* cover story calls for a stronger military to respond to hurricanes *generally*, without context or consideration of the particularities of *this* climate change–intensified storm or the many possible alternative, community-led responses.

These military-led responses that are privileged in American media inherently require a clearly demarcated enemy as a foil to the U.S. military as the Earth's savior. In U.S. climate journalism, this enemy formation is repeatedly forged through very familiar Cold War logics.[64] When climate change is linked to extreme weather like Hurricane Irma, other nations—most often China—are often positioned as the *real* threat and the *real* cause of climate change as opposed to the U.S.'s fossil fuel–dependent economy. As opposed to the U.S.'s subsidizing of the fossil fuel industry and exploitative global economic policies that incentivize destructive extraction practices, China's communist state policies are frequently blamed as wholly complicit, thus negating any U.S. efforts to reverse the impacts of climate change so long as China's economy keeps booming. As we saw in Chapter 1, climate change is often repositioned through a discourse of "total war" akin to World War II (WWII) in climate news reports. In order to retain claims of American superiority, *other* nations are thus framed as the *real* climate villains. This vilification not only elides accountability, but it also quells momentum for international cooperation and more robustly democratic climate responses within and across borders.

It is precisely here where abstract renderings of an imperiled planet are leveraged to assert the need for American interference to combat enemies threatening the nation *and* the whole Earth. On the cover of the December 11, 2015 issue of *Newsweek*, for example, a bold and bright colored image of a disembodied gas mask is pictured with a communist red flag of the People's Republic of China forebodingly reflected through the eyes of the mask.[65] It appears as though the mask looks out and sees this flag in the near distance. The image can be interpreted as representing a dystopian, post-apocalyptic scenario where China won the "war on warming" and is now the global superpower, not the U.S. Written across the gas mask in big, red, bold lettering—signaling urgency—is the headline "**BREATHTAKING.**" Written in yellow and in a smaller print under this fear-inducing main headline is the assertion: "YOU CAN'T FIGHT CLIMATE CHANGE WITHOUT CHINA'S HELP."[66] Strikingly, the subheadline's use of the personal address of "you" renders the Chinese Other as a very close and intimate threat to the reader. Despite the claimed necessity, however, a Chinese and American partnership is described as nearly impossible in the accompanying cover story's text. A U.S. show of force, therefore, is the only option to avoid personal peril and the dystopian image portrayed on the cover of *Newsweek*. This representation of climate change thus sustains a feeling of individual futility and a lack of personal agency in preventing a dystopian scenario that will impact "you" without a U.S. military intervention and American saviors capable of crushing the enemy nation of China.

This blaming of China is often attributed to its Communist Party rule. The Chinese state is reported on through a Cold War lens whereby communists are anti-American enemies and thus must be stopped. As discussed in the previous chapter, the U.S. since WWII has cast itself as the great global stabilizer and as exceptional due to its supposed unparalleled immunity from social upheaval at home (except for today's momentary rupture wrought by "extremists" in an age of "total crisis"). In contrast with this image of a timeless and transcendent American stability, the May/June 2020 issue of the centrist *Foreign Affairs* magazine shows an hourglass with the Earth turning into fiery lava, falling into the bottom half of the vestibule. On the top of the cover is written: "THE COMING UPHEAVAL IN CHINA," and right above this anxiety-inducing image showing how time—and the Earth—are slipping away into oblivion is written: "**The Fire Next Time.**"[67] Smaller text below it offers "How to Prevent a Climate Catastrophe."[68] The catastrophism of total planetary annihilation and fearmongering of a communist/Chinese

Other is combined here to elevate militarized calls for securitizing the globe and thus reclaiming American relevancy as the global peacekeeper. Indeed, the entire issue is dedicated to methods and means for securing this American dominance and centrality in global affairs—framed as for the overall benefit of the planet currently at risk with an unchecked Chinese economy and state.

The reduction of climate change, its threats, and impacts through a planetary-scale lens and Cold War optics eliminates complexities that need to be grappled with in order to fundamentally address the root causes of it. Representations of climate change via GCMs and WMDs forge the false perception of mastery and control on a planetary scale that dangerously simplifies the problem. Through a militarized gaze, political complexities, different perspectives, and historical contexts are cut out of sight. In addition to satellite images, the aerial view of drones—another military technology— is a common representational trope in news coverage of climate change stemming out of a whole Earth way of seeing. These aerial images work to further erase particularities in exchange for a sense of power via a "God's eye view" of the world from above. On the cover of the special climate issue of *TIME* published on September 23, 2019 (see Figure 2.4), for example, an aerial image taken by a drone shows an outline of planet Earth etched into the dry, tan soil of what appears at first glance to be a desert landscape. Around the etched outline of the globe, people are congregated—appearing like tiny figures absent of any distinction or identifying facial or other personal features. The people depicted are not posing or arranged and therefore appear unaware of the photo being taken. The identities and characteristics of the different people are thus irrelevant and merely an aesthetic feature. In contrast with the vibrant colors of a Chinese "enemy" and urgent calls for action decipherable in the previously discussed cover stories, this cover photo is dull in coloration. Images of drought reflect an already dead landscape—quelling action to address what is perceived as already lost.

Moreover, the image on this cover of *TIME* is striking because of its similarity to the wartime images taken by military-operated drones during the Iraq War. Critical scholar Simone Browne details how aerial images like this are an optic of war that strip people of their own subjectivity while emboldening the drone's distant operator to do what they please as an absent force/"as a god."[69] The headline accompanying the cover image is "2050: **HOW EARTH SURVIVED.**"[70] With a similarly absent subject and referent

76 APOCALYPTIC AUTHORITARIANISM

Figure 2.4 Cover of *TIME*. © [September 23, 2019].
Courtesy of TIME USA LLC. All rights reserved. Used under license. https://time.com/

as the September 25, 2017 *TIME* cover story on Hurricane Irma, the question of *who* survives and *how* is ambiguous, but the list of prominent American figures including Al Gore implies the answer. This is in contrast with the faceless people pictured in the cover image. Once more, the elevation of American saviors offers a sense of comfort for the privileged, middle-class readership of *TIME* within an overwhelming moment of perceived "total crisis" by promising that current structures of power—including their own personal privilege—will not be upended now or in 2050 for those who are gazing from above. *Other* people down below will be lost, but the enlightened readership of *TIME* positioned "as gods" via the drone's aerial view will be among the saved.

The Anthropocene Gaze

The visual pleasure of control accrued through aerial photos that are captured by drones operated by men "as gods" is taken to an extreme when these images are consumed as art. Here the militarized and masculinized gaze melds with the "Anthropocene gaze"—where imagemakers create "beautiful" visuals of destruction and bask in the sublime pleasure of their own power. Pictures of total destruction are abstracted from a referent and context to be enjoyed for their compositional style and arrangement of vibrant colors and patterns. Demos critiques these Anthropocene aesthetics as "beautifying" environmental destruction and enabling "the military-state-corporate apparatus to disavow responsibility for the differentiated impacts of climate change, effectively obscuring the accountability behind the mounting eco-catastrophe and inadvertently making us all complicit in its destructive project."[71] It is here where the causes of climate change are erased by the very smart men who are empowered by the military-state-corporate apparatus and who now claim to be the Earth's saviors despite their role in its continued destruction.

As communication scholar Bryan Taylor and his coauthors point out in an analysis of nuclear discourse and images, this obfuscation allows for claims of global "guardianship" by an elite few often at the helms of the U.S. military as opposed to a more bottom-up and robustly democratic form of governance.[72] This asymmetrical dynamic of power is reflected on the cover of the May/June 2017 climate change issue of *Foreign Policy*.[73] In this photorealistic cover image reflective of the aerial aesthetics of drone images, a small group of—once again—featureless human figures are pictured from above, but here on a lone iceberg in a vast blue sea below. Turning the polar bear trope on its head, in this image people are pictured as the precarious beings floating on an iceberg and in desperate need of saving. The people shown in this image lack agency and are represented as totally helpless. The only solution to "save" these tiny, faceless, and doomed humans appears to be through the will and power of a guardian (as a god) from above—that is, the drone operator and the "military-state-corporate apparatus" that empowers him.

These militarized optics and patriarchal logics of the Cold War are at the crux of a planetary way of seeing that drives the Anthropocene gaze. The Anthropocene gaze serves to prop up the assertion that God-like American men are Earth's keepers who solely possess the capacity to save Earth's "human children."[74] Carruth and Marzec explain how these optics and logics were promoted by agents from the CIA and Pentagon following the Cold War in an attempt to shift the former global risk of communism to the planetary risk of climate change in an effort to secure their own relevancy.[75] It is here where "the Pentagon and other security institutions invest[ed] in projects to visualize and also simulate climate change scenarios seen as the next threat to the nation's security."[76] In other words, the abstract and planetary rendering of the whole Earth embedded within GCMs and circulated across climate journalism serve to propagate and legitimize brutal modes of U.S. military power that keep the national security state solidly in place and historically privileged men solidly at the center of global affairs at the expense of *actually* addressing the root causes and impacts of climate change.

The wide and high vantage of the September 1, 2016 cover of *Foreign Policy* (see Figure 2.5) and the accompanying images inside the issue, for instance, decontextualize climate change to little more than an abstraction with little room for imagining political responses to it beyond a guardian or God-like savior. With the headline "**PARADISE LOST**" and subheadline "THREE ARTISTS CAPTURE THE DESTRUCTION OF EARTH'S BEAUTY—AND THE BEAUTY OF ITS DESTRUCTION," the ecological devastation of a destroyed environment pillaged by mineral extraction is declared dead and "lost" at the same time it is declared sublime and "beautiful."[77] Moreover, in the case of Anthropocene images of dead and lost landscapes, there is no historical contextualization, nor are there on-the-ground perspectives to informationally fill in what is obscured visually. Different vantages are missing in image and text. Instead, the optics of drones flying high in the sky and gazing down below obscure and blur the particularities of harm, specifics of impact, and the causes of destruction. Abstract geometries and striking color palettes replace particular conditions and contexts. The Anthropocene gaze inspires ocular enjoyment and pleasure through the evacuation of all contexts and empowering a (false) sense

AMERICAN EARTH: PLANETARY OPTICS OF CONTROL   79

Figure 2.5 Cover of *Foreign Policy*. © [September 1, 2016].
Image by Overview, source imagery © Maxar.

of mastery and control of Earth from above. Pleasure is derived when the gazer is in full ocular possession of the object of his desire—but from a distance. The Anthropocene gaze is fundamentally voyeuristic and requires a separation between the gazer and the Earth. The gazer is safely flying above and is not a part of the world below crawling with mere mortals who may be saved or not depending on the will of very smart men "as gods".

The Anthropocene gaze has become a strong precedent for climate photography. Zelizer underscores that the aesthetic appeal of vibrant colors and beautiful images "often works against the information that news depictions can provide."[78] The Anthropocene gaze cloaks the historical contexts of climate change and muddies differences in the degree of impact, intention, and complicity. Concerningly, textual news accounts of climate change also frequently fail to fill in these details by constructing narratives through a whole Earth discourse. Photos taken by people on the ground and the lived experiences of those actually being impacted by climate-intensified storms are better able to depict the particularities of climate change. Drones flying high in the sky and operated by men virtually parachuting in from faraway places cannot do this.

On-the-ground perspectives contest the claims of mastery and control among GCM modelers and drone operators. Crucially, different accounts and lived experiences weaken claims of dominion and omnipotence by just a few very smart men "as gods." Demos describes how, conversely, "Anthropocene visuality tends to reinforce the techno-utopian position that 'we' have indeed mastered nature, just as we have mastered its imaging—and in fact the two, the dual colonization of nature and representation, appear inextricably intertwined."[79] If histories and contexts and different experiences are recognized and centered in climate journalism as opposed to being cut out or shrouded, then the fast and slow violences of colonial and capital accumulation will be recognized as the central drivers of climate change. Demos goes on to clarify how the aerial aesthetics and the beautification of ecological destruction wrought by fossil capitalism that characterize an Anthropocene way of seeing, however:

> merges with nature, unified aesthetically, composing a picture that is, monstrously, not only visually pleasurable, but also ostensibly ethically just—an image of American 'freedom' whose historical progression, according to the familiar patriotic narrative, is necessary, inevitable, even—as pictured here—beautiful.[80]

Here, once more, history is transformed into nature[81] but this time under the depoliticized purview of the Anthropocene gaze.

Notably, the Anthropocene aesthetics of aerial photos of the "World from Above" were also featured in the 1968 issue of the *Whole Earth Catalog* and once more reflects the *Catalog*'s celebration of American male superiority above all Others and the lingering legacy of this celebration. Called "mystery shots" in the *Whole Earth Catalog*, the satellite images of Earth taken far above the ground's surface were admired for their abstract allure. These abstract aesthetics were (and continue to be) appreciated by the *Catalog's* middle-class male audience for their "mystery"—in other words, for the very fact that context and details are absent from view. Indeed, context and complexity aren't desired. Similarly, the contemporary photographer featured in the *Foreign Policy* special issue (see Figure 2.5) champions his abstract renderings of "lost" and drought-stricken desert landscapes destroyed by industrial mining for their "mystery." The photographer states in *Foreign Policy*:

> I know I have succeeded when I show someone a final composition and they excitedly ask me, 'What is that?' By stitching together numerous high-resolution satellite images to form one single view, I elevate my audience from their usual line of sight and allow them to see our Earth like never before.[82]

He congratulates himself for allowing his audience of mere humans to join him above and in the realm of gods for a moment by "elevat[ing]" them "from their usual line of sight" on the lowly ground below. The photographer goes on to add that the "abstract feel" of his work through his "emphasis on cropping, crispness, and color" is what makes it so powerful and profound. In other words, the "beauty" of contextless spectacle is enjoyed as art and celebrated for its "mystery." Moreover, drones and satellite technologies that allow men like him to create and consume images of the world from above are embraced as God-like feats of innovation.

The "Good" and "Bad" Anthropocene

The 1960/1970s embrace of rugged individualism in the countercultural back-to-the-land movement paired with the techno-libertarianism that fostered Silicon Valley decades later is described by Demos as "sickly sweet with optimism."[83] This sickly optimism is derived from the notion of perpetual progress via endless economic growth that keeps the engines of the myth of Manifest Destiny going. And according to the church of the frontiersmen celebrated by figures ranging from Stewart Brand to Steve Jobs to Al Gore, "a major principle of laissez-faire individualism is that general well-being is best served when individual self-interest is left free to maximize personal gain."[84] Progress and the "inevitable" flourishing of an exceptional America, therefore, are understood as possible only through unfettered individual freedom.

These libertarian impulses are combined with the deep cultural roots of a high energy economy at the crux of American identity. The social theorist Ian Barbour and coauthors highlight an important consequence of the expansion of the nineteenth-century myth of Manifest Destiny while the U.S. transitioned into a fossil fuel–dependent nation—namely, concepts of patriotism and material growth were tied to the fossil fuel industry.[85] Following this, contemporary questioning of the high-energy economy and calls for limits to growth are often perceived as unpatriotic and even sacrilegious. Because the American ideals of liberty and individualism are so strongly linked with energy and industrial production,[86] it is very difficult for the realities of environmental destruction caused by U.S. enterprise to be conceived of as even possible. This impossibility in part explains the embrace of abstraction through the Anthropocene gaze and GCMs. An aerial vantage cuts the violence and suffering caused by an "American way of life" from view at the same time as it allows for the sustained notion of perpetual progress through technological innovation and a singularly powerful U.S. national military and capitalistic economy to address planetary threats. As Barbour and coauthors state: "Americans saw in the prodigious use of energy […] the means to material growth. A mechanized society, with seemingly infinite sources of energy symbolized permanent and progressive human progress."[87] The myth of perpetual growth without limits in U.S. contexts gives "special attention to the importance of material improvements by linking it with belief in individual rights, freedom of opportunity, progress, and a superior quality of life."[88]

Consequently, responses to climate change are deemed good or bad by patriotic rugged individualists, depending on whether or not they are perceived as promoting or impeding this perpetual progress. Strikingly, the *Whole Earth Catalog* was reanimated and used by *New York Magazine* in the mid-2010s to illustrate these good and bad responses through visions of a "Good" and "Bad" Anthropocene. Visions of a "Good" Anthropocene propagate a green capitalist and techno-libertarian image of the future where unabridged economic growth is fueled by green technologies that are developed by visionary sages who are revered "as gods." The September 7, 2015 issue of *New York Magazine* reflects this image of the future with a globe model of the whole Earth being joyfully tossed around by members of the

1960s/1970s counterculture (notably all young and white) like a beach ball playfully being passed from one to another in a crowd at a music festival.[89] The cover story's headline is written in the *Whole Earth Catalog*'s distinct font, bolded style, and white color with the declaration: "**Maybe the Planet Isn't Doomed After All.**"[90]

On the flip side, visions of the "Bad" Anthropocene leverage apocalyptic images of a dead and uninhabitable planet following years of decline and depravity in a dystopian scenario made so because visionary sages were not revered and were thus impeded from doing their Earth-saving work. The July 10, 2017 issue of *New York Magazine* reflects this vision and reverses the optimism expressed two years earlier (before the "total crisis" and supposed decline of the U.S. deepened) to offer a foreboding image of a brown and charred planet and a headline written in the same distinct *Whole Earth Catalog* font and style, stating: "**The Doomed Earth Catalog.**"[91] Through a predictive discourse of apocalypse, the cover story's author David Wallace-Wells (who is well known for penning *The Uninhabitable Earth*) foretells a "Doomed Earth" if "the people" do not follow the lead of visionary sages and rapidly implement green innovations on a planetary scale.

As gleaned from a comparison of these two *New York Magazine* cover stories that recenter the *Whole Earth Catalog*, innovative "breakthroughs" in technology, geoengineering, and design are celebrated by traditional journalists as the way forward to secure a Good Anthropocene—as evident with the plethora of news stories on new and novel work done by "brilliant" entrepreneurs and engineers. These very smart men are positioned as visionary sages who can ward off the Bad Anthropocene and prevent a doomsday future scenario. Stories and images of the Good Anthropocene offer a vision of the future not only where the centrality of historically privileged men is secured but also where these men reach even higher levels of power. In a letter from the editor for the September 2018 issue of *Fortune* with the headline "MAKE THE WORLD GREAT AGAIN," for instance, the editor asserts that the Earth can be saved (and the market can be too) through investment in innovative new technologies that will accrue vast "profits for progress."[92] The transformation of Trump's authoritarian call to "Make America Great Again" into "Make the World Great Again" casts a different, planetary vision of American dominion via the guise of entrepreneurism amid "total crisis." According to this logic, profit equals progress equals technological innovation equals a strong and secure nation led by very smart men who are singularly capable of saving both the U.S. and the whole Earth.

Figure 2.6 Cover of *Bloomberg Businessweek*. © [June 10, 2019].
Used with permission of Bloomberg L.P. © 2024. All rights reserved.

Planetary-scale geoengineering projects are here singled out as particularly "exceptional" across the U.S. climate beat. Demos aptly describes geoengineering as "neo-Promethean."[93] One of these neo-Promethean projects is featured on the cover of the June 10, 2019 issue of the centrist news magazine *Bloomberg Businessweek*, which celebrates the technological

Figure 2.7 Cover of *The New Republic*. © [December 2015].
Courtesy of *The New Republic*. All rights reserved. Used under license. https://newrepublic.com/

prospect of moving an iceberg from the far north to the equatorial regions to kickstart the cooling functions of manipulated oceanic circulation patterns (see Figure 2.6). Demos offers a critical view and explains how visions of a Good Anthropocene place "technocrats and scientists in the role of bringing about a great awakening regarding climate change and then conveniently puts those same figures in the position of being the only ones that can fix the problem—via geoengineering."[94] Like the dubious industry of economic forecasting that claims the ability to predict where growth will occur, the "Futurists of the Anthropocene" (a self-selected group that includes Stewart Brand) also assert the ability to predict the future and thus develop technologies to interfere and prevent a Bad Anthropocene scenario. The December 2015 cover of the special issue on climate change for the left-leaning *The New Republic* (see Figure 2.7) reflects the neo-Promethean fantasy of Anthropocene Futurists. The cover image shows a snowcapped mountain imprisoned in a glass box with solar lamps above it. The mountain is not a part of a wider landscape or system—it is isolated and contained. The headline reads "**FUTURE PROOFING THE PLANET.**"[95] This "future proofing" is understood as derivative of the genius of Futurists and geoengineers who are able to manage and control the planet "as gods."

The trope of perpetual progress is here again advanced as good, green, desirable, and secured through a flourishing market of unabridged innovation. As one of the subheadlines for the December 2015 cover of *The New Republic* articulates: "Fighting climate change for fun and profit."[96] Crucially, this Good Anthropocene vision of the future is presented as within reach if only the technological innovators are left to their own devices—unfettered and with free "access to tools." It is within this vein that an additional subheadline asserts: "A better future doesn't have to be science fiction"—implying the immediate possibility of a Good Anthropocene if geoengineers are allowed the tools and freedom to do their innovative and "fun" work.[97] Similarly, the June 10, 2019 issue of *Bloomberg Businessweek* is titled "THE SOONER THAN YOU THINK ISSUE"[98]—indicating that "daring feats of innovation" (including moving an iceberg to the tropics) are totally possible and within reach if geoengineers are celebrated, fully supported, and given free rein of the whole Earth.

The prospect of geoengineering a Good Anthropocene is imperial in nature. The Anthropocene is even explicitly named as the final frontier by the astrophysicist Adam Frank in an opinion piece published by *The New York Times*.[99] The Good Anthropocene is thus seen as a "new" New World where rugged individualists can build their own superior civilization. Through a colonialist, frontier logic and the language of conquest, both the whole Earth and the whole universe are understood as under the domain of visionary sages. As described earlier in this chapter's discussion of Stewart Brand and Elon Musk's shared infatuation with developing their own space colonies, the containment, control, and mastery of *all* planets are understood by these men as both possible and desirable. Political and social complexities are erased through the fantasy of planetary dominion. Images of the final frontier—both in the "new" New World of the Anthropocene and in space—require a blank slate through which men like Brand and Musk can imagine and construct their own fiefdoms. The desire for total control and the comfort and pleasure of men "as gods" obstruct the necessary political-economic transformations required to address climate change in a robustly democratic way.

Conclusion

Returning to the edited volume *American Earth* this chapter began with, Al Gore elevates the mythical power of the frontiersman by citing Thoreau and Whitman and celebrating the "vitality of American growth and progress via the 'unseen moral essence of all the vast materials of America' transforming into a 'new society proportionate to Nature.'"[100] Climate change is depoliticized and decontextualized in an ideology of rugged individualism where the embrace of perpetual progress propagates fantasies of American men's dominion over the whole Earth. Green capitalism and planetary technologies such as geoengineering that are developed by these men are imagined as required to "save the Earth" as opposed to collective action and robustly democratic decision-making processes. In fact, diverse collectives and strong democracies are deemed impediments to the Earth-saving work of very smart men like Musk who see themselves "as gods" and thus above the rules and restrictions of the mortal world. This neo-Promethean fantasy emboldens and empowers hyper-capitalistic market and military responses to climate change that thrive when democracies are weak.

Ultimately, the planetary scale is a unique (and uniquely dangerous) form of universalism that elevates and advances the image and myth of a containable Earth managed by American men "as gods." This perspective is advanced by powerful adherents hailing from Silicon Valley to the Pentagon to Wall Street united as *visionary sage figures*. The next chapter unpacks the discursive construction of these figures in climate news stories and reveals how their construction and the media's reverence for them fans the flames of apocalyptic authoritarianism.

3
Tyrant of a Trope: Visionary Sage Figure

Images and stories of planetary "prophets"[1] and "saviors"[2] color the pages of some of the most prominent newspapers and news magazines in the U.S. Cult-like leaders who claim to possess prophetic knowledge from an unexplained, divine-like origin retain a peculiarly enduring appeal in American culture.[3] This chapter shows how this enduring appeal is recurrently activated through the *visionary sage figure* in climate journalism. In the U.S. climate beat, the visionary sage figure contributes to the formation of a simple binary of hero versus villain in a universal tale of American goodness that transcends the present, particular, and proximate. This binary flattens the complexity and dynamism of different subject positions as it buttresses reverence for all-knowing authorities above democratic collectivities. Admiration of and deference to prophetic figures close off meaningful engagements with a plurality of lived experiences, knowledges, and possible responses to climate change. At the same time, it expands the legitimacy of antidemocratic claims to power. This chapter illuminates how these antidemocratic claims are naturalized through the privileged centrality of the visionary sage above all Others in U.S. climate journalism.

The American Jeremiad

The 1630 sermon by the Puritan preacher John Winthrop is cited as an important initial text that laid the groundwork for the development of the myth of American exceptionalism—a myth that requires visionary sage figures as conduits of God's will.[4] Winthrop proclaimed the Massachusetts Bay Colony a "city on a hill" and its new settlers—if they followed this will as Winthrop decreed it—a shining example of goodness from which other peoples of the world could model their own communities. Winthrop's speech is significant as an original American jeremiad—the prophet's form of speech.

The jeremiad relies upon a unidimensional construction of time whereby the complexities of the present are subsumed by the certainty of a predetermined future—a future understood as ultimate, universal, and foreseeable by a visionary sage figure such as Winthrop. Time is understood in transcendent terms and less value is placed on the political, particular, and present. Moreover, within this temporal prism of transcendence, the visionary sage holds a great deal of power. Communication scholar Casey Schmitt elaborates on how the jeremiad form is "modeled on the exhortations of the biblical prophet Jeremiah."[5] Schmitt clarifies how the prophet moves "the people" to action through three appeals that characterize the jeremiad form: "first, it establishes the great or divine potential of a people; next, it laments how the community has strayed from its sacred responsibilities; and finally, it then rallies its audience to rededicate itself to a communal cause, achieving their destiny."[6] It is here where Winthrop casts the Puritans as pilgrims in a preordained religious odyssey. The Puritans were lost and wayward in the sinful Old World. Now in the New World, they can live in purity and goodness—but only if they follow God's will as proclaimed by Winthrop as a visionary sage. Importantly, according to the sermon, the pilgrims must protect their city on a hill from forces that will try to defile it. Catastrophe is portended if the hierarchical power structures of the new religious settlement are toppled. In other words, if the social stratum that secures Winthrop's position of authority is altered, total civilizational collapse will ensue—an apocalyptic prediction that undergirds apocalyptic authoritarianism.

The narrative of renewal through the reclamation of an inherent "American goodness" holds sway across party lines in the U.S. but with very different political goals. The Biden administration, for instance, called for renewal through a *re*newed American exceptionalism in order to reignite America's once vibrant light since dimmed by the violence of Trump, his enablers, beneficiaries, and advocates (who, it is important to note, also rallied around calls to "Make America Great Again" but with Democrats positioned as the sinful threats imperiling the nation). Notably, Biden—through the jeremiad form—placed climate action via his Inflation Reduction Act as a central route for national reclamation and renewal as discussed in Chapter 1 of this book.

The jeremiad form accommodates different aims and is easily co-opted for violent ends because it removes focus on the complexities, differences, and specificities of the present through a transcendent and abstract notion of time. The jeremiad therefore has clear political appeal for those who resist progressive movements for social change or who have authoritarian aspirations. It has been especially taken up by the Republican Party since the 1970s/1980s when Ronald Reagan reanimated the notion of American exceptionalism by proclaiming that "there was some divine plan that placed this great continent between two oceans to be sought out by those who were possessed of an abiding love of freedom and a special kind of courage."[7] In the decades since, the Republican Party has increasingly centered the notion of the U.S. as a "city on a hill" under siege by threatening outsiders who wish to dim America's greatness.[8] Strikingly, QAnon takes the Republican jeremiad of "Make America Great Again" to a violent extreme. The conspiracy touting anonymous 8chan (also known as 8kun) netizen "Q" declared themselves a prophet and retains a large, cult-like following of believers keen to cast blame on a "cabal" of evil liberal elites and "woke" social and climate justice "warriors" who have corrupted the nation and who must be purged in order to reclaim their beloved city on a hill. Drawing upon apocalyptic imagery and religious iconography, QAnon exemplifies the dangers of the celebration of a visionary sage figure taken too far. If the jeremiad can be so easily reversed and used to justify violence and intolerance by, for instance, QAnon conspiracy theorists, what are the risks in using it to orient and structure climate news stories?

The Genius Complex

The desire for an enlightened and far-seeing prophet holds significant sway in American culture—but especially among those who perceive societal change as a threat to their own social status and power. The trope of the visionary sage figure and his[9] jeremiad cuts a deep divide between an in-group and out-group and therefore a right and wrong way of thinking and being. Through claims of genius, omnipotence, and prophetic knowledge, there is very little room or ability to contest the visionary sage and his followers. The trope of the visionary sage figure is therefore deeply exclusionary and can be used to elevate and legitimize antidemocratic modes of governance—as seen, for instance, with planetary-scale projects of geoengineering discussed in the previous chapter.

It is notable that among the followers of a visionary sage, there is often a search for peers, which is, in turn, used as evidence to bolster the sage's legitimacy. Again, Stewart Brand exemplifies this strategy. Media studies scholar Anna McCarthy points out how "Brand made himself at home in sites as diverse as the Fluxus happening, the Hippie commune, and Los Alamos National Laboratory."[10] McCarthy underscores how Brand's movement across groups of fellow historically privileged American men united these disparate factions together via a shared techno-libertarian and techno-utopian ideology that the communication scholar Fred Turner refers to as "New Communalism."[11] Turner delineates how "like the communards of the 1960s, the techno-utopians of the 1990s denied their dependence on any but themselves. At the same time, they developed a way of thinking and talking [...] from within which it was almost impossible to challenge their own elite status."[12] Through a network of utopian-minded ecomodernists and techno-libertarians, the antidemocratic and "profoundly apolitical (or more accurately, anti-radical)" notion of the pioneer-man and his "free-thinking" rugged individualism barred the possibility for opposition and engagement with different points of view outside of their insulated and privileged group.[13]

Notably, the architect Buckminster Fuller became an icon and hero among the New Communalists.[14] Fuller's ideal of a "Comprehensive Designer," or a creator who embodies the "synthesis of artist, inventor, mechanic, objective economist and evolutionary strategist," reflects the techno-libertarians' celebration of the power of individual genius.[15] The Comprehensive Designer is imagined as able to solve the toughest problems of the world—like climate change—through his mind alone. It is through a critique of these techno-utopian visions of a controllable Earth managed by a network of Comprehensive Designers that the political scientist Cara Daggett laments how environmentalism became masculinized "as a result of the dominance of science and security frames for understanding climate change."[16] Daggett clarifies how "these 'hardened' framings" of a planet that was imagined to be totally malleable by the genius of Comprehensive Designers resulted in a preference for "the kinds of solutions that are the traditional domain of men and hegemonic masculinity," which reject "ethical concerns" such as "justice, health, or economic equity."[17]

It is important to note that Comprehensive Designers have a very real stake in the status quo because it is in their personal best interest to maintain the hegemonic authority of historically privileged men like themselves. There is little perceived relevance or value for them in engaging with those deemed outside of their network of peers. Energy tycoons, venture capitalists, and Silicon Valley engineers comfortably commingle and devise planetary technologies together without any qualms. This is because technological "solutions" are understood as transcendent and somehow above and exempt from the Earthly realm of everyday politics. Just like the equation "1 + 1 = 2," the "solution" to climate change is imagined as neatly solvable by very smart men and very smart men alone without the need for democratic processes or procedures. In the words of the writer Anna Wiener: "What a luxury it is to be released from politics—to picture it all panning out."[18]

The genius complex of men as all-knowing and all-seeing "gods" further entrenches the binary of an in-group and out-group characteristic of the jeremiad form and is at the crux of apocalyptic authoritarianism. This stark division is achieved through declarations of genius and the predictive power of select individuals. Comprehensive Designers—as visionary sages—are presumed capable of stopping climate change if they are granted unfettered freedom to activate and perform their profound individual potential without societal constraints. It is through this prism of rugged individualism that technological solutions to climate change—designed by a network of "visionaries"—are elevated as the *only* way to "solve" climate change.

The April 2020 issue of WIRED reflects this rigidity around the idea that technology is the only "solution" to climate change capable of "saving" the whole Earth with the headline: "We have one Earth—and the technology to save it. Go!" (see Figure 3.1). The cover story's author celebrates an array of technological designs that, according to the writer, can "solve" climate change but laments the lack of public support for these designs—essentially shifting blame onto "the public," that is, everyone besides the visionary sages and their loyal followers.[19] Strikingly, the cover image for this issue of WIRED is visually quite intense. A rendering of *The Blue Marble* is placed at the center of the image within a rainbow of vibrant neon colors. The colors are arranged in a way that creates an optical illusion. This illusion can be physically distressing to look at for longer than just a few seconds. It is, quite viscerally, alienating. This off-putting cover image and the story's reverent embrace of technological "solutions" designed by Silicon Valley geniuses demonstrate how antidemocratic logics are amplified in U.S. climate journalism through the visionary sage figure.

Transcendent Figures of the Long Now

Because the visionary sage is positioned as a transcendent figure of great genius in stories like the WIRED special feature,[20] the everyday politics of

Figure 3.1 Cover of *WIRED*. [April 2020]. Alvaro Dominguez/Wired; © Condé Nast.

everyday people here and now are deemed irrelevant and banal from a temporal perspective. Visionary sages work within the "Long Now"—as the network of "Anthropocene Futurists" including Brian Eno, Danny Hillis, Jeff Bezos, and Stewart Brand, among others, call it—and are elevated above and beyond the present. This transcendent position absolves the visionary sage of responsibility or obligation to address historical injustices and current inequities because they are above it all "as gods." Indeed, Hillis and Brand cofounded a nonprofit organization focused on "'long-term thinking,' [that] counts Peter Norton and Pierre Omidyar among its funders," which they aptly named "The Long Now Foundation."[21] Wiener describes how "the organization hosts a lecture series, operates a steampunk bar in San Francisco's Fort Mason, and runs the Revive & Restore project, which aims to make species like the woolly mammoth and the passenger pigeon 'de-extinct.'"[22] The Long Now Foundation also boasts about its project to erect a series of 10,000 Year Clocks with forty-two million dollars of funding from Jeff Bezos and the go-ahead to build the first clock in West Texas where he owns vast tracts of land.[23] Wiener writes how the "gigantic monument" is imagined to "tick, once a year, for a hundred centuries." She adds how when she first heard about the 10,000 Year Clock project, it struck her "as embodying the contemporary crisis of masculinity."[24]

The 10,000 Year Clock as "embodying the contemporary crisis of masculinity" is an apt description. Like the ardent support for geoengineering and techno-utopian designs most vocally advanced by men such as Bezos and Brand, the 10,000 Year Clock reflects a deep desire for the sustained relevancy of historically privileged white American men for many millennia to come. Suggesting an odyssey to be embarked upon by future men of their caliber, the vision of the Clock reads like a script akin to *Indiana Jones*.[25] The Clock's designers and funders imagine that the object will be discovered and revered by men who happen upon it thousands of years into the future. This discovery mimics the plotline of adventure tales featuring usually European or American men navigating "exotic" lands to uncover long-lost treasure and the secrets of extraordinary men like them from the past. By constructing these elaborate Clocks and placing them in mountains across the globe, the men of the Long Now are essentially erecting permanent monuments in commemoration of the importance of their own lives.

This desire for a permanent and central presence on Earth also drives the "petro-masculinity" of American fossil fuel tycoons. Daggett points out how: "appreciating the historic relationship between fossil fuels and white patriarchal rule is helpful in terms of understanding the authoritarian desires and anxieties aroused by the Anthropocene."[26] She adds how critical attention to the mechanisms of "petro-masculinity alerts us to those perilous moments when challenges to fossil-fueled systems, and more broadly to fossil-soaked lifestyles, become interpreted as challenges to white patriarchal rule."[27] Fears of irrelevance are conjured in reaction to growing movements for climate and social justice in the U.S. and prompt "authoritarian desires and anxieties" among historically privileged white men from both ecomodernist and fossil fuel circles united through their privilege. Despite the perils of climate change that the fossil fuel industry has propagated, more and more extreme measures are sought to extract every last drop of profitable oil—from tar sands to offshore drilling to "miraculous" discoveries of wells after extensive subterranean explorations. This is because campaigns to divest from fossil fuels are interpreted as a threat to the traditional authority of white patriarchal rule and, according to these men, the stability of the nation *and* whole Earth.

Ideological parallels can be seen in the techno-libertarian imaginary that defines visions of the 10,000 Year Clock and fossil fuel extraction—each of which celebrates powerful technologies as magnificent examples of white American men's virtue and prowess. A critical analysis of the discursive mechanisms of apocalyptic authoritarianism reveals these parallels. In a strikingly similar compositional style, images from Bezos' website[28] dedicated to the 10,000 Year Clock and the December 3, 2018 cover image of the conservative magazine *National Review* with the headline "**AMERICAN POWER**: The West Texas energy miracle" (see Figure 3.2) showcase "man-made" machinery in extreme environmental conditions. The supposed strength and ingenuity of American men are celebrated and advanced through these images of "mastery" over harsh conditions through their technological designs—whether through machinery on the side of a steep Texan mountain or machinery in the vast and unforgiving desert. These landscapes have been conquered and subdued by the technological innovation that supposedly makes these very smart American men so great.

Notably, the December 3, 2018 cover story for the *National Review* was published following the midterm elections and the Republican loss of the House of Representatives that year.[29] The post-election issue was published when bitterness over the loss was still fresh and features a cover story dedicated to the celebration of the fossil fuel industry as both the embodiment of "American power" and masculinity (i.e. petro-masculinity). This cover story is written in the jeremiad form. It laments the loss of American masculinity with the rise of social and climate justice warriors and proclaims the need to reinvest in American oil to regain men's rightful and natural position of authority. The rising sun on the cover behind the horsehead of the

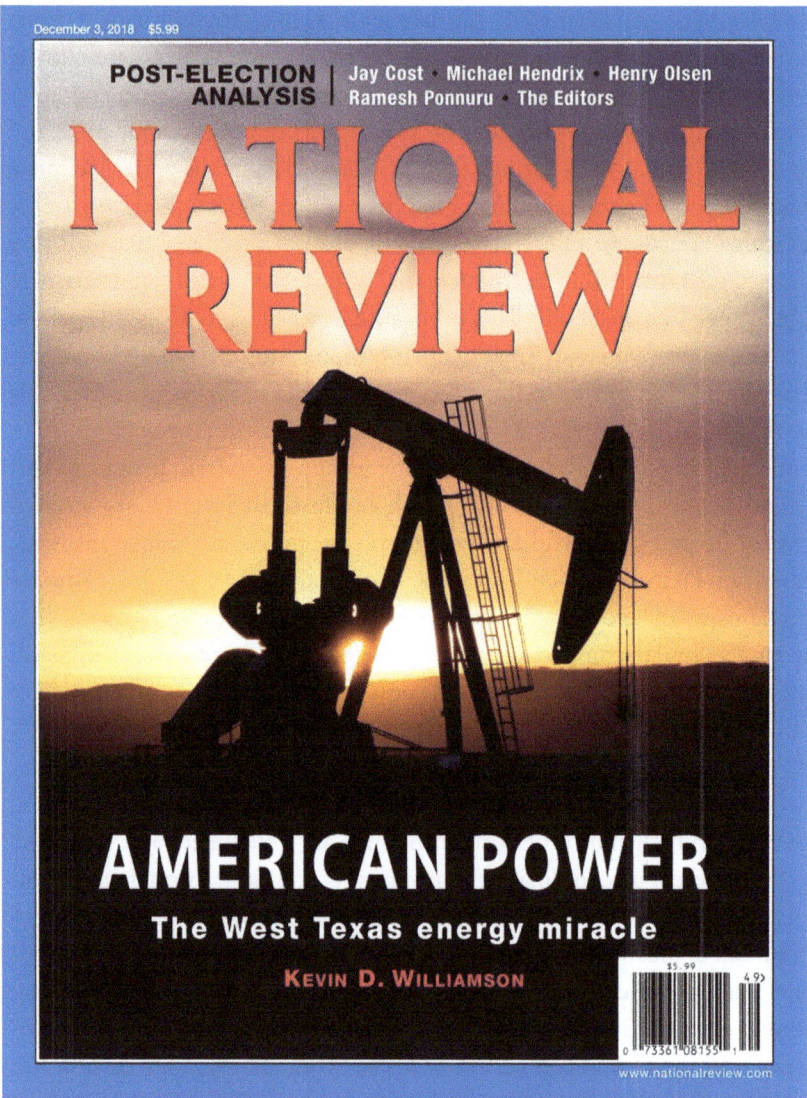

Figure 3.2 Cover of *National Review*. © [December 3, 2018].
Courtesy of National Review.

oil rig in the West Texan desert reflects this notion of the dawn of a new day via the renewal of "American power" and, thus, the oil industry's and men's centrality.

The climate social scientist Martin Hultman clarifies how the ideology of ecological modernization that propels the celebration of green tech and the ideology of American petro-masculinity that propels the celebration of fossil fuels can both "be understood as attempts to incorporate and deflect criticism in order to perpetuate hegemony, to ensure 'business as usual' [so that] modern society can continue unchanged."[30] Both ecomodernist-masculinity and petro-masculinity preserve the status quo and thus protect existing hierarchies of power and privilege. "The Long Now" can be understood not so much as long-term thinking in the sense of recognizing and resolving the slow violence[31] of climate change, but rather as a vision of the everlasting relevance of Comprehensive Designers. Techno-libertarians and their utopian embrace of technological "solutions" as a panacea for all problems on Earth can be interpreted as an attempt to secure the power and privilege of American men amid widespread calls for social and climate justice. The currents of apocalyptic authoritarianism span across different ideologies but are united through a common desire for the safeguarding of the historical privilege and centrality of just a few "very smart men." These men are exploiting apocalyptic anxieties amid a period of social change to justify their own claims to power via assertions that they alone are singularly capable of "saving the Earth." In turn, these men and their admirers vehemently contend that they must not be impeded or else the whole Earth will be doomed.

Predictions and Claims of "I Told You So"

"Anxieties aroused by the Anthropocene can augment desires for authoritarianism"[32] because progressive social change and calls for social justice are cast as threats to the relevance and authority of men like the 10,000 Year Clock's designers, tech-bros, and oil tycoons alike. If the status quo—and by proxy the visionary sage's relevance—is rattled, then total civilizational collapse is portended by these men in response. Critical scholar Betsy Hartmann observes how "apocalyptic thinking distorts our sense of time and history. Whether of the religious or secular variety, it predisposes us to invest the current moment with prophetic intensity as the cataclysmic rupture that portends the end times."[33] Apocalyptic prophecies—through a discourse of fear—are thus used to bar more equitable forms of governance from taking hold while elevating the unabridged authority of an "enlightened" few.

Following from these prophetic assertions, claims of "we don't have time for that" are frequently heard along with calls for the suspension of democratic procedures among would-be apocalyptic authoritarians.

Over and over again, the so-called uniformed/ignorant/unenlightened masses/public/people are blamed as *the* reason for civilizational collapse because they obstruct the world-saving technologies designed by very smart men. In turn, calls for the elimination of social and climate justice advocates and young progressives' democratic rights are often advanced by doomsday prophets as necessary in order to "save the Earth." In place of historical context and an engagement with the root causes of climate change and societal injustices, crises and conflicts of all kinds are cast as a cartoon-like battle between good and evil and an in-group and out-group.

This cartoon-like battle of good versus evil is particularly beneficial for those with a stake in preserving the status quo. For this reason, claims of prophetic knowledge are problematic because they can be co-opted by a variety of opportunists and used to bolster political projects of exclusion that legitimize authoritarian-aspiring figures. In his book *Apocalypse Man*, communication scholar Casey Ryan Kelly argues, for instance, that many Trump supporters blame "radical leftists" and "Antifa" for the catastrophic collapse of America and thus as existential threats that must be eliminated with violence.[34] Claims of civilizational decline and the prophecies that portend it are frequent features of white nationalism and are used to justify appalling acts of brutality and bloodshed—as seen during the January 6, 2021 Capitol insurrection. Despite this, apocalyptic prophecies proliferate across climate journalism in more "moderate" centrist publications as traditional journalists similarly vie to regain their own privileged positions as gatekeepers and truth-tellers. This has led to climate news stories that portend total chaos and catastrophe as more or less inevitable due to both a lack of "public will" and to "militant" progressive activists who are preventing very smart men from saving us all.

A concerning outcome of this form of climate reporting is the assumption that the opportunity to mitigate climate change has passed due to both "the masses" and "radical leftists" who are blamed for impeding "climate action." *The New York Times Magazine*'s special climate issue released on August 5, 2018, for instance, includes a cover feature by Nathaniel Rich titled "Losing Earth," which employs this trope (see Figure 3.3). The cover's headline is written in small white text atop a black background, almost like the prophetic text of a Magic 8-Ball appearing in the void, and ominously declares: "Thirty years ago, we could have saved the planet."[35] This headline implies that "we" *could* have but ultimately did *not* save the planet because visionary sages were impeded then and continue to be impeded now. The

Figure 3.3 Cover of *The New York Times Magazine*. © [August 5, 2018].
Courtesy of The New York Times Company. All rights reserved. Used under license. https://www.nytimes.com/

prophecy of a planet in peril that scientists like James Hansen warned about, according to Rich, went unheeded due to the careless "masses" duped and manipulated by fossil fuel executives, lobbyists, and the Republican politicians who benefited financially from Big Oil. The out-group is the Republican Party and Big Oil, but Rich elevates the prophet—climate scientist James Hansen—without much interest in anyone else. Climate activists, environmental justice campaigns, and the many people who have been organizing in response to climate change for decades are sidestepped and even blamed as part of "the masses" who did not follow Hansen's call soon enough. The main focus of the article is on Hansen's prophecy and the peril of "the people" ignoring very smart men like him. Once more, the visionary sage is elevated to the highest pulpit while "the masses" are blamed for civilizational decline.

Interestingly, the left-leaning news magazine *In These Times* employs this "I told you so" trope in its May 2019 issue, but positions its environmental journalist, Dick Russell, as the unheeded visionary sage as opposed to Hansen.[36] The article shows an excerpt from its January 11, 1989 issue. In this 1989 issue, Russell paints an apocalyptic scenario for the year 2010 if global warming is left unchecked and if green technologies and green energy designed by visionary sages are not implemented immediately. *In These Times* tuts: "**WE'VE KNOWN FOR 30 YEARS**"[37]—thus implying that the magazine's editors and journalists knew and told you (as one in the crowd), but you did not listen. This "tut-tut" and shaming of "the people" who failed to follow the journalists' lead is a strategic move to reassert and reclaim the publication's own authority. In other words, the magazine is saying: "you need us, we are a guiding light and this time you must listen to us and very smart men like James Hansen or the Earth will be lost for good!"

The Centrality of the Visionary Sage Above All "Others"

Within this prism of apocalypse and prophets, all context and complexity are elided: "there is often no place for interstitiality in the apocalypse."[38] Very different people are represented as either good or bad/right or wrong in prophetic tales of the end times as opposed to multidimensional, dynamic, and complex. During her initial rise as an environmental icon across media in 2018/2019, the renowned youth climate activist Greta Thunberg, for instance, was reduced to the unidimensional image of a pure and holy prophet figure and left with very little room to express her more systemic and particular critiques.[39]

Across U.S. news media, Thunberg was repeatedly portrayed—both visually and discursively—as transcendent of historical time and above the material world.[40] Like the Pope—with whom she was frequently pictured alongside in early media accounts—Thunberg was depicted as capable of seeing beyond the shortsightedness of the material present. "If I were like everyone else," Thunberg is quoted saying in the 2019 *TIME* Person of the Year issue, in which she was selected and honored, "I would have continued on and not seen this crisis."[41] Compared to Joan of Arc, Thunberg is further declared a prophet by *TIME*: "Where others smile to cut the tension, Thunberg is withering. Where others speak the language of hope, Thunberg repeats the unassailable science: Oceans will rise. Cities will flood. Millions of people will suffer."[42] Expanding upon this prophetic representation and framing of Greta as a "moral" voice, the *TIME* Person of the Year cover story also quotes Al Gore, saying: "Throughout history, many great morally based movements have gained traction at the very moment when young people decided to make that movement their cause."[43]

The 2019 *TIME* Person of the Year cover photo also *explicitly* portrays Thunberg in the image of a prophet (see Figure 3.4). Wearing her long blonde hair unstyled and flowing in the wind, Thunberg is pictured looking up and out across the ocean while paying no mind to the natural elements and tumultuous waves beside her—indicating her elevation above the physical world and up into a purer, holier, and more spiritual plane.[44] She is cast in a heavenly light and appears to be seeing into the great beyond—evidently viewing what can only be witnessed by her as the enlightened one.[45] This pure and holy representation of Thunberg starkly contrasts with the overtly sexualized portrayals and images of Rep. Ocasio-Cortez as a siren and demagogue discussed in Chapter 1. Thunberg—a white European girl—is here cast as a sort of foil to the sultry, racialized, and radicalized Ocasio-Cortez.

At the same time as it deepens the moderate versus militant binary along racial lines, the religious portrayal of Thunberg also evacuates her own dynamic subject position while lumping together and belittling other youth climate activists from other parts of the world who are referred to by the journalists writing for *TIME* as "hundreds of thousands of teenage 'Gretas,' from Lebanon to Liberia."[46] These young female activists' distinct and diverse subject positions are melded into just one mass of mindless followers or "fangirls," as detailed in Chapter 1 of this book. Young female climate activists from the Global South are literally transformed into "Gretas" and stripped of their own complexity and agency. At the same time, the lingering threat of the fangirl "masses"—a fear-laden construct identified in Chapter 1 that is racialized as well as gendered and aged—percolates across news stories.

102 APOCALYPTIC AUTHORITARIANISM

Figure 3.4 Cover of *TIME*. © [December 23, 2019].
Courtesy of TIME USA LLC. All rights reserved. Used under license. https://time.com/

Thunberg has repeatedly rejected the label of prophet on social media and has clearly articulated her desire to be represented along with and not above or in place of climate activists "from Lebanon to Liberia." Taking control of the narrative, Thunberg used Twitter to express her critiques of these news media portrayals of her and her peers. She also used Twitter (before it was bought by Elon Musk and turned into "X") to push back against the hatred and misogyny spewed out against her by Trump and his supporters. Trump and the right-wing media sphere repeatedly labeled Thunberg as a "puppet" being manipulated by "liberal elites." This representation is paired with news stories in the conservative press that cast her as inept and irrational due to her autism, young age, and gender. Whether as a puppet or prophet, across media, Thunberg is denied a dynamic and full speaking position. Thunberg is transformed into an Other even in stories that seemingly celebrate her. Within the discursive bounds of apocalyptic authoritarianism set by historically privileged groups of men, young female climate activists are repeatedly relegated to the margins. "Gretas" and "fangirls" are always portrayed as outside of the realm of rationality and reason. As with Rep. Ocasio-Cortez, Thunberg is reduced to a caricature and is cast as something markedly different and distinctly Other.

Fallacies and False Equivalencies

Ultimately, this preoccupation with prophecies and sages entrenches an in-group and out-group. This paradigm makes it difficult to accommodate systemic critiques, on-the-ground experiences, and a diversity of perspectives on how to respond to climate change. So-called visionary sages are regarded as credible because of their supposed special and unique status as "geniuses" while the knowledges and lived experiences of "the people" are met with suspicion and animosity. The narrative of apocalypse and prophet is extremely limiting because it greatly restricts the number and types of subject positions given representational space and recognition as legitimate/worthy of voice. The visionary sage figure is frequently given the primary position as the legitimate authority/expert in climate media discourse—but this figure is a myth. And like the militant Other/climate justice warrior stereotype that young progressive women of color are repeatedly reduced to, the visionary sage trope subsumes very different perspectives within its confines, as seen with Thunberg's portrayal as a holy, pure, Joan of Arc-type figure as opposed to a multidimensional, irreducible, and dynamic subject. Divergent experiences and positionalities are made thin to the point of erasure through tales and characters of apocalypse.

A focus on prediction, moreover, obscures actual sight. The desire for more models, prophets, and stories of a doomsday to come prevents engagement with the complexities of the present. For example, the November/December 2020 cover of *Foreign Affairs* pictures an incoming asteroid about to hit a man in a business suit who is looking elsewhere through binoculars, totally unaware of his impending doom.[47] This image can—on the one hand—be read as a critique of the dangers of prediction and the hubris and inherent limitations of a proclaimed prophet and the search for absolute truths of the future. But the headline instead reifies the desire for prophecies and the ability to "predict the next crisis" by asking **"What Are We Missing?"**[48] This frames the problem as one of currently unsophisticated, unclear, or unheeded foresight as opposed to the limitations of revering the predictions of just a few very smart men above the experiences and perspectives of everyone else. *Foreign Affairs* sidesteps the opportunity for critique and instead reinforces the authority and necessity of prophet-like figures and "smart" predictions.

Predictions, however, are incredibly easy to contest. Inaccurate future claims are used to cast doubt on climate science and the reality of climate change. For example, the May 1, 2017 issue of the conservative news magazine *National Review* turns the label of "denier" on its head and casts climate "believers" as the dangerous out-group promoting a hoax.[49] With a post-apocalyptic image of New York akin to images from the famous dystopian cli-fi film *The Day After Tomorrow* (2004), the headline for this issue of *National Review* asks: **"WHO'S A DENIER NOW?"** with the subheadline "CLIMATE APOCALYPTICISM IGNORES THE SCIENCE."[50] The *National Review*'s claim of false prophecy is difficult to counter within a discourse of prediction where the in-group and out-group can easily be reversed. Indeed, deniers and believers are either good or evil depending on the prophet doing the predicting. This extends the problem of false equivalencies. To this end, communication scholars Pieter Maeseele and Daniëlle Raeijmaekers discuss the political theorist Chantal Mouffe's work in critique of Cold War binaries by clarifying how Mouffe[51] "predominantly takes aim against how, in the discursive processes of achieving consensus, the us/them discrimination is no longer defined in political terms, but in rationalist and/or moralist terms."[52] Maeseele and Raeijmaekers lament how this move towards morality and consensus threatens robustly democratic processes by framing struggles as universalized battles between good and evil as opposed to necessary conflicts between different political positions.[53] They add how these "moralistic terms operate as discursive mechanisms of exclusion" because viable political critiques and conflicts are condemned, and dissent is viewed as immoral/wholly bad.[54] Prophetic tales of good and evil make all complexity and context moot. This restricts more robust media engagements with climate change outside of depoliticized stories of heroes and villains.

Anti-Politics of Captain Planet: American Heroes and Villains

The popular Cold War era American environmental hero/icon Captain Planet is an influential example of the enduring appeal (and danger) of the construction of clear-cut heroes and villains in climate stories.[55] *Captain Planet and the Planeteers* first premiered at the tail end of the Cold War in 1990 following years of media fearmongering about villainous enemies from the Soviet Union. Following the 1986 Chernobyl disaster in the Soviet bloc, the environmental sins of the U.S.S.R. were extensively featured across U.S. news reports.[56] And with the fall of the Berlin Wall in 1989, Captain Planet came to embody the fantasy of a victorious U.S. as the heroic and sole superpower now capable of bringing back order (and a clean environment) to the whole Earth.

The buff Captain Planet has a group of sidekicks (i.e., the Planeteers) from various geographical regions from Africa to Asia to Latin America—signaling the dream of a U.S.-led post-1989 world. The villains that Captain Planet pummels often change in each episode, but a recurring one is named Hoggish Greedly who is a portly half-man/half-pig monster that destroys nature as he greedily seeks to make more and more money from his dirty enterprises. Captain Planet ultimately fights off Hoggish Greedly with his superior strength and good values to save the planet from harm. Only the heroic and good Captain Planet can destroy the morally flawed and bad enemies that threaten the health of the world.

Notably, within this schema, Hoggish Greedly is cast as the ultimate evil and primarily blamed for all ecological crises. The problem is not capitalism, according to this logic, but villainous individuals who give capitalism a bad name. Drawing upon literary theorist Kenneth Burke's work on societal guilt and quoting Casey Schmitt's concept of "scapegoat ecology,"[57] communication scholar Emma Frances Bloomfield underscores how in climate discourse "attending to an individual is 'easier to comprehend and reconcile than blaming systemic factors' and 'offer[s] an immediately satisfying moral tale.'"[58] Accordingly, cartoon-like environmental villains are also constructed in news media accounts of climate change and are positioned as scapegoats to effectively sidestep more critical and contextualized media engagements with the actual root causes of climate change.

Even though these "villains" often do commit egregious acts of environmental harm, their supposed immorality and evilness as individuals are not the reason for climate change—a fact that is often absent from the Captain Planet/Hoggish Greedly narrative dynamic. For example, Scott Pruitt—the climate-denying and anti-environmentalist former head of the Environmental Protection Agency appointed by Trump during his first presidency—was consistently cast as the villain by journalists in a cartoon-like battle between good and evil. Pruitt is the **"TOXIC AVENGER"** in the March/April 2018 issue of *Mother Jones*[59]—decked out in the garb of a supervillain, green cape and all, in a cartoon rendition that accompanies the story. Similarly, the February 16, 2018 issue of *Newsweek* features Pruitt among a frantic pack of cartoon animals—straight out of a Disney forest—running from him in fear. In both of these magazine features, Pruitt is *literally* portrayed as a supervillain.[60]

In addition to the problem of oversimplifying more systemic issues of environmental destruction that go beyond just one man, these cartoon representations also remove any and all political context from view. This context is erased and replaced by a superhero universe. In this transcendent realm of the superhero/villain, everyday politics don't matter. Indeed, the superheroes in *The Avengers*—to which the March/April 2018 issue of *Mother Jones*[61] alludes to in its "Toxic Avenger" feature—move in and out of time periods and realms to fight off evil threats to the universe. Superheroes supersede Earthly affairs and are a part of a larger battle of good versus evil. In this way, superhero narratives obstruct meaningful engagement with the lived experiences and everyday hardships of people here and now.

While Pruitt is consistently portrayed as a particularly terrible environmental villain, his "super" villain status stems from his association with the biggest and baddest of all: Trump. Trump is portrayed as the ultimate supervillain and Pruitt is cast as one of his henchmen—or one of his **"HORSEMEN of the TRUMPOCALYPSE,"** as *The Nation* states in the headline of its September 11, 2017 issue (see Figure 3.5). In this cover story, the trope of apocalypse is reframed as the "Trumpocalypse," with the collapse of American civilization ushered in by Trump and his villainous

Figure 3.5 Cover of *The Nation*. © [September 11, 2017].

Courtesy of The Nation Company. All rights reserved. Used under license. https://www.thenation.com/

underlings.[62] Once again, the larger systemic issues that brought Trump into power are left out of this cartoon rendition of current affairs. In this way, accountability is shunted beyond the named scapegoats. A focus on particularly bad individuals may offer a sense of collective relief and comfort amid an overwhelming "total crisis," but the punishment of scapegoats leaves a corrupt system unperturbed. There is no limit to the number of villains that can be named and shamed—and the status quo remains secure so long as the cartoon battle continues.

The "Trumpocalypse" is also depicted by cartoon illustrations on the cover of the Winter 2017 issue of the leftist news and politics magazine *Jacobin*.[63] While this cover image does portray Trump as the embodiment of evil at the center of Earthly catastrophe, it also offers an entry point for critique of this representational form. A more complex and symbolically rich image—with references to QAnon, white nationalism, evangelical ideology, and more—the cover of *Jacobin* requires a deeper understanding of political context in order to be understood.[64] The stories featured in the issue expand on and clarify this context by critiquing the normalization of white supremacy and hate in American politics under Trump, but still often fall into the trope of an in-group and out-group amid a more generalized "total crisis."

The comfort afforded by a degree of abstraction from these generalizations is understandable during a time of such upheaval. But the mythical tale of superheroes and supervillains directs attention away from the root causes of climate change and the particular impacts of it. Although the stories printed in the Winter 2017 issue of *Jacobin* challenge readers to navigate the cover image's symbolic meanings, the stories still fall short of moving beyond a narrative of good and evil. In turn, the desire for a visionary sage figure is still elevated by *Jacobin*.[65] In stories where Trump is represented as the ultimate supervillain, there is more often than not a superhero that appears as his foil. In centrist magazines ahead of the 2020 election, this superhero was usually Joe Biden, and in left-of-center magazines like *Jacobin*, Alexandria Ocasio-Cortez or Bernie Sanders often appeared as Trump's foil. The May 6, 2019 issue of the center-left *The Nation*, for example, featured an Arlen Schumer comic book image of Ocasio-Cortez as "Lady Lantern" and a new superhero in the DC universe.[66] Ocasio-Cortez is pictured as a comic book hero with green hair, green eyebrows, green earrings, green eyes, green mask, green lipstick (here green replaces her signature red lipstick often featured in other media representations of the Congresswoman), and a tight-fitting green turtleneck jumpsuit.[67] Evidently, climate politics and climate change are easily interpreted through the lens of a comic book tale across the ideological spectrum.

Environmental communication scholar Steven Schwarze calls this rhetorical form of environmental heroes and villains an "environmental melodrama."[68] Schwarze argues that environmental melodramas "can transform ambiguous and unrecognized environmental conditions into public problems" adding that this presents "an enticing rhetorical strategy for environmental advocates."[69] Schwarze here pushes back against critiques of environmental melodramas and highlights how this narrative style may be useful because it can inspire an initial interest in a reader who will then seek out further information on climate change. The problem with Schwarze's argument in the case of climate journalism is that the news media are a prime source for this further information.[70] Traditional journalists' repeated elevation of certain subject positions over others in climate stories thus has a great impact on surrounding discourse. When the visionary sage is repeatedly placed at the center of climate journalism, different perspectives and experiences are persistently excluded within and outside of the climate beat.

Indeed, just like in superhero stories, "the masses" are understood as irrelevant and are interpreted as either doomed to perish at the hands of a supervillain or destined to be saved by a superhero and their valiant strength. The binary of hero/villain therefore limits the representational space allowed for "the masses"/"the people"/"the public" when it brings just a few select saviors to the fore. A deep desire for order once again surfaces here—as we have seen elsewhere—and ignites a quest for moral truths and the comfort of a simple binary of right and wrong with clear-cut enemies and a legible in-group and out-group. Once again, within this paradigm, all-encompassing solutions designed by visionary sages are advanced as the "correct" and *only* way forward. A very limited number of visions for how to navigate climate change are advanced when a visionary sage is placed at center stage.

The hero and villain narrative, therefore, comes with major risks when adopted by the democratic left. This is because the core problem remains: If Trump is cast as the supervillain and ultimate harbinger of apocalyptic chaos, then climate discourse is limited to a melodramatic tale of good versus evil with only two possible endings—either the hero or villain triumphs. There is little space allowed for imagining different futures beyond the visionary sage's prophecy—whether that be a dystopian hellscape/"Bad" Anthropocene discussed in the previous chapter or a more utopic/"Good" Anthropocene designed by just a few very smart men.

Furthermore, Trump's removal from office is advanced as the ultimate resolution to a very long and dark story. Hartmann calls this ultimate scapegoating of just one man "Trump exceptionalism" and warns that a singular focus on Trump as the source of all present-day conflict and strife has "deflected attention from the country's hyper-militarization in recent decades."[71] Hartmann further laments how "many Americans now look to military and intelligence agencies as saviors that will protect us from Trump and restore America's rightful place as the greatest and most powerful nation on earth."[72] As discussed in the previous chapter, military action is often advanced in climate news stories as necessary to stave off the harms of climate change and other threats impeding American leadership and centrality in the world. Because Trump is portrayed as the ultimate supervillain akin to Hoggish Greedly and a threat to American power and economic centrality, Captain Planet and the strength of the American military are positioned as required to fight off this present danger. Once Hoggish Greedly is defeated, the U.S. will be secure and all will be good in the world again.

This is where Joe Biden was often cast as the ultimate hero across centrist media following his presidential victory in November 2020. Notably, President Biden was regarded as a conduit for renewal and redemption to "build back better" after the devastation of the first Trump presidency. The November 2020 cover of *Rolling Stone* reflects this notion asserting "**Biden's Moment**" and portraying him as the "right leader to rebuild America."[73] The cover story's illustration of Biden looking forward amid a background of blue sky and heavenly clouds portrays him as a good and holy figure capable of bringing peace back to the land.[74] Only Biden's head and upper torso are pictured. He is shown squinting slightly as his bright vision for the future comes into view. Biden is depicted wearing a shirt and blazer but no tie—signaling that he is a distinguished and seasoned leader but not too far removed from the "average" American. He is both a man of the people and a Godsent leader who will shepherd America out of the chaotic and undignified Trump years and into a glorious future. This story of renewal and rebirth is typical of the jeremiad form and risks the further entrenchment and obfuscation of larger systemic issues. To this point, Hartmann warns that:

> we should resist the temptation to see [Trump's] demise in apocalyptic terms: the death of the Antichrist and the birth of a new golden age. The forces that produced Trump will persist after he is gone. […] Trump's end will not be the end of history.[75]

The Winter 2021 cover of *Jacobin* pokes fun at this heroic representation of President Biden as the ultimate savior and the media's portrayal of his election as the "birth of a new golden age."[76] In the cover image, Biden is portrayed as Jesus, and Democratic leaders and journalists appear as angels.[77] Everyday people gaze above and celebrate the miracle of his being. Although *Jacobin*'s parody is pointed, critiques need to go beyond this. There must be a breakage of unidimensional caricatures, not a reinforcement—even if in a parodied form. This can be done through more nuanced coverage of the root causes, present harms, and different responses to climate change from a plurality of dynamic subject positions and lived experiences. But because systemic critiques and contexts often do not accompany news stories where the hero/villain binary is leveraged, good/bad positionalities and claims of right/wrong are easily reversed to serve very different political ends.

This dualism of hero and villain poses the risk of co-optation and the eventual elimination of the ability to make viable critiques of the political economy and exploitative governance structures. Fossil fuel lobbyists and conservative media, for example, ubiquitously cast critical figures fighting for political-economic change, such as Ocasio-Cortez, as the villains—as seen in the March 11, 2019 cover image of *National Review* (see Figure 3.6). In this cartoon image, Ocasio-Cortez is cast as "sinful" and villainous—in stark contrast with her superhero portrayal as "Lady Lantern" by the cartoonist Arlen Schumer featured in the center-left *The Nation*. Ocasio-Cortez is drawn with exaggerated features including an elongated face and nose with gigantic ears, eyes, eyebrows, teeth, and red lips from her signature red lipstick.[78] She is also shown adorned in a suffragette-inspired white pantsuit like the one she wore at her Congressional inauguration along with other female members of Congress in protest against Trump, a statement that is here mocked along with her "absurd Green New Deal."[79] With the headline **"SINS OF EMISSION"** and images of cow butts, the cover story ridicules Ocasio-Cortez's concerns regarding greenhouse gas emissions from massive industrial agriculture operations.[80] According to the reporters for this magazine, the *real* supervillains are Democratic leaders who support the "absurdity" of Ocasio-Cortez, not Trump and his allies. False equivalencies abound. In tales of heroes and villains, reversals of character are extremely easy to pull off. For example, and as we have seen in Chapter 1's discussion of the October 2019 issue of *The New American*,[81] right-wing media reverse the horsemen of apocalypse portrayal of Trump and his cabinet members to instead cast Ocasio-Cortez and "The Squad" as the four horse*women* of the apocalypse.

Figure 3.6 Cover of *National Review*. © [March 11, 2019].
Courtesy of National Review.

Discursive Mechanisms of Exclusion

It is difficult to distinguish particularities in apocalyptic narratives of prophets and tales of good and evil. That is because particularities do not matter in these stories. Nuanced critiques of exclusionary structures of power from progressives are silenced at the same time as they are co-opted and evacuated of meaning by the right.[82] In the realm of the transcendent where present particularities are overshadowed by universal truth claims, opposites cease to be opposites and systemic critiques are lost within a contextless void. Trump is a hero and Ocasio-Cortez is a villain just as easily as they are not. The role of hero and villain can be appropriated, manipulated, and assigned to one or another public figure with little effort or justification. Historically privileged figures thrive in these conditions of decontextualization and depoliticization. As Bloomfield underscores, the construction of scapegoats and a temporality of transcendence "create and maintain order."[83] Belief in heroes and villains provides a sense of comfort and control while elevating just a few "very smart men" to the highest helms of power because it eliminates the need for navigating complexities and imagining how politics and society could be otherwise.

Universal tales with clear-cut outcomes as opposed to complex stories with uncertain futures maintain the status quo and protect traditional figures of power. Venture capitalists are declared prophets and saviors as opposed to being questioned and critiqued for their role in weakening democratic decision-making processes and bolstering an exploitative economic system. For example, the financier Jeremy Grantham is celebrated as "An Investing Prophet" who "[Took] on Climate Change" in *Bloomberg Businessweek*.[84] Geoengineers who want to move an iceberg from the Arctic to the equator in order to cool the oceans and "solve" climate change (and make some cash via highly lucrative and privately operated geoengineering technologies along the way) are similarly celebrated as climate heroes by *Bloomberg Businessweek* in the June 10, 2019 issue.[85] Photographic portraits of this "investing prophet" and "genius" geoengineers appear in *Bloomberg*—each of which shows a man who is older, white, and well-dressed. These portraits work towards elevating these men to a position of greatness as powerful, authoritative, dignified, and important visionary sages. Portrait photos like these are common in climate journalism. Originally commissioned by the royals and aristocracy to reflect their prestige and long-lasting influence even after death, portrait images have historically been used to commemorate individuals of great wealth, power, and significance. In climate news stories, the portrait image usually depicts an older, well-dressed, white man doing "very important" work—like Grantham at his office desk in *Bloomberg*. These genius portrait photos that accompany many climate news stories are usually a headshot or a full body shot of a man looking right at the camera in their office, lab, or place of business. The proliferation of this type of image reinforces and legitimizes the superiority of these men as *the* authority on climate change now and forever.

Within this regime of representation where just a few superior and select sages dominate, different subjectivities and forms of expertise and knowledge are either totally denied or disparaged. Once more, dynamic positionalities are flattened while unidimensional caricatures are elevated. This flattening, as we have seen, can be accomplished through either subsuming social conflict into a universal story of hero versus villain or through casting very different people as cartoon-like characters. Additionally, certain people and their voices are removed from the story altogether. Ocasio-Cortez and Democratic Socialists are, for example, consistently portrayed as outside of the transcendent realm of heroes and their perspectives are often elided or ridiculed in news stories. Even in her superhero portrayal as "Lady Lantern,"[86] *The Nation* editorializes this image in a parodical manner—poking fun at the reverence Ocasio-Cortez garners from young progressive female "masses"/"fangirls" who supposedly lack the vital critical thinking skills and basic understanding of political strategy to be taken seriously. "**The Socialist Moment**," according to the headline for the June 2019 issue of the left-leaning *The New Republic*, reflects the sentiment that Ocasio-Cortez's appeal among young Democratic Socialists may just be a *momentary* blip within an unusually chaotic present.[87] Unlike her male counterparts who are cast as far-seeing geniuses, young women like Ocasio-Cortez are dismissed as shortsighted and unable to see beyond the mere present. Young progressive women of color are, therefore, dismissed as outside of the realm of the transcendent and thus deemed irrelevant even in publications that are more sympathetic to leftist causes.

The cover image for the June 2019 issue of the left-leaning *The New Republic* (see Figure 3.7) reveals the embedded gender and racial stereotypes that often shape this distinction between farsighted men and shortsighted young women who don't deserve to be heard. Ocasio-Cortez is cast as the wife in the cover image's adaptation of Grant Wood's 1930 painting *American Gothic*, and is shown in a darker light, looking off to the side, distracted, and unfocused—reproducing exactly the wife's gaze from the original painting. Bernie Sanders, portrayed as the husband and cast in light while holding the Democratic Socialist rose in place of a pitchfork, stares right back at the painter/viewer of the magazine cover, retaining a higher

Figure 3.7 Cover of *The New Republic*. © [June 2019].
Courtesy of The New Republic. All rights reserved. Used under license. https://newrepublic.com/

level of authority than Ocasio-Cortez. Sanders is thus positioned as the image's central figure. Ocasio-Cortez is once again dismissed as misguided, shortsighted, and somehow below "exceptional men" even in a left-leaning publication. Because the visionary sage figure is given such a central representational space in climate journalism across the ideological spectrum, the repeated portrayal of Ocasio-Cortez as a myopic young woman effectively delegitimizes her speaking position. Ocasio-Cortez is consistently portrayed as Other and as irrational, shortsighted, and potentially dangerous.

"Rational speech," according to the social theorist Jürgen Habermas, is deemed essential for ensuring "quality" political and media discourse that is vital for "democratic deliberation."[88] This rational speech criterion, however, problematically bars certain communication forms that lie outside of the moderate ideal established by the old boys' club of Enlightenment-era European men.[89] Ecofeminist scholars highlight how women and especially women of color are repeatedly represented as below men who are positioned as the default "rational" subject through claims of female "irrationality" and "immoderation" entrenched via the exploitative binary of nature/culture.[90] Tellingly, women and especially women of color are heavily involved in the environmental movement, and their activism often echoes ecofeminist critiques of the interrelationship between environmental exploitation and the exploitation of women and marginalized groups more generally.[91] Despite their dynamic critiques, media representations of female environmental activists—like Ocasio-Cortez as an alluring siren or Thunberg as a pure and holy prophet—often draw upon essentializing tropes that obscure and silence their actual voices. Limited by strict claims of morality and goodness, the binary of moderate versus militant entrenches these tropes and relegates women and especially Black, Brown, and Indigenous women as Other and outside the realm of moral reason and thus justifies their exclusion from deliberations and decision-making.

It is through this binary where longstanding gender, racial, and generational stereotypes are drawn upon by traditional journalists dedicated to "quality information"[92] to especially exclude or denigrate young progressive women of color in climate news stories. With clear right and wrong modes of speech delineated and with historically privileged American men consistently celebrated as the default "rational" and "good" subject, a plurality of dynamic and complex subjectivities that differ from this rigid, liberal democratic one are deemed "wrong."

Conclusion

The visionary sage figure is a main character in climate journalism. The centrality of the visionary sage in media accounts problematically flattens dynamic histories, experiences, and speaking positions. Through narratives of prediction and clear-cut solutions, systemic critiques are cut from view. Only one vision of the future—as portended by the visionary sage—is demarcated as correct. Responses that contest or critique these sages are demonized as obstructionist and impeding the "right" path forward. Very little space is given to proposals for change that question or seek to disrupt longstanding dynamics of power and exclusionary decision-making processes. Different contexts and perspectives are subsumed by a tale of good versus evil. This decontextualization and depoliticization prevents meaningful consideration of responses to climate change that lie outside of the purview of just a few very smart men.

In the chapter that follows, these limitations are examined further through a critical analysis of representations of race in U.S. climate journalism. Chapter 4 illuminates how racist stereotypes and neo-Malthusian claims of "population bombs" and out-of-control "hordes" of climate migrants coming from the Global South severely restrict climate news stories. This fearmongering of racialized Others, in turn, works to animate reactionary movements that propel apocalyptic authoritarianism.

4
Climate Death-World and Life-World

Discursive processes of Othering play a central role in U.S. climate journalism. In addition to the discursive construction of militant Others at home, predictions of climate chaos are also often paired with striking images of Black and Brown climate migrants and refugees from abroad who are fleeing the Global South—a region of the world that is consistently framed in U.S. news reports as unstable and dangerous. These images direct climate fears and anxieties towards often racialized Others portrayed as hailing from *other* "uncivilized" parts of the world. Scenes of violent disorder are constructed through sensational claims of mass migrations paired with stories detailing how climate change is a threat multiplier that will bring social unrest to the U.S. from outside if protective actions are not taken to keep "them" out.

Apocalyptic authoritarianism leverages xenophobic sentiments to blame a designated group of Others for causing global climate chaos. This chapter reveals how journalists construct an essentialist dualism between a "civilized" and "uncivilized" world to justify the U.S.'s economic and military interference abroad. In addition to claims of national security, this interference is framed by journalists as a noble act that will *give* the freedoms of an American way of life to those who currently do not possess "liberty and justice for all." In turn, this framing legitimizes U.S. global expansion as a necessary response to the "total crisis" of social and climate breakdown.

Othering and American Empire

Postcolonial and cultural studies scholars including Edward Said, Stuart Hall, and Gayatri Chakravorty Spivak reveal how stereotypes of corrupt, unstable, violent, and uncivilized Others have been forged and leveraged by imperial nations—including the U.S.—to legitimize their claims to power. Said argued that the identity of nation-states in the "West" has for centuries depended on their unique legibility and distinction from the "Orient."[1] Said explained how fabricated and exoticized images of the Oriental

Other are reinforced through cultural stereotypes that denigrate the people who live in places outside of Europe and the settler nation-states of the "West." [2] Stuart Hall clarified how through repetition across art, films, news stories, and other modes of cultural representation a dualism of the "West" and the "rest" has been entrenched to the point of common sense.[3] To this end, Spivak argued that through discursive processes of Othering, imperialists and neo-imperialists "world" (used here as a verb) the "rest" via the totalizing image of the "Third World"/"Global South."[4] This "worlding" constructs the "Global South" as a distinct and separate realm from the "First World"/"West"/"Global North" and as an innately inferior and less stable one.[5] It is within this divided set of worlds where the position of "self" in relation to a distinctly foreign "Other" is fashioned and preserved via racist tropes. An essentialist dualism of an American self at odds with an anti/un-American Other draws upon these tropes and fundamentally shapes how climate change is reported on by traditional journalists writing for national news publications.

The assertion that the U.S. is *giving* the advantages of an American way of life to the Global South is for example used to justify calls for protecting this "gift" from those who seek to steal or destroy it. For instance, in his study of development institutions following World War II (WWII), critical anthropologist Arturo Escobar details how the breakup of formal European colonial holdings in Africa, Asia, and Latin America did not mean the end of imperial rule.[6] Instead, via a discourse of poverty and economic underdevelopment, postcolonial nations were represented as particularly wanting and in need of experts from the U.S. and Western Europe to help "modernize" economies and political institutions.[7] Escobar identifies the construction of new terms like gross domestic product (GDP) that were crafted as an "objective" measurement and used to assess the stability and economic health of a nation.[8] Measures of GDP became and continue to be used as a tool for determining whether certain nations are "advanced" or not based on levels of economic production and consumption. In turn, "poor" nations with low measurements of GDP are positioned as both desperate for economic development and also financially risky for businesses to invest in. This creates the impression of a limited route forward where only loans, aid, or expertise can be *given* to the Global South from the Global North—but with many strings attached. The predominance of global projects of green tech transfer and climate loans *given* to the Global South from wealthy nation-states in the Global North are celebrated across national news stories as heroic and reinforce these asymmetrical relations of power.

The vast apparatus of post-WWII global economic and development institutions led by the U.S. depended on a permanent state of underdevelopment in the Global South to legitimize interference by Global North nation-states in newly independent postcolonial nations. Escobar clarifies:

> The objects with which development began to deal after 1945 were numerous and varied. [...] Everything was subjected to the eye of the new experts: the poor dwellings of the rural masses, the vast agricultural fields, cities, households, factories, hospitals, schools, public offices, towns and regions, and, in the last instance, the world as a whole. The vast surface over which discourse moved at ease practically covered the entire cultural, economic and political geography of the Third World.[9]

Through "worlding" and a dualism of developed and underdeveloped, the U.S. and nations of the Global North justified their presence in the Global South as existing for the greater good of *giving* poor and "backwards" nations the "advanced" technologies they needed to "modernize" their economies and states. Problematically, however, the so-called developed nations took—and continue to take—advantage of "cheap" labor and "cheap" natural resources in the Global South (often referred to as the "Third World" during the Cold War time period) to the detriment of both the environment and democratic decision-making processes.[10] Awareness of this exploitation and the hypocrisy of contemporary calls for Global South nations to curb their industrial activities and greenhouse gas emissions because of climate change often leads to suspicion of global environmental initiatives or outright animosity—as seen with the right-wing nationalism of former president Jair Bolsonaro's antiglobalist and anti-environment platform in Brazil. Concerningly, the Bolsonaro regime leveraged these suspicions of the Global North while leaning into a strong embrace of nationalism to legitimize the violent removal of Indigenous Amazonians and the purposeful burning of the rainforest in which they lived for the development of cattle ranching operations in the name of "national prosperity."

Despite these and other problematic implications of worlding, development discourse, and strong nationalist responses to both, the U.S. and Global North continue to draw upon essentialist tropes and stereotypes to advance new reasons for interference in the Global South—including around climate change. The deployment of "sustainable development experts" to Africa, Asia, and Latin America is validated as required for the health and well-being of economies, states, and the natural environment in the Global South as well as for overall global security. Sustainable development experts often pay less attention to the murders of Indigenous Amazonians, however, than to the peril of the fires and smoke suffocating the "lungs of the world" (i.e., the Amazon rainforest) and thus choking the Global North too. While the burning of the Amazon is an important concern, the manner in which these threats are described by both sustainable development experts and journalists in the U.S. elide the underlying (neo)imperial systems and inequitable structures of power that bring the likes of Bolsonaro (and Trump) to the helms of government.

Despite the longstanding postcolonial critiques of Othering and development discourse, climate stories in some of the most prominent American news publications continually position the U.S. as distinct and superior to financially "poor" nations in the Global South. For example, a special issue of *Bloomberg Businessweek*, published on November 5, 2018 (see Figure 4.1), features stories on the potential climatic *perils* of economic growth in the Global South. The prospect of increased meat consumption and the demand for more consumer products as more people move out of poverty are positioned as a climatic threat. The cover image for this special issue of *Bloomberg Businessweek* features a headline written in large bold text—"**Growth Engines**"—with a GDP map of the globe.[11] A subheadline states: "The world as we know it is about to change."[12] This cover image reflects the construction of "underdevelopment" that Escobar identifies.[13] Namely, through the GDP map, Africa, the Middle East, parts of Asia, and Latin America are pictured as strikingly misshapen because they are compressed by a low GDP. The nations of the Global South look skinny and starved—literally portrayed as lacking. Meanwhile, the U.S. and Western Europe look disproportionately larger than the typical Atlas image—they are robust and plump with large GDPs. The weight and mass of the map are pulled upward—into the "developed" Global North. Strikingly, the foreboding subheadline "The world as we know it is about to change"[14] signals that "growth" in the Global South is an imminent threat to this robustness and dominance of the Global North as well as to the world's climate. In other words, a more equitable globe where material wealth is more evenly distributed is, in an ironic twist of the stated goals of development projects, represented as a potentially dangerous prospect.

The GDP map on the cover of *Bloomberg* is essential to the cover story's construction of the Other. An economically robust Global North is

Figure 4.1 Cover of *Bloomberg Businessweek*. © [November 5, 2018]. Used with permission of Bloomberg L.P. © 2024. All rights reserved.

demarcated as distinct from an economically starved Global South. Postcolonial scholars point out how maps have been used as tools of power to demarcate and naturalize "centers" and "peripheries" since Mercator's *Atlas* was published in the late 1500s.[15] Postcolonial scholar José Rabasa explains how:

along with an ideological stance, [Mercator's] the *Geographie and Historie of the Atlas* convey a planetary strategy wherein knowledge and representation indissolubly institute and erase territories. If specific political configurations establish boundaries and national identities for a European geographic space, then the rest of the world acquires spatial meaning only after the different regions have been inscribed by Europeans.[16]

Notably, in the case of the *Bloomberg* cover image, GDP is the marker that inscribes and makes certain areas legible or not. GDP—as Escobar points out[17]—is a Global North invention, and the legibility of nations, according to this map, wholly depends on a European/U.S. design and the ideological construct of economic growth. Parts of the globe are shrunken or entirely erased via the limited lens of GDP, the consequences of which include the entrenchment of Global North claims of legitimacy, sovereignty, and centrality in global affairs.

At the same time, however, the obvious manipulation of the standardized world map image on the cover of *Bloomberg* also opens up the possibility for potential critiques of the constructed nature of the map and Atlases in general, which are positioned by their creators to be more or less objective and true. Rabasa emphasizes how "nothing keeps the *Atlas* from being translated into a non-European idiom as its ultimate irony within a historical horizon."[18] Indeed, the blatancy of U.S. interests in demonizing the "Growth Engines" of China and India[19] as global environmental threats especially emboldens anti-Western critiques of the cartographic and statistical data advanced by the U.S. This, in turn, can be—and is—used to foment Chinese and Indian nationalism to the detriment of potential transnational coalitions and partnerships required to address climate change. From either direction, the essentializing binary of East/West and North/South is challenging to break and move beyond.

Escobar, in his more recent work, argues that it is essential to chisel apart dualisms in order to move away from a polarizing form of politics and towards a more pluralistic form that can contend with the complexities of climate change in a just and transformative manner.[20] Escobar observes that since the Enlightenment, the Cartesian model of nature/culture has shaped the way Europeans interpret the world—including the "New World."[21] Through a contemporaneous imperial project, Escobar contends that Europeans exported and reinforced the Cartesian model elsewhere through economic, cultural, and political institutions of the "modern" nation-state including traditional journalism.[22] Despite the brittle binaries forged through an imperial discourse that deemed non-Europeans as Other and lesser, Rabasa underscores how "the empire has always been writing back."[23] "Master narratives" and dominant "regimes of representation" are always resisted, contested, and negotiated.[24] These negotiations, however, are often relegated to an ideological battlefield between two camps. Stories of enmity limit an engagement with difference, nuance, and complexity beyond a binary formation.

It is extremely difficult to break free of an entrenched dualism of good and evil/right and wrong. In U.S. media and politics, this difficulty has been compounded since the Cold War. As discussed in the previous chapters of this book, during this contentious period of ideological jousting and American empire-building, U.S. journalism doubled down and reactivated stark, binary divisions of the world with the U.S. on one end and the U.S.S.R. on the other—a trend that continues to shape journalistic accounts of global crises, wars, and catastrophes[25] including climate change. Through the separation of the "free world" (i.e., the U.S.) from the "slave world" (i.e., the U.S.S.R.),[26] the illusion of a "One-World World"[27] where one way of organizing a society is deemed absolute was entrenched through stories that framed communism as a direct threat to an American way of life and thus to the whole Earth. Through one-sided accounts of the Soviet Union and of postcolonial socialist movements in the Global South, American Cold War discourse drew upon longstanding colonial tropes to advance notions of a zero-sum game—where the flourishing of socialism was interpreted as a direct threat to American lives.[28] Through the construction of a postcolonial and socialist Other, Cold War media discourse integrated racist stereotypes together with red-scare fearmongering to generate a sense of existential peril. This fearmongering continues to validate American state, economic, and military interference abroad as necessary for keeping the free world free.

The maps and figures included in the feature stories inside this special issue of *Bloomberg*, for instance, are editorialized and colored by an Americentric positionality that paints climate change as a zero-sum game according to Cold War logics. A binary representation that portrays China and India as both inferior to the U.S. and as environmental threats entrenches an oppositional divide between the "West" and the "rest."[29] The title of one of the editorialized maps featured inside *Bloomberg* is "Mapping the Miasma."[30] This title contains a surprising reference to "miasma"—a medical theory disproven in the nineteenth century that hypothesized the spread of disease and death via "bad air." This is a striking reference not only because miasma is an obsolete medical theory but also because it was a discriminatory one—used to demonize, police, and purge supposedly unclean or otherwise undesirable people from the community. In Greek mythology—from which the word originates—"miasma" was understood as "a contagious power" that until "purged by the sacrificial death of the wrongdoer, society would be chronically infected by catastrophe."[31] This "wrongdoer" is represented as innately Other, foreign, and a threat to society. Accordingly, the green dots on the "Mapping the Miasma" graphic that are placed over major cities in China and India indicate areas where "catastrophic" pollution pervades. In order to remediate and cleanse these problematic areas of "bad air" (for the sake of global air quality and greenhouse gas emissions levels), a fundamental upheaval of the currently "unsustainable" and "bad" economic practices and ways of life in India and China is promoted as essential for the overall health and stability of the "global commons."

In this feature story published in *Bloomberg*, the "traditional ways" of people in the Global South who live in the demarcated "bad" areas wrought by environmental wrongdoing are demonized as an overwhelming threat that must be contained and eliminated. The domestic cooking traditions and rural farming practices of Indians, for example, are constructed as a large contributor to the impending catastrophe of global warming. The *Bloomberg* article states:

> Now that Indian farmers have harvested their fall crops, they will clear their fields the traditional way—by burning them. The soot-thick air hangs over northern India during the winter, dramatically exacerbating the cloud of toxins already spewed by power plants, factories, vehicles, and stoves.[32]

Nothing short of a total change to Indian society—from the home to the economy to land use—is therefore required. The echoes of colonial and development discourse are strong. "Clean technologies" and "clean-air policies" introduced by the Global North are elevated by *Bloomberg* as a desperately required solution to quell toxic air pollution and climate change.[33] Once again, a clearly delineated "right" response of clean/green tech transfer via "expert" economic and sustainable development institutions is advanced by visionary sage figures from the U.S. as the one and only way forward to "solve" the *crisis* of climate change. The unaddressed biases and imperial roots of these solutions are easily spotlighted and pointed out by opportunistic leaders in India and China to demonstrate the hypocrisy of the U.S. and the West and to assert their own supreme authority. In turn, more comprehensive and robustly democratic climate initiatives supported by transnational coalitions of climate justice activists in China, India, and the U.S. are demonized in each nation-state. Critical humanities scholar Eddie Yuen underscores how consequential this is and argues that "the impulse to blame the masses of the Global South for the environmental crisis is especially damaging, because they are often on the cutting edge of ecological activism and are looking for allies."[34] The blaming of a racialized group as the cause of a global "miasma" closes off the possibility for alliances and instead legitimizes a "militarized lifeboat ethics"[35] where only some can survive the incoming "climate apocalypse." According to this logic, all undesirable Others must be kept off the boat and killed for "us" to be saved. Critical scholar Betsy Hartmann calls this lifeboat ethics the "greening of hate"[36]—others call it ecofascism[37] or biopower.

Biopower/Population Control: Saving Ourselves from the Population Bomb

It is advantageous for the U.S. to continue to maintain a binary of self/Other through essentialist logics that espouse often racist claims of innate cultural superiority/inferiority because it legitimizes what Foucault calls "biopower"—defined as the regulation of and control over populations of people.[38] The concept of biopower is highly relevant to climate discourse because it helps explain policies that claim to "save" and "protect" human lives on Earth from, for instance, overconsumption and toxic pollution in the Global South and "population bombs"[39] of undesirable Others. The U.S. nation-state, in other words, retains its legitimacy and power if it upholds the promise of securing the health and safety of American lives and an American way of life from these Others.

Economic and population growth in the Global South—that is, "Growth Engines" in *Bloomberg*'s lingo[40]—are framed as dangerous to American lives. All people from the Global South are Othered as existential threats—for example, as a "miasma"[41] that must be contained and purified. Whole populations are framed as potential "bombs" that could spread this miasma and bring down the global climate and the U.S. with it. In *History of*

Sexuality, Vol. 1, Foucault underscored how the advancement of biopolitics in the late eighteenth/early nineteenth centuries through statistical social sciences like demography reduced humans to mere bodies defined by their biological functions (such as fertility and procreation), with "an explosion of numerous and diverse techniques for achieving the subjugations of bodies and the control of populations."[42] It is here where Foucault argued that "the discipline of the body and the regulations of the population constituted the two poles around which the organization of power over life was deployed."[43] To "make life live," in turn, became a state's rationale for its existence and justification for its authority.[44] Intellectual historian David Macey clarified that biopolitics is concerned with "the level of life itself."[45]

It is within these biopolitical dynamics of power that a discourse of overpopulation in the Global South is advanced as an existential threat that requires a sovereign power (i.e., the U.S.) to step in, control, and securitize. Climate media discourse in the U.S. is often shaped by fearmongering of an out-of-control increase of primarily poor populations in the Global South. Poor people from poor places are imagined as a contagion or "miasma" wreaking havoc and causing climate chaos. A solution to this chaos, therefore, is the containment of these Others. For example, in a feature in the May/June 2017 issue of *Foreign Policy*[46] titled "**Is There a Case to be Made Against Baby Making?**," two philosophers from the U.S.—Travis Rieder and Rebecca Kukla—"discuss the morality of deciding to have children in a world threatened by environmental degradation."[47] Couched in a discussion of morality where there is a "right" and a "wrong" way of making a family, these two U.S. philosophers from Johns Hopkins and Georgetown University call for a "culture shift" where "small, active city spaces with tons of possibilities" are the utopic model for a future society.[48] People who live in *these* kinds of places (i.e., wealthy urban centers with highly educated and privileged residents) tend to make more "ethical" and "rational" decisions about family planning and their "carbon footprint." Rieder clarifies how:

> it's not my job to tell people what to do procreatively. Instead, what I do is I carry people through a deliberative process that my family has gone through because they're relatively like me—wealthy high emitters with control over reproductive decisions. And we got to have a child—we did it. We understand that comes with a massive cost that the world's worst-off will be the ones to bear. Would it be selfish, or troubling, or irresponsible, or problematic to do it again? And the answer we came to—in our very contextualized and specific situation—was yes.[49]

In other words, although it's not Rieder's "job to tell people what to do procreatively"—after all, he can't force anyone to abstain from having children—he can encourage them to be more like him: rational and ethical (i.e., more "advanced"). This division of American men like Rieder as rational and moral and entirely distinct from the irrational and inevitably doomed "worst-off" Others is highly classed, gendered, and racialized. Rieder's elevation of his deliberative capabilities as a well-educated, well-off, moral, and responsible white male positions himself among those who *should* have children after careful reflection and planning, separating Rieder from those who should not. These Others require what Rieder calls a "culture shift" in order to be on the same intellectual level as him. He ominously adds that this "culture shift," however, "will take time we don't have"—implying that more heavy-handed measures may be warranted to combat population growth and the climate "emergency."[50]

Rieder's discussion partner, Rebecca Kukla, pushes back against some parts of Rieder's argument (the article is set up as a debate as much as a discussion between these two American philosophers)—in particular, against his recurrent and core focus on women's reproductive decisions as opposed to a more fundamental analysis of patriarchal dynamics and oppressive conditions of poverty. Despite this critique, however, Kukla remains in agreement that a "culture shift" is absolutely necessary. This agreement reinforces the blame on less educated and poorer Others. The scholar and environmental activist Vandana Shiva points out how poor women and especially poor women of color are most often the ones demonized and targeted by men and women like Rieder and Kukla from the Global North who want to control the supposed overpopulation of Others in the Global South.[51] The historian and political theorist Achille Mbembe further explains how "biopower, in Foucault's work, appears to function by dividing people into those who must live and those who must die [...] This control presupposes a distribution of humans into groups [...] Foucault refers to this using the seemingly familiar term 'racism.'"[52] Young Black and Brown women are repeatedly blamed for overpopulation and framed as a global environmental threat. At the same time, women's access to birth control is used as a marker of development[53]—along with GDP[54]—to signal how advanced a nation is.[55] In other words, women and girls are reduced to mere bodies as well as to statistical indicators of development that the Global North claims the authority to regulate—whether from birth control or everyday bodily functions.

Instead of a focus on systemic shortcomings and entrenched policies of imperial exploitation, environmental degradation and economic underdevelopment are blamed on Black and Brown women who are represented as Others and as the source of societal and environmental chaos. Take, for instance, another feature article published in the November 5, 2018 special issue[56] of *Bloomberg Businessweek* titled "A simple way to advance women."[57] The story features a lead image of three young Indian girls wearing school uniforms and carrying books and backpacks. The image's caption is "Schoolgirls in the village of Kachhpura in northern India."[58] Gender studies scholar Chandra Talpade Mohanty details how images of young girls and women from the Global South are often appropriated by Western humanitarian organizations to justify their interventions.[59] This appropriation, in turn, lumps all women and girls from the Global South together into a monolithic caricature of oppressed females devoid of agency.[60] Here, the image of young schoolgirls is leveraged as a visual indicator of their "advancement" thanks to the "simple," yet effective, technological interventions introduced by Global North "humanitarians" into the bodily lives of young women in India.[61] Namely, the article discusses how young Indian women are "empowered" by the installation of latrines near their homes. Instead of needing to leave the home in the early morning or late at night and walk far distances due to the embarrassment of relieving themselves where someone could see them near their home, women and girls can now go to the bathroom in privacy and comfort in their own dwelling space. This change in the location of where young women relieve themselves is championed by the writers of *Bloomberg* as a superb way of controlling environmental pollution and disease while also empowering girls by *giving* them more time and dignity to do other things (like go to school). This emphasis on the bodies of girls once again focuses on young women's biological features as the source of their own disempowerment. In turn, girls' and women's bodies are cited as the necessary location for intervention and regulation.

The supposed benefit of U.S. interference in the bodily lives of Others is repeatedly used to legitimize certain responses to climate change that are discriminatory and often highly invasive at the most intimate of levels for people in the Global South—from the bedroom to the bathroom to the kitchen table. The kitchen, implicated in fearmongering about the overconsumption of food and water resources, is another frequent talking point in narratives of overpopulation. Hartmann points out how:

the relationship between population growth and human and environmental health can be negative, positive, or non-existent. It's not subject to one universal logic or law. What makes Malthusianism so dangerous is not only its claim to universalism, but its appeal to apocalypse. In the policy realm, from family planning to the environment to national security, it convinces many otherwise well-meaning people that it is morally justified to curtail basic human and reproductive rights of poor people at home and abroad in order to save ourselves and the planet from otherwise certain doom.[62]

The Malthusian blaming of large families of poor people for environmental and societal degradation is highly problematic. After all, Thomas Malthus, who was an English aristocrat, frequently expressed explicit contempt for working-class people and leveraged racist tropes to denigrate the imperialized Others of the British Empire.[63]

Notably, Malthusianism gained traction and widespread popularity in the U.S. during the Cold War with Paul and Anne Ehrlich's book, *The Population Bomb*, published in 1968. Hartmann points out how the Ehrlichs expanded a Malthusian mode of apocalyptic fearmongering by directly blaming the rapid procreation of poor and racialized Others as the ultimate demise of the "civilized" world.[64] Hartmann argues that the Ehrlichs were "one of the first, but hardly the last, environmentalist[s] to tap directly into the Book of Revelation, associating the threat of overpopulation with the Four Horsemen of the Apocalypse: War, Famine, Pestilence, and Death."[65] Despite the highly suspect roots of the Ehrlichs' underlying premise and claims, their Malthusian theory of the exponential rise of undesirable Others as an existential threat continues to be elevated as an objective fact in many climate news stories published across the ideological spectrum of the U.S. press.

The October 20, 2015 issue of *Newsweek* (see Figure 4.2), for instance, demonstrates how Malthusian tropes shape climate journalism in the U.S. The headline on the outside cover is: "**THE FUTURE OF FARMING**: THE NUTS AND BOLTS OF HOW WE WILL FEED THE WORLD,"[66] and the story's secondary headline printed inside the magazine asserts: "To Feed Humankind, We Need Farms of the Future Today: If we keep farming like we've been for the past century, we'll end up with millions starving and a planet denuded of trees." These two headlines reflect Malthusian fears of resource depletion and environmental degradation as a consequence of unregulated population growth. The blame is placed squarely on the Global South—China, in particular:

Figure 4.2 Cover of *Newsweek*. © [October 20, 2015].
Courtesy of *Newsweek*. All rights reserved. Used under license.

Right now—at this very moment—there are over 7 billion humans crawling on the Earth. That's a lot of mouths to feed. […] Unfortunately, meat is a luxury item, and as more and more people are pulled from poverty in places like India and China, the demand for meat is increasing enormously […] The growing demand [for meat] might just be the death knell of the

Amazon rain forest [...] The demand for soybeans to feed China's hogs is driving a soy revolution in Brazil, which, in turn, is incentivizing farmers there to chop down the rain forest to plant more soy. And, of course, cutting down the rain forest releases carbon into the atmosphere, which speeds up global warming, which gives us less arable land, which makes our upcoming land versus food problem all the worse.[67]

The complexities of the relationship between China and Brazil as well as land-use practices are flattened and erased. Indeed, the long histories of U.S. interference in Latin America and the introduction of monoculture— including soybeans—to the detriment of indigenous crops are sidestepped.[68] Instead, visionary sage figures from the U.S. and their technological "solutions" are advanced as required to curb the "irresponsible" farming practices of China and Brazil.

U.S. technologies and engineers are elevated as absolutely essential. The cover story promotes the idea of "modernization" through U.S. aid stating how:

> increasing the yield of staple crops to the point where we can feed 9.6 billion people likely won't involve anything as glamorous as greenhouse clusters seen from space; it might be as simple as making the whole farming world more modern. "A lot of poor farmers in underdeveloped countries are still farming as though it's 10,000 B.C.," says Dan Glickman, former U.S. secretary of agriculture, now consulting with several nonprofits that hope to solve world hunger. "There's no crop rotation, no irrigation; people are still using animals for plows. Just exporting modern farming practices globally will do a lot to feed a lot more people."[69]

The binary of "developed" and "underdeveloped" is here again leveraged in a way that entrenches U.S. claims of superiority and legitimacy in the affairs of other nations. Notably, the advancement of biopolitical surveillance technologies in China and India is celebrated as "modernizing" their "backwards" farming practices with "data-driven farming" that supposedly will also bring more and better jobs "along with new fields of study and new careers for those willing to crunch a lot of numbers."[70]

Interestingly, the *Newsweek* cover story celebrates U.S. technologies as solutions to global environmental problems while also admitting past failings. The U.S.'s heavy use of chemical pesticides to grow monocrops is cited by *Newsweek* as generating problematic shortcomings that are inefficient, toxic, and rely on heavy inputs of fossil fuel energy. In a striking twist of logic, however, these failings are turned upside down and strategically leveraged to carve out a position of American centrality in global environmental affairs. The U.S.'s culpability is, in this way, used to further legitimize American interference in other nations to "fix" their own past mistakes and, more importantly, to deter, prevent, and police the "backwards" Global South from foolishly making these very same mistakes again today. The cover image reflects this contradictory logic (see Figure 4.2). The cover image shows an orangey, apocalyptic sky with two robots positioned in the foreground—here again mimicking the painting *American Gothic* (as also seen in *The New Republic* cover story[71] discussed in the previous chapter). This image reflects a Frankensteinian dynamic where the technology invented by the scientist is the source of the nightmare itself. Just as Dr. Frankenstein sought to destroy his monster, the U.S. is represented as now seeking to manage its own. Both Dr. Frankenstein and the U.S. are, however, positioned squarely in the center of their own respective tales—reaffirming the U.S. as the protagonist facing a hellish predicament.

This dynamic of the U.S. as the creator of monstrous environmental crises and also as the world's savior from them is a notable feature of climate news stories. For instance, in the April 2020 issue of *Fortune*,[72] the U.S. is critiqued for dumping large amounts of plastic waste in the Global South in a story titled "Vicious (Re)Cycle: With the world drowning in plastic, the need for recycling is more acute than ever. But the industry that handles all that waste is on the verge of collapse." Despite its past mistakes, the U.S. is again elevated as the only possible hero capable of getting the world out of this mess. Drawing upon images of chaos and out-of-control populations of poor people, the Global South—as a whole—is portrayed as corrupt, disorganized, and totally unable to deal with the "plastic flood" that is placing the entire "planet in crisis."[73] American intervention, therefore, is declared as the only possible way forward and as the ultimate solution to fix "the global waste trade [that] is essentially broken."[74] More specifically, a savvy American business enterprise dedicated to sustainable waste management is declared as the ultimate solution. Through fearmongering of heavily polluted waters in other places spreading toxins across the world's oceans and onto American shores, the dire need for U.S. interference is heightened. One striking image of a low tide along a Malaysian shoreline with loads and loads of garbage floating in the water accompanies the article and has the caption "Toxic Tide"[75] which specifically directs anxieties regarding pollution squarely onto villages in the Global South. Instead of a nuanced analysis of U.S.-backed international trading policies that incentivize environmental and labor exploitation abroad for profit maximization at home, an apocalyptic image of a "Toxic Tide" coming over from the East to the West dominates the story and steers proposed responses.

The fundamental problem with news stories of "toxic tides" and "population bombs" is that they often lack the context, nuance, and analysis required to understand and comprehensively respond to climate change and other distinct and intersecting environmental and social issues. Through the image of a "population bomb," coined by the Ehrlichs, and the image of swarms of people and trash imperiling the planet across climate news stories, the trope of apocalypse is reinforced while invasive policies of control and containment of Others through U.S. economic and military actions are celebrated. Contempt, racism, and Othering proliferate, and a nuanced understanding of climate change comes up short. This shortcoming closes off the necessary analytical and critical space required to move beyond both a colonial imaginary and the discursive practices of worlding and dualisms that entrench chauvinistic tropes of American exceptionalism and that legitimize the politics of apocalyptic authoritarianism. Considerations of climate justice fall by the wayside in climate news stories while fearmongering and Othering are extended.

Biopower/Security State: Saving Ourselves from the Invasion of an "Epic Climate Migration"

Notably, Malthusian-influenced climate media discourse often features a plethora of numbers and statistics that reinforce fears of an overwhelming swarm of threatening Others from the Global South via seemingly uncontestable facts and figures. For example, *Newsweek* asserts how there are "7 billion humans crawling on the Earth."[76] In addition to the citation of vast numbers of people in general, vast numbers of climate migrants are highlighted in particular. Illustrative of this, the January/February 2015 issue of the centrist magazine *Foreign Policy* wrote in all-caps and large text how "2.2 MILLION PEOPLE COULD BE DISPLACED FROM SMALL ISLAND NATIONS BY THE END OF THE CENTURY."[77] And in the May 2019 issue of the left-leaning magazine *In These Times*, bold and large text declares how

"**143,000,000** people [will be] displaced by climate change in sub-Saharan Africa, South Asia and Latin American by 2050, without climate action."[78]

Moreover, shocking statistics of extinction rates are leveraged to demonstrate the grave toll of increased human populations, consumption, and waste production. Above the climate migrant statistic, *In These Times* also features an animal's skull and highlights how "**16%** [of] Species [are] expected to go extinct at 4.3°C."[79] Through this fearmongering, the migration of people into the Global North from the Global South is often framed as an invasion that threatens local human and nonhuman lives. Stories of Others fleeing from the Global South to the U.S. are often constructed via images of desperate/uncivil/violent/destructive climate migrants in climate news reports published by publications from across the political spectrum. This threat, in turn, is framed as requiring the power of the U.S. nation-state (and military) to protect and save American lives and local environments. These stereotypes are leveraged in a way that projects fears and anxieties about impending climate chaos and mass extinction directly onto climate migrants. This fearmongering can contribute to far right, ecofascist talking points. Indeed, ecofascist ideology is constructed via the image of dirty, destructive, and undesirable Others who are invading and degrading the environment, economy, and culture of "Western civilization."[80]

The media image of "the climate migrant" is shaped via discriminatory tropes of representation that tap into racist and nativist ideologies. The stereotypical climate migrant—seen for example in the July 26, 2020 Climate Issue of *The New York Times Magazine* (see Figure 4.3)—is often described as poor, desperate, and Black or Brown. Moreover, as *The New York Times Magazine* headline proclaims: "AS WARMING MAKES PARTS OF THE PLANET LESS AND LESS LIVABLE, AN EPIC CLIMATE MIGRATION HAS BEGUN"[81]—the image of desperate flocks of Others heading "our" way invokes a sense of insecurity and anxiety about hordes of migrants traveling to the U.S. in an "epic climate migration" that seemingly cannot be stopped without extreme force.

Anxiety regarding impending swarms of desperate climate migrants is compounded by the entrenched stereotype of the Global South as an inherently unstable, corrupt, and uncivilized world. Climate change is represented as in part a consequence of the overpopulation of Africa, Asia, and Latin America as well as a "threat multiplier" that worsens already-existing problems in these supposedly unstable places. A story in the May/June 2017 issue of *Foreign Policy*,[82] for instance, claims that "**Environmental** changes

Figure 4.3 Cover of *The New York Times Magazine*. © [July 26, 2020].
Courtesy of The New York Times Company. All rights reserved. Used under license. https://www.nytimes.com/

spark violence [in Africa], and violence leads to **FURTHER** environmental **DESTRUCTION**."[83] Additionally, according to an article titled "Why Climate Change Matters More Than Anything Else" in the July/August 2018 issue of *Foreign Affairs*,[84] what makes "climate change all the more frightening are its effects on geopolitics. New weather patterns will trigger social and economic upheaval."[85] The idea of climate change as a threat multiplier that contributes to civil wars in the Global South, incites global upheaval, and spreads chaos across borders is a recurrent claim that shapes many U.S. news stories on climate migration.

This predominant mode of climate journalism spans from print to screen formats. For example, the U.S. television company Showtime produced a popular documentary series titled *Years of Living Dangerously* in 2014 that advanced the idea that contemporary war and civil unrest are in part caused by climate change. In a famous segment in this series, *New York Times* columnist Thomas L. Friedman elevated the claim that "a long drought in Syria was one of the primary causes of that country's civil war."[86] International relations scholar Jan Selby and his coauthors strongly oppose and challenge this claim and, in their study, show how there is "little merit" and "no solid evidence that drought migration pressures in Syria contributed to civil war onset."[87] Selby's research team therefore advises that "policymakers, commentators, and scholars alike should exercise far greater caution when drawing such linkages or when securitizing climate change."[88]

Despite this advisement by Selby and his collaborators as well as the direct contestations of many Syrian people who argue that it is a much more complicated situation than how Friedman tells it, *The New York Times* and other publications still tout this line and frequently report on climate change as a source of civil war and violence. This reporting strategy, for instance, undergirds the July 26, 2020 special Climate Issue of *The New York Times Magazine* (see Figure 4.3). Asking "where will they go?" in reference to the "billions of people" that will be forced to migrate due to climate change, *The New York Times Magazine* plays upon this established trope and invokes anxieties about the potential unrest migrants from war-torn countries will bring with them.[89] After posing this question in large and bold print on an inside page of the special issue, *The New York Times Magazine* shows a series of images of Black and Brown climate migrants from various nations in Latin America, Africa, and Asia—reinforcing the image of desperate and poor people of color fleeing "unstable" and "underdeveloped" Global South nations for more "stable" and "developed" places such as the U.S., or at least what *was* more stable and developed prior to the onset of these "mass migrations."

Longstanding racist media tropes that frame young Black men as having a natural propensity for violence[90] shape journalistic representations of climate migrants and propagate claims that they are destabilizing forces that imperil previously stable places. For example, a story in the May/June 2017 issue of *Foreign Policy*[91] tells the tale of aggressive and violent Somalians who kidnapped an English environmental scientist named Murray Watson. This story positions climate change as a harbinger for more kidnapping and general mayhem in the Global South—and via the movement of migrants, the whole world. The headline for this article is "**The WATSON FILES**: What if there were a blueprint for climate adaptation that could end Somalia's civil war? An English scientist spent his life developing one—then he vanished without a trace."[92] This article's headline not only entrenches fear about climate-induced violence but also here again *blames* people from the Global South—represented as militant and dangerous—for stalling "climate adaptation that could end [...] civil war" and thus end both climate and societal chaos too.

While women from the Global South are framed as overly fertile and therefore threatening, men from the Global South are framed as overly violent. The combination of these representations forms an overarching image of a dangerous Other that must be contained and kept out of the U.S. The climate social scientist Hedda Ransan-Cooper and her collaborators argue that "the conflation of development and military intervention has long been an element of defense policy that helps to justify a security response to environmental migration."[93] Ransan-Cooper and coauthors add how "the supposedly rational North tends to be positioned normatively in a position of control in relation to 'chaotic' Southern states through agendas of military intervention, development and modernisation."[94] Moreover, the construction of climate migrants as threatening and violent Others legitimizes militarized U.S. borders and discriminatory policing practices. The national security state is upheld as absolutely necessary for protecting the lives of American citizens within today's "total crisis" that is beset with violent Others.

This demarcation of citizens from noncitizens and fearmongering of a dystopian world wrought by climate and societal chaos in an unprecedented moment of "total crisis" is an increasingly dominant form of "worlding" akin to the (neo)colonial discursive practice identified by Spivak following WWII.[95] The July/August 2018 cover story for *Foreign Affairs* titled "Which World Are We Living In?" reflects this worlding whereby any opposition or threat to the hegemony of U.S. democratic liberalism and postwar capitalism is visualized as ushering in an all-encompassing disaster on a planetary scale.[96] Possible disaster worlds of climate chaos, corporate corruption, socialist revolution, tribal warfare, and illiberal states are described by

Foreign Affairs.[97] Ultimately, according to *Foreign Affairs*, the only "good" world is a liberal democratic one led by the U.S. and a "bad" world is an illiberal one where radicalized and racialized Others proliferate. If the U.S. is dethroned as the world's superpower, then the doomsday prophecy of *Bloomberg Businessweek's* "Growth Engines"[98] will result.

It is through this disaster worlding that U.S. citizenship is made legible across the ideological spectrum.[99] In the July 16, 2018 issue of the left-leaning *The Nation*, this demarcation of "citizen" from "noncitizen" is clarified.[100] In calling for a "**Citizen Intervention**" and a "**New Foreign Policy**" to combat everything from "**CATASTROPHIC CLIMATE CHANGE**" to a "**RISING REFUGEE CRISIS**" to "**ENDLESS WARS**,"[101] *The Nation* extends the biopolitical imagination through claims that a stronger U.S. nation-state with a "new foreign policy" that is capable of managing these planetary threats is absolutely essential for protecting the lives of American citizens amid "total crisis." Climate migrants who are cast as Others are inherently excluded from this protected citizenry. It is here where Foucault argues that "it is now not so much sex as death that is the object of taboo […] it is only natural that death should now be privatized, and should become the most private thing of all."[102] The national security state and borders are represented as "life giving" protections.[103] Images of citizens' deaths therefore have no place in the public sphere and are rarely included in news stories that detail the threats of climate change. Borders are "life giving," not "life taking."[104] Within this regime of representation, therefore, only certain images of death are shown—namely, the bodies of those who are excluded from the protected citizenry. This demarcation of certain populations as outside of the citizenry and therefore outside of the realm of protected lives and the living is what Mbembe calls "necropower."[105]

Necropower: Demarcating the Already Drowned and the Inevitably Damned

Necropower refers to how certain populations of Others are not only demarcated as potentially threatening to a designated citizenry but also as absent of life itself. Mbembe elucidates how "the ultimate expression of sovereignty resides, to a large degree, in the power and the capacity to dictate who may live and who must die."[106] In contrast with the supposedly protected and secure citizenry, therefore, Others are represented as perpetually precarious and assumed to be already doomed and inevitably dead.[107] Expanding upon Foucault's work and theory of biopower, Mbembe emphasizes how those deemed to be among the inevitably dead are almost always represented as poor, of color, and from the Global South.[108]

Fundamental to this necropolitical marginalization of Others is the representation of racialized communities from the Global South as dwelling in a state of constant depravity and decline. People from the Global South are often demarcated—or "worlded"—by journalists writing about climate change in the U.S. through the image of a "death-world," defined by Mbembe as a "new and unique" form of "social existence in which vast populations are subjected to living conditions that confer upon them the status of the *living dead*."[109] The October 5/12, 2020 issue of *The Nation* (see Figure 4.4), for instance, demonstrates this worlding and discursive demarcation of a climate "death-world" and "life-world." The cover image shows a stormy sky above a dark ocean with crashing waves in the foreground. A heavenly white light from the sun is breaking behind the clouds and cuts a small path of brightness across an otherwise dark and foreboding sea. The headline is written in dark, bold text: **"The Drowned and the Saved,"** with a smaller headline underneath stating: **"Why real climate justice is so hard."**[110] This necropolitical worlding and division of the "drowned" and the "saved" reinforces the discursive bounds of a death-world where people of color and people living in poverty are doomed to remain. *The Nation* paints a portrait of a future where primarily white and wealthy people living in the Global North will be "saved" from climate disasters—made secure through the fortitude of militarized borders that will keep the life-world and death-world separate.[111] *The Nation* reports a pessimistic prediction with little room given to imaginings of a different future. In turn, the cover story entrenches the claim that "climate justice is so hard" *because* the borders dividing and separating the life-world from the death-world are so strong.

Moreover, *The Nation* contributes directly to the discursive construction of the death-world as distinct from the life-world by leveraging and expanding claims of the inevitable deaths of poor people and people of color where disaster strikes. This representation of the already dead and drowned, in turn, casts doubt on the possibility to do anything about the fast and slow violences of climate change and the injustices therein. The lead image in the cover story printed inside the October 5/12, 2020 issue of *The Nation* (see Figure 4.5), for instance, shows a Black woman in what appears to be a night dress and Crocs with her arms stretched out in a

Figure 4.4 Cover of *The Nation*. © [October 5/12, 2020].
Courtesy of The Nation Company. All rights reserved. Used under license. https://www.thenation.com/

gesture of desperation amid piles of wood and debris where her home once stood before Hurricane Dorian, described as "a monster that pummeled the Bahamas's Haitian minority." The woman's facial expression is one of total despair. The caption below the image reads "**Trapped and bereft:** A Haitian

142 APOCALYPTIC AUTHORITARIANISM

Figure 4.5 Photo by Al Diaz/The Miami Herald via Getty Images, as appeared in *The Nation*, October 5/12, 2020 issue, with the caption: "Trapped and bereft: A Haitian woman stands on what remains of her home in the shantytown known as the Mudd, September 5, 2019."
Courtesy of Getty Images. All rights reserved. Used under license.

woman stands on what remains of her home in the shantytown known as the Mudd, September 5, 2019." The photo's caption fails to identify the woman's name, merely calling her a "Haitian woman"—therefore stripping her of her specific subjectivity and casting her as merely one of many similar Other women living in poverty and desperation. She is also determined to be "trapped and bereft"—represented as lacking the power and agency to change her own circumstances. The scene of total destruction around her is therefore demarcated as her inevitable future—she is relegated to the climate death-world. The Christ-like positioning of her hands as if nailed to a cross further indicates her inevitable fate—a sacrifice deemed necessary for the life-world to remain intact. Through this portrayal, her suffering and death as a drowned Other (i.e., "them") is represented as both preordained and essential for the salvation of the living (i.e., "us"). Journalism scholar Barbie Zelizer argues how news images of the *already* dead often discourage political intervention to prevent similar deaths from war, catastrophe, and crisis from happening.[112] The relegation of the "Haitian woman" and all Others like her to the death-world, therefore, impedes transformative political change that could prevent her own and future climate deaths in the Global South from occurring.

It is here where U.S. news stories and images of climate justice are often limited by an entrenched binary of doomed Others and saved selves where people of color within and outside of the Global South are consistently assumed to be condemned to the climate death-world and as always and forever "trapped" there.[113] This binary is leveraged by journalists in a way that distinguishes these Others' fate as distinct from "yours and mine." The "Haitian woman's" death, therefore, is represented as required for "our" own salvation (as the presumed predominantly white, financially well-resourced, and American readership of this U.S. news magazine). The consistent representation of people of color in general as doomed victims of climate change entrenches and expands the latent racist assumption that "full" U.S. citizenship and rightful protection by the state are reserved for only certain (white and well-off) people. In a striking example of this death-worlding within the bounds of the U.S. itself, the cover of the August 2, 2020 issue of *The New York Times Magazine*[114] shows a gray, polluted sky above a rusty, metallic refinery with the headline "BLACK AMERICANS ARE 75 PERCENT MORE LIKELY THAN OTHERS TO LIVE NEAR FACILITIES THAT PRODUCE HAZARDOUS WASTE. CAN A GRASS-ROOTS ENVIRONMENTAL JUSTICE MOVEMENT MAKE A DIFFERENCE?" By posing this as a question following a daunting statistic, the implication is that action to remediate this injustice is impossible and will therefore *not* make much of a difference. Black Americans, according to this media representation, are forever condemned to the death-world.

Through questions and statements such as the one posed by *The New York Times Magazine*,[115] movements for climate justice are portrayed as essentially pointless. This closes off even more space for imagining alternative, robustly democratic, and vibrant futures that contest an apocalyptic authoritarian vision.[116] For instance, in the January/February 2015 issue of *Foreign Policy*,[117] there are two scenarios described for climate refugees forced to flee their homes: Either refugees are saved and accepted into the life-world of the Global North, or they are drowned and will forever remain in the death-world with the Other nameless and forgotten victims. The headline is "**EXILE BY ANOTHER NAME**" with a subheadline "FOUR YEARS AGO, **IOANE TEITOTA** BARELY KNEW WHAT GLOBAL WARMING WAS. TODAY, THE MIGRANT FARMER FROM

THE TINY ISLAND NATION OF KIRIBATI IS A TEST CASE FOR DETERMINING WHETHER MILLIONS OF PEOPLE, PUSHED FROM THEIR HOMES BY CLIMATE CHANGE, WILL BE ACKNOWLEDGED OR FORGOTTEN."[118] The headline is placed next to a full-page, black and white portrait of Ioane Teitota. The choice of a black and white photo is telling. Absent of color and life, the image of Teitota implies a sense of historicity—he is, indeed, doomed to a most certain erasure from the present and from the living and therefore will inevitably be "forgotten." The cover story goes on to paint a bleak scenario for Teitota and other climate refugees—a common trope. Indeed, cultural geographer Carol Farbotko and environmental anthropologist Heather Lazrus highlight how islanders are consistently reduced to "fearful climate refugees" across news media and framed as at the mercy of richer nations in the Global North.[119] Farbotko and Lazrus critique how this media representation propagates claims of "environmental determinism" and closes off the consideration of how politics could be different and national policies could be more just and hospitable for refugees and migrants.[120] This doomed representation of climate refugees from the Global South—and of small island nations, in particular—condemns them to a most certain death and ultimate irrelevancy, thereby eliding calls for their inclusion in politics and policymaking as full—and fully alive—speaking subjects.

The June 24, 2019 cover of *TIME*[121] also leverages this trope of the doomed climate refugee to imply that large-scale climate action in the Global North is essentially pointless because the U.S. will ultimately be saved and small island nations will ultimately be lost. The cover image shows the United Nations (U.N.) Secretary-General António Guterres "off the coast of Tuvalu, one of the world's most vulnerable countries." Guterres is shown in a business suit standing in the ocean with water up past his knees. The headline "OUR SINKING PLANET: RISING SEAS, FLEEING RESIDENTS, DISAPPEARING VILLAGES"[122] along with this image of Guterres further advances the notion of the inevitable drowning and disappearance of Others who lie outside of the protected borders of the U.S. Comprehensive climate policies developed by international bodies like the U.N., therefore, are framed as destined to fail because Tuvalu is already lost.

The people of Tuvalu, however, strongly reject these doom-laden media representations. Farbotko and Lazrus emphasize how "rather than being the expression solely of crisis, population mobility is at the core of islanders' pasts and presents."[123] Ursula Rakova of the Carteret Islands in Papua New Guinea and her coauthors add that "journalists put us on the 'frontline of climate change'" and lament that islanders "do not need labels but action."[124] Rakova adds that her people are "tired of empty promises" and tells of how "the Carterets Council of Elders formed a non-profit association in late 2006 to organise the voluntary relocation of most of the Carterets' population of 3300."[125] This political initiative explicitly rebuffs the "labels" ascribed to islanders by journalists from the U.S. The people of the Carteret Islands in Papua New Guinea vehemently reject claims that they are fated to a certain death caused by climate change. The labels of drowned Other and doomed denizen of the climate death-world are imposed *on* people.[126] Casting someone into the death-world legitimizes their exclusion from national and international bodies deciding how to respond (or not) to the threats of climate change. Mbembe crucially points out how political agency within contemporary conditions of necropolitics implies the ability to be recognized as alive and thus among the living in the future, not condemned to a category of the inevitably dead and soon to be of the past.[127]

The binary of Global North and Global South divides the climate lifeworld and death-world and legitimizes the further marginalization and exclusion of people from Southern nations. This planetary division deepens chauvinistic and racist visions of superior and inferior cultures while it propels the morbid fantasy of the total demise of Others for the sanctity of the U.S. The cover image of *New York Magazine*'s main feature story by the journalist David Wallace-Wells published in November 2021 demonstrates this latest iteration of neo-imperial worlding through the necropolitical imagining of climate change with clear divisions between a death-world and life-world (see Figure 4.6). The headline "The Guilty and the Damned" is placed above the image of a globe floating in a black void.[128] The word "Guilty" is placed over the top half of the globe (i.e., the Global North/life-world) and the word "Damned" is placed over the bottom half (i.e., the Global South/death-world).[129] Strikingly, this bottom half of the globe is totally engulfed in flames—evidently consuming the entirety of the Global South in a hellish inferno. The only visible part of the Global South left that is not burned entirely is the word "South" written on the continent of South America—thereby making it explicitly clear where the death-world is and who will be killed by climate change.

Notably, this image of the Global South on fire parallels with the 1989 first edition cover of Bill McKibben's famous book *The End of Nature* published by Random House,[130] a book widely regarded as the first popular climate change text written by an American journalist for a popular audience, but

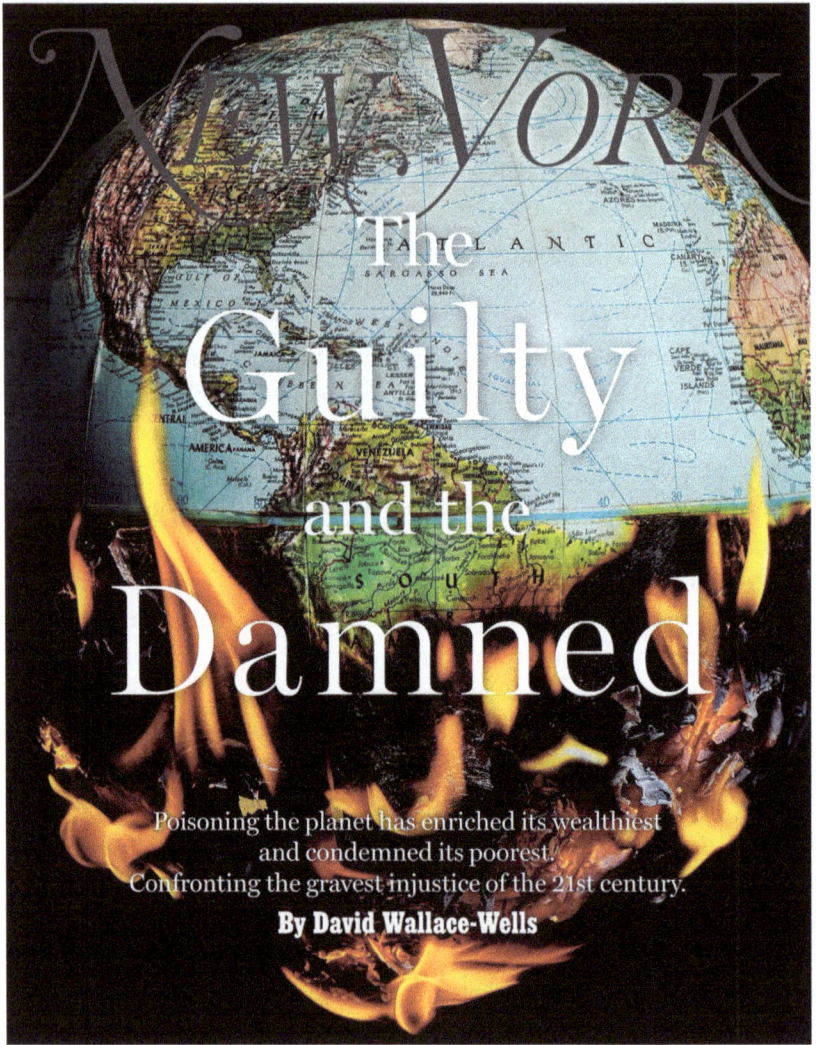

Figure 4.6 Cover of *New York Magazine*. © [November 8/21, 2021].

Courtesy of Hannah Whitaker, *New York Magazine*, Vox Media, LLC ©. https://nymag.com/magazine/toc/2021-11-08.html

with one crucial difference: McKibben's cover shows the *entire* globe on fire, not just the Southern Hemisphere. McKibben's cover reflects Cold War–era anxieties of nuclear apocalypse circulating across popular culture and the news media at the time. On the one hand, the Blue-Marble-on-fire image demonstrates the conceptual link made between nuclear and climate imaginaries. Indeed, as discussed in the previous chapters, beneath these apocalyptic imaginaries is the lingering fantasy of either planetary-scale destruction or planetary-scale salvation at the hands of an elite group of very smart men (i.e., visionary sages). On the other hand, the image of a burning Earth opens up the discursive space for an anti-nuclear/antiwar global peace movement and a global environmental movement that contests the national security state and U.S. development of both Earth destroying and supposedly Earth saving technologies (such as nuclear weapons and geoengineering). What is so consequential about the Global-South-on-fire image, therefore, is the closing-off of this discursive space. Now the visionary sage is on more solid ground with the edict: "follow me, keep them out, and stay in line, or the whole Earth will burn along with the Global South." Implicit here, then, is the buckling down on a right and wrong way to "solve" climate change with only one path forward—a path with limited space reserved for the enlightened, civilized, and inevitably "saved" as determined by the visionary sage. The goal then is not to "save the Earth," but to "save an *American* Earth"—as detailed in Chapter 2 of this book. This, evidently, was always the goal—but the explicit separation of a death-world from a life-world makes this necropolitical fantasy of planetary dominion and control by just a few very smart American men all the clearer.

The labeling of the Global North as "Guilty" is another extension of the Dr. Frankenstein dynamic whereby the U.S. knows and admits it created the monster, but nonetheless asserts that American genius-men are the only ones capable of controlling it. In the *New York Magazine* article, Wallace-Wells goes on to describe how:

> Warming is often described as an ecological crisis. But there is another way to conceive of climate change: as a moral catastrophe, engineered by the sheltered nations of the global North in the recent past, and suffered by those, in the global South, least responsible for it and least prepared. The rich are rich today because of development powered by fossil fuels; the poorest today are those who have produced practically none of that pollution. But the atmosphere is as indifferent to the location of emissions as it is to motive; what matters is the tally of damage. Climate policy concerns itself primarily with future emissions trajectories: what can be done. But we have a climate crisis in all its urgency and brutality now because of legacy emissions: what has been done.[131]

Here, Wallace-Wells acknowledges past injustices. He does not shy away from the fact that the U.S. is the richest of the "sheltered nations of the global North" wholly dependent on a high-energy fossil fuel economy.[132] The U.S. is not innocent or pure. But by positioning the climate *crisis* as a "moral catastrophe" and entrenching the binary of a life-world and death-world (i.e., "The Guilty and The Damned"), Wallace-Wells carves out an even larger space for the visionary sage to stake his authoritative claims via appeals to American morality and moderation and the reclamation of U.S. global leadership via a *re*newed American exceptionalism. Pointedly, Wallace-Wells quotes the controversial climate social scientist Holly Jean Buck in his story:

> "The moral case is pretty basic," says Buck. "The question is, 'What sort of people do we want to be?'" Contemplating the damage already done in the developing world by the global North, it might be hard to answer that question optimistically, though Buck does. "I think that most Americans want to be people that clean things up," she says. "They don't want to have their legacy be one of trash."[133]

In other words, the U.S.'s global climate leadership is still needed even if just to protect the nation's legacy as a moral example.

As evident from the cover image and inside pages of this *New York Magazine* feature story, the article takes the life-world and death-world as givens. This necropolitical imagining implicitly assumes that although the U.S. should certainly try to save poor and helpless Others in the "developing world" through clean tech transfer, aid, and experts, these valiant efforts will inevitably be a little too late. Wallace-Wells underscores how:

> By the end of the century, even moderate warming could increase the number of Africans exposed to dangerous urban heat by a factor of 20. The Institute for Economics and Peace recently identified three belts of impending ecological disaster especially vulnerable to conflict and collapse: one stretching from Mauritania to Somalia, another from Angola to Madagascar, and a third from Syria to Pakistan. Meanwhile, the global North may benefit in certain ways. Impacts in Europe are expected to be significant, but in Canada, Russia, and parts of Scandinavia, even high-end warming could more than triple per capita GDP, according to some economic analysis. Research by Marshall Burke and Noah Diffenbaugh shows that climate change has already exacerbated global inequality by as much as 25 percent. In India, they found, per capita GDP is 30 percent lower today thanks to warming.[134]

Economic growth and "adaptive projects like seawalls in the developing world" are doomed to fail, according to Wallace-Wells, because the crisis is so vast, and the death-world is so violent and all-consuming. A larger, planetary-scale solution is, however, described by Wallace-Wells as a bit more promising to try and save at least some poor people from their most certain demise. It is here where Wallace-Wells grapples with the neo-Promethean[135] potential of carbon capture and removal technology developed by visionary sage figures. He muses:

> Removal could in theory restore more comfortable conditions, pulling the most vulnerable parts of the world back from the brink of ecological disaster and undoing some of the punishment that warming promises to layer on top of earlier legacies of brutality and extraction.[136]

Even though Wallace-Wells expresses some concerns with the techno-utopianism of carbon capture and removal, he nonetheless underscores the technology's importance "in theory" by reaffirming the moral duty of the U.S.—a flawed yet still exceptional nation—to at least try and "pull" some of the damned out of the death-world to join "us" in the life-world via technological feats of innovation.

According to this embrace—even if just "in theory"—of planetary-scale technological fixes, a few very smart American men "as gods" are elevated once more to the supreme position of *the* planetary authority fully capable and rightfully empowered to determine who will live and who will die. People living in the Global South dwell in the death-world and have no agency or free will, according to this necropolitical embrace of the demise of Others by self-declared visionary sages as "sovereign individuals."[137] Only these visionary sages "as gods" can select and save a few worthy victims from the deadly flames of climate chaos and pull them up and into the life-world. Through this representational prism, the U.S. and historically privileged American figures resecure their self-proclaimed status as life-giver and life-taker as part of their Manifest Destiny. To this end, the repeated appeal to the moral duty and authority of the U.S. as a climate leader and savior is leveraged in a manner that legitimizes calls to keep the so-called militant Others and climate justice warriors *within* the Global North/life-world in line. Wallace-Wells notes:

> In 1988, when James Hansen first warned Congress about the risks of global warming, all that was required to keep temperatures below 1.5 degrees was gradual decarbonization unfolding over more than a century. We probably wouldn't have even had to hit net zero by 2100. Now, given how much

carbon has been blithely added to the atmosphere since, we only have until 2050, and we are staring out at the prospect from the vantage of an emissions peak almost twice as high.[138]

The message is clear: "you better listen to and follow the visionary sages like Hansen this time or you in the U.S. who don't comply may also be condemned to the death-world's inferno." The inevitably "saved," therefore, are not "the masses" or climate justice "warriors" in the Global North, but only the visionary sages and their inner circle of followers who, if all else fails, can escape to apocalypse bunkers in New Zealand and space colonies on Mars. Within the discursive confines of apocalyptic authoritarianism, there is little room for imagining worlds and futures otherwise. There is either a right or wrong, good or bad, life-world or death-world. There is no room for complexity, uncertainty, hybridity, or interstitiality.

Conclusion

News stories and images of climate chaos amid a "total crisis" carve out a clear binary of the "drowned" and the "saved."[139] Through this binary, the entirety of the Global South and its people are presumed to be "damned" despite not being "guilty" of causing climate change. Stories of the life-world and death-world elevate false claims that this damnation is inevitable and that nothing can be done about it. Who will live and who will die from the impacts of climate change is *not*, however, predetermined. Likewise, while the risks of apocalyptic authoritarianism are profound, they too can be prevented. As critical communication scholar Catalina M. de Onís contends: "Unmaking oppressive relations for major power shifts in all forms requires historicizing and illuminating the tenacious presence and communicative enactments of empire, colonialism, white supremacy, and other entwined lethal patterns and structures amid struggles for a good life."[140] With this call to action at the fore, the Conclusion chapter of this book that follows reimagines what climate journalism *could* be by asking: What forms of climate journalism are required to contend with and contest the discursive "techniques and tactics"[141] of apocalyptic authoritarianism?

Conclusion
Alternative Climate and Journalism Futures

During a critical juncture or "hot moment" in historical time, such as the first and second presidential elections of Donald Trump in the U.S., how crises are defined by various groups—including the news media—is pivotal for determining what types of responses will follow and what types of figures will be empowered and emboldened. Through the identification of a new, reactionary mode of antidemocratic politics termed *apocalyptic authoritarianism*, this book shows how a post-2016 apocalyptic mood or "structure of feeling," in the words of cultural studies scholar Raymond Williams,[1] problematically hardened into a U.S. media pulpit where historically privileged figures can amplify their claims of authority in possession of *the* moral, moderate, and "right" way to respond to the "total crisis" of climate and societal breakdown.

At its core, apocalyptic authoritarianism entails the construction of a "right" and "wrong" way of knowing and responding to climate change that exploits national anxieties and fearmongers that an all-encompassing, apocalyptic collapse is imminent if a historically privileged group of *visionary sages* is not heeded and followed. In turn, exclusionary modes of governance are legitimized as necessary within what is described by journalists as an "unprecedented" moment of chaos. Traditional centers of power are elevated "as gods" capable of "saving" the nation, global commons, and planet amid this "total crisis." Playing upon fears of national and planetary precarity and fulfilling patriarchal fantasies of total control, the supreme authority of just a few "very smart men" is amplified by climate news stories published by some of the most prominent publications of record in the U.S.

Notably, since this post-2016 apocalyptic mood set-in, there has been an intense yearning for the return to a supposed "golden age" of post-World War II (WWII) America in many climate news stories—a time when both U.S. journalism and the U.S. nation-state were imagined to be at their pinnacle and fulfilling their God-ordained mission of guiding the world out of darkness and into the light. It is not inconsequential that this pre-Civil Rights, postwar era is also yearned for by some members of the MAGA right. This was an era when white men's personal privilege, relevancy, and centrality in American culture and politics were less up for public debate. The molten brew of apocalyptic anxieties among the far right and moderate center both bubble up around the same reactionary fear that the nation and "Western civilization" will fall *because* their own authority is being questioned by young progressives of the "new" New Left. In particular, this book has shown how young progressive women of color who advocate for climate and social justice are especially demonized. Instead of a reckoning with the antidemocratic and reactionary responses to shifting dynamics of power in American society, prominent U.S. newspapers and news magazines are adding fuel to the apocalyptic fire by amplifying derogatory representations of young women of color as militant, threatening, and anti-American Others.

Ultimately, this book has detailed how traditional journalists at prominent news publications in the U.S. cast climate change as an all-encompassing, totalizing, and amorphous crisis but with clear boundaries between right and wrong/good and bad ways of responding that entrench and expand the centrality of a historically privileged few. Across national news media, representations of climate change as a "total war" amid a "total crisis" almost morbidly *celebrate* the "war on warming" as an opportunity through which both the embattled press and the U.S. led by an imagined cohort of visionary sages can regain their historical positions of moral, economic, and political leadership and control. But news stories do not *need* to maintain these rigid notions of right and wrong, self and Other, good and bad, American and anti-American. More robustly democratic futures, dynamic subjectivities, and transformative ways of seeing, knowing, and responding to climate change are possible and are already in motion.

Robust Democracy, not Apocalyptic Authoritarianism

The dissolution of an exclusionary regime of climate journalism and the contestation of apocalyptic authoritarianism begin with the articulation of more robustly democratic futures and the elevation of vibrant, dynamic, and intersectional subjectivities. Radically different reimaginings of climate change can move beyond the specter of an all-consuming apocalypse and beyond the necropolitical dualism of a life-world and death-world. A notable alternative news magazine named *Hammer & Hope*, for example, sees the post-2016 "hot moment" in very different terms than traditional news media do. In their inaugural Winter 2023 issue, the cofounders of *Hammer & Hope*, Jennifer Parker and Keeanga-Yamahtta Taylor, write that "we live in a time of catastrophe" and lament how "millions of bereaved children have lost a parent or caregiver to the coronavirus, while capitalism accelerates the climate crisis—as flash floods wash away towns, and the elderly and disabled people die first during otherworldly heat waves."[2] Parker and Taylor crucially underscore how:

> we also live in a time when there is enormous potential for change. Millions of people rebelled after the murder of George Floyd in 2020, demanding a new kind of politics, one that attends to people's basic needs and establishes a sense of common purpose. [...] Mainstream media and the political class shrugged off the rebellion, and multinational corporations tried to co-opt it, but the conditions that propelled millions into the streets are still with us. People still yearn for a radical new future. [...] We created *Hammer & Hope* out of the urgency to make a practical contribution toward those efforts, from Brooklyn to Bahia to Botswana. "If there's a book that you really want to read, but it hasn't been written yet, then you must write it," Toni Morrison counseled in 1981.[3]

Notably, in Parker and Taylor's description of today's "time of catastrophe," there is no explicit or latent fear of "the masses," militant Others, or climate justice warriors. Unruly and uncivil Others are not blamed for impeding post-pandemic recovery or disrupting national stability. The moderate versus militant/saved versus damned binaries are dissolved. This dissolution opens up a much richer space for defining and responding to the complexities and disparate impacts of climate change. Indeed, there are no attempts to reassert historically privileged positions of power within *Hammer & Hope*'s problem-definition of and response to present-day catastrophe. Instead, this privilege is directly contested. "Mainstream media," the "political class," and "multinational corporations" are identified as the architects of catastrophe that are obstructing today's "enormous potential for change." To address these inequitable dynamics of power and elite-driven mechanisms of obstruction, then, different modes of expertise are required to adequately identify, understand, and grapple with climate change within a "time of catastrophe."

Although *Hammer & Hope* gestures towards a death-world (i.e., "as flash floods wash away towns, and the elderly and disabled people die first during otherworldly heat waves"), the magazine does not inscribe it with permanent ink or assign a victim-status to racialized Others. Parker and Taylor directly contest the necropolitical imaginary of the inevitably drowned and damned by underscoring how "a radical new future" is possible and the written word—here in the form of a news magazine with a stated commitment to Black politics and culture as well as "a sense of common purpose" across groups—plays a central role in facilitating this change. Redefining who an "expert" is entails expanding the realm of legible subjectivities beyond the default white, male, liberal democratic subject position. Through this redefinition and expansion, elite panic and apocalyptic authoritarianism are replaced with radical hope and robustly democratic decision-making processes.

Environmental sociologist Dorceta Taylor crucially illuminates how from the start, the environmental justice movement was—and continues to be—led by people of color in the U.S. who have been working for decades to combat the necropolitics and environmental racism of mainstream environmental discourse and politics.[4] Taylor delineates how when the environmental justice movement emerged in the 1980s, it looked very different from previous decades of nature conservation initiatives primarily led by upper-middle-class white men and women inspired by early American icons such as John Muir, Teddy Roosevelt, and Henry David Thoreau.[5] Environmental justice advocates and organizations, in contrast, were/are still primarily led by women of color and motivated by figures of the Civil Rights movement such as Martin Luther King, Jr. and Malcolm X.[6] Despite the "fact that women form the overwhelming majority of the [environmental justice] movement's leadership," according to environmental sociologist David Pellow, they have been historically "less politically visible because they tend to work for smaller, community-based organizations that rarely make the headlines and survive on volunteer labor and small grants."[7] In this way and in contrast with the large national environmental organizations such as the Sierra Club and Nature Conservancy that are run like corporations and have been historically led by primarily well-resourced and highly visible white men who are also featured extensively across traditional news media, environmental justice organizations and their leaders are often relegated to the margins.

Like the movement itself, proposals and calls for environmental justice are diverse, divergent, and always changing. Pellow underscores how "while the *experiences* of various groups [of people] are qualitatively distinct (they are not equivalent), the *logic* of domination and othering as practiced by more powerful groups against them provides a thread of intersectionality through each of their oppressions."[8] In tangible terms, American studies scholar Julie Sze clarifies how this means that environmental and climate justice movements "eschew the marketization and cheapening of life, labor, and land" and thus reconceptualize and "reframe their problems and center their lived experiences."[9] In other words, the intentional act of centering the diverse and irreducible "lived experiences" of women, young people, working-class folks, communities of color, Indigenous people, the disabled, and the unhoused, among other historically marginalized groups, motivates and unites a vibrant climate justice movement comprising "qualitatively distinct" yet also "intersectional" subjects. This expansion of recognizable subjectivities beyond binary formations or "rational" speech criteria is central to the environmental and climate justice movement's resistance to existing oppressions and exclusions. Centering the knowledges and lived experiences of historically marginalized people directly contests the visionary sages' assertion of planetary mastery and control. To this end, the "typical" climate expert is turned on its head in *Hammer & Hope* with bylines and expertise from women of color featured centrally across the magazine's pages.

The climate justice podcast and digital newsletter *Hot Take* similarly took aim at visionary sages' stronghold in U.S. climate media and politics. The two women of color who formerly wrote *Hot Take*—Amy Westervelt and Mary Annaïse Heglar—conducted hard-hitting investigations and news analyses, but through sardonic humor, informal language, and a personable style that poked holes in the rational speech criteria and unattached/unemotional/one-step-removed positionality of the "traditional journalist."[10] For example, Westervelt and Heglar referred to their readers as "Hot Cakes," added emojis to their text, shared personal details about taking time off from writing for vacation, and peppered self-declared "dad jokes" into their prose.[11] This expansion of legitimate climate speech beyond the domain of visionary sages' rationality and a detached press powerfully counters the rigid bounds around expert/nonexpert used to exclude women and young women of color in particular from the climate beat.

Despite this expansion of recognizable subjectivities and legitimate modes of speech, historically privileged figures within the U.S. media space responded to Westervelt and Heglar by tightening their claims (and purse strings) around what good versus bad climate reporting is and what "quality information"[12] entails. As discussed in Chapter 1, Heglar and Westervelt allege that their critiques of the Inflation Reduction Act were in large part what led to *Hot Take*'s subsequent cancelation by their producers.[13] Evidently, violation of the visionary sage-set bounds around "appropriate" speech is grounds for censorship. Once again, this journalistic boundary-making occurs through fearmongering that is directed at climate justice activists who are described as "idiot"[14] Others and are positioned as threats to national stability. A full contestation of apocalyptic authoritarianism requires a fundamental reckoning with these exclusionary binaries of moderate versus militant/American versus anti-American that are repeatedly leveraged and entrenched by the "protectors" of traditional journalism within a broader culture of U.S. chauvinism and myth of exceptionalism.

Reimagined Communities

When appeals to nationalism are combined with apocalyptic imaginaries in climate media and politics, robustly democratic decision-making processes are impeded through unbending visions of an inevitable future and just one "right" solution to "save the Earth." Apocalyptic authoritarianism legitimizes the exclusion of a diversity of knowledges and proposals for change through claims of good and bad ways of responding to the post-2016 "total crisis" of national and planetary disarray. Within the bounds of apocalyptic authoritarianism, there is only one right answer to climate change as designed and determined by a select few visionary sages. Nationalism grounds apocalyptic authoritarianism through a clearly demarcated American self/us and anti-American Other/them. These Others are discursively demonized and physically policed. This policing is legitimized as necessary to control and purge "them" from the national body for "our" sake. Longstanding racist, misogynistic, and xenophobic tropes animate and color images and narratives of an "out-group" of anti-American Others. This Othering is not just a project of ecofascism and the far right—although, antidemocratic logics are more explicit among these groups. Discursive processes of Othering are also leveraged to reestablish historical centers of power among the "old guard" of the Democratic Party and traditional journalists[15]—both currently under question by young progressives. A desire for a return to a national "golden age" when their own centrality, relevancy, and authority were on more solid ground links these historically privileged groups from the center to the right around a common enemy of the "new" New Left.

Dreams of a *re*newed American exceptionalism and the yearning for the glorious return of the nation's imagined former prestige propel assertions of a right and wrong way of "solving" climate change as determined by just a few very smart American men "as gods."[16] The nationalistic pillars of the U.S. climate beat buttress emergent strands of apocalyptic authoritarianism by elevating and legitimizing the authority of traditionally privileged figures. Climate journalism does not *need* to propagate antidemocratic claims to power. The centrality of just a few very smart American men is not an inevitable endpoint or fate. But what would a "non-nationalist"/"counter-nationalist" mode of climate journalism look like that contests this centrality and privilege?

The philosopher Judith Butler in conversation with postcolonial theorist Gayatri Chakravorty Spivak muses how: "If we were to ask the question: what makes for a non-nationalist or counter-nationalist mode of belonging?—then we must talk about globalization."[17] This is partly because global capitalism depends on clearly demarcated nation-states to protect assets, secure trade deals, and provide infrastructure for industry. Sociologist Neil Davidson underscored how:

> the capitalist class in its constituent parts has a continuing need to retain territorial home bases for their operations. Why? Capitalism is based on competition, but capitalists want competition to take place on their terms; they do not want to suffer the consequences if they lose.[18]

This is where the discursive demarcation of an "in" and "out" group materializes in very real, tangible ways. Davidson highlighted that "if everyone is protected [by the state] then no-one is: unrestricted market relations would prevail, with all the risks that entails."[19] Davidson further emphasized that "the state therefore has to have limits, has to be able to distinguish between those who will receive its protection and those who will not."[20] And this is where nationalism comes into play because "the state cannot simply be the site of particular functions, with no ideological attachment; capitalists have at least to try to convince themselves that what they are doing is in a greater 'national' interest, even if it is plainly in their own."[21]

It is precisely here where notable contradictions emerged during the Cold War and the post-1989 era of hegemonic neoliberalism ushered in by U.S.-led globalization. Free market ideology, deregulation, and the defunding of public institutions disparaged the state at the same time as capitalists inordinately depended on it.[22] More and more, the capitalist class in the U.S. and elsewhere in the Global North fanned the flames of nationalism to keep "the people" in line amid the alienating currents of shrinking public institutions and declining job opportunities at home amid rapid globalization and the search for "cheap" labor in the "underdeveloped" world to maximize profits even further.[23] Davidson explained how "nationalism is the necessary ideological corollary of capitalism" because it offers a "form of collective identity with which to overcome the alienation of capitalist society."[24] Conveniently, this allows multinational corporations with home bases in the U.S. to continue largely unabridged in the name of "national interest" and "national prosperity" despite less working-class jobs at home and greater labor and environmental exploitation worldwide under an elite-captured state's strong protection of the capitalist class.

Post-WWII (neo)liberal projects were, therefore, marked by the political and cultural manufacturing of patriotic fervor to unite and suppress an alienated work force for the benefit of a small group of very wealthy elites at the expense of both the climate and robust democracies. How can global capitalism and (neo)liberal ideologies be dissolved in favor of a plurality of identities and collectivities that are more just and transformative? Critical geography scholar David Harvey highlights how the embrace of even stronger and more inward-facing and exclusionary modes of nationalism only makes the problem of globalization worse because it can lead to "the spread of neoconservative, if not outright authoritarian, power."[25] Harvey warned two decades ago that a neoconservative and reactionary turn could lead to the "descent into competing and perhaps even warring nationalisms"—a reality that is now true in a post-2016 present.[26] Harvey also mused that "to avoid catastrophic outcomes therefore requires rejection of the neoconservative solution to the contradictions of neoliberalism. This presumes, however, that there is some alternative"[27]—and that this alternative is not suppressed or cast as anti-American or dangerous by the national press.

As we have seen through this book's critical analysis of U.S. climate journalism and identification of apocalyptic authoritarianism, the buckling down on images and narratives of a postwar American "golden age" and nostalgic calls for a "new"[28] or renewed American exceptionalism among both "moderates" and traditional journalists obstruct a meaningful engagement with alternatives to the violence of the "neoconservative embrace of a national moral purpose."[29] The U.S. news media's post-2016 reactivation of the myth of Manifest Destiny to guide journalistic interpretations of climate change and to determine what "sensible" solutions to today's "total crisis" are prevents this reimagining of alternatives.

Stemming out of a frustration with this dearth of different national visions and the continued embrace of U.S.-centric and hyper-capitalistic responses to climate change across the American press, the Democratic Socialists of America and allied climate justice activists are working to highlight and combat the "contradictions of neoliberalism"[30] through the development of viable alternatives. The actually-existing-state has become the prime focus for many radical reimaginings that aim to counter what Chantal Mouffe calls a new authoritarian form of neoliberalism[31] that propels both climate change and "the rise of antidemocratic politics in the West"—in the words of political theorist Wendy Brown.[32] Mouffe stresses how the "state needs to be a significant actor in a 'Green Democratic Revolution' because, as many activists and scholars recognize, it will not be possible to achieve the necessary transition to renewable energy without planning."[33] Fundamental to this project of reimagining and proposing compelling alternatives to a chauvinistic and capitalistic U.S. nation-state is to build a sense of community and belonging capable of usurping the myths of American exceptionalism and Manifest Destiny that uphold a violent, exclusionary, and antidemocratic state for the benefit of a wealthy and privileged few. It is here where the Green New Deal (GND) seeks to resolve the contradictions of globalized neoliberalism by fostering belonging and inclusion through a reimagined state for a reimagined community committed to climate justice as opposed to American exceptionalism.

The youth-led climate justice coalition that formed following the shock of Trump's 2016 election, called the Sunrise Movement, for instance, centers its campaigns for a GND around the capacity for bottom-up organizing and more transformative climate decision-making to foster more robust and connected communities. The GND is described as an alternative to the violence and hate of Trump's America, the alienation and inequality of neoliberalism, and the elitism and exclusions of democratic liberalism. The Sunrise Movement stated ahead of the 2024 presidential election how their goal was to "bring the Green New Deal to our communities all across the country."[34] They add how:

> fascists and fossil fuel billionaires will attempt to keep their power. Still, we will commit to the project of deeply organizing our communities and building the power we need to get a Green New Deal that serves our communities, our future, and the lives we deserve.[35]

By building a compelling alternative with and for "young people from all walks of life" that invests in "the Black, brown and working class communities that have long held our country together, and have been overlooked by our politicians," climate justice activists campaigning for the GND offer a route out of today's environmental and political challenges by contesting apocalyptic authoritarianism in favor of something more robustly democratic.[36] As leading thinkers of the GND Kate Aronoff, Alyssa Battistoni, Daniel Aldana Cohen, and Thea Riofrancos contend: "the Green New Deal has the capacity to mobilize a truly intersectional mass movement behind it—not despite its sweeping ambition, but precisely because of it."[37]

The GND in many ways provides a sustained sense of belonging via prior years of movement building. Most notably, many prominent supporters of the GND—including Rep. Ocasio-Cortez—first glimpsed an alternative path for the U.S. through their time at Standing Rock in 2016. "Making new identities was central to Standing Rock," according to Sze, as was the "sense of community and optimism, the making of a temporary home in the face of violence and destruction."[38] The GND builds off this powerful sense of community and belonging felt at Standing Rock during the #NoDAPL movement through a shared commitment to Indigenous rights and climate justice as an alternative national identity. In this way, the GND demonstrates how the U.S. could be different if the capitalist class and historically privileged figures are no longer at the helms of power. The nation's "imagined community"[39] can be reimagined in ways that center the irreducible lives of those currently cast aside as Others. Focusing on housing, public healthcare, public transit, childcare, healthy schools, and more fulfilling jobs, the GND shows how the future could be much *better* than the past and present for many more people. Crucially, the GND also illustrates how state responses to climate change do not need to be top-down, one-size-fits-all models developed by a few very smart men who assume the position of supreme experts in possession of the only correct climate "solution." Different responses developed by different subjects with different lived experiences and expertise are instead placed at the center of decision-making processes under the GND.

With a reimagined community committed to climate justice as opposed to unrivaled American glory and economic power, journalism in the U.S. can also be reimagined. Zelizer, Boczkowski, and Anderson argue that "although democratic liberalism has long fueled unmarked assumptions about what good journalism could look like, a revolutionary view holds it responsible to much of journalism's unnecessarily narrowed positionality."[40] A reimagined journalism for a reimagined community would thus center and serve a plurality of different subjects beyond a singular default white, male, liberal democratic citizen. Zelizer, Boczkowski, and Anderson add that "challenging the default assumptions of democratic liberalism invites in its stead other kinds of emancipatory political arrangements to the table" and highlight how "such practices already live everywhere in the world, and it is through that world that journalism needs to find its path forward to relevance."[41]

As detailed in this book, vibrant and intersectional movements committed to social and climate justice exist and are strong and growing despite violent reactionary responses to them. Returning to the example of *Hammer & Hope*, the magazine's cofounders explicitly state their alliance with these movements and underscore their anticapitalist commitments. As opposed to adhering to the liberal democratic principles of the modern capitalistic nation-state, *Hammer & Hope* demonstrates how this "path forward to relevance" means attending to the people and politics on the ground. By learning from "the people" as opposed to fearing, suppressing, and trying to enlighten/civilize "them," news magazines like *Hammer & Hope* retain the powerful potential to reimagine journalism as a terrain for disrupting and contesting apocalyptic authoritarianism as opposed to a tool for entrenching the exclusionary politics of a violent U.S. nation-state even further.

Reimagined Climate Journalisms

Drawing upon Spivak's postcolonial critiques of the nation-state, postcolonial literary scholar Peter Sjølyst-Jackson asserts how the "task for the imagination, literary or otherwise, is to re-invent the abstract structures of the state beyond nationalism and national sovereignty."[42] The expansionist myth of Manifest Destiny and the image of an "American Earth" discussed in Chapter 2 of this book must be dissolved through a reckoning, reimagination, and reinvention. The long and rich history of Indigenous movements in the Americas within and beyond the U.S. demonstrates how this can be done. In contestation of a "One-World World"[43]—a vision that is brutally advanced and entrenched by imperial nations like the U.S. and its totalizing image of just one "American Earth" with just one, superior "American way of life"—geography scholar Levi Gahman describes how the "Zapatistas are working towards constructing what they refer to as '*Un Mundo Donde Quepan Muchos Mundos*' ('A World Where Many Worlds Fit')."[44] Gahman adds how the "Zapatistas are also careful to stress Zapatismo does not seek power, is not a model or doctrine, and should never be imposed."[45] This refusal of concreteness and certainty is at odds with the rigid absolutes of liberal democratic rationality and the temporality of inevitability and fate that drives the U.S. myth of Manifest Destiny. The historian Jeanette Charles underscores how it is essential to understand how the Zapatistas in Mexico do not consider their antiglobalization and Indigenous-led movement to be one that is "consummate or static," but ever-changing and transforming.[46] This is not to say that their movement is defined by the kind of "flexibility" akin to a neoliberal vision of free-market globalization or a libertarian ideological commitment to antiregulation, but rather that their movement rejects the forceful institution of one culture and one way of life. This rejection inherently contests the illusory vision of a singular "mass" and instead celebrates a vibrant plurality of ever-changing collectivities of people. The desire for "a world where many worlds fit" embraces an array of different subjectivities as opposed to fearing an unruly crowd/unpoliced "mass" that must fit within one orderly and bounded nation-state.

Visual studies scholar T. J. Demos details how radical futurisms like the Zapatistas' vision for "a world where many worlds fit" recognize "that past violences are not only past, but continue in present conditions" and must be contended with as opposed to sidestepped when reimagining what the future could look like.[47] Demos specifically draws upon Afrofuturism and centers Afrofuturist scholars, writers, artists, and media-makers who also advance very different images of what the future could look like beyond a techno-utopian or necropolitical imaginary repeatedly elevated across U.S. climate news stories.[48] Visions of both Big Tech green-capitalist fiefdoms and climate death-worlds are rejected and replaced by Afrofuturist visions of Black life and liveliness as alternative compasses for the future.

CONCLUSION: ALTERNATIVE CLIMATE AND JOURNALISM FUTURES 163

In this way, radical futurities powerfully disrupt the necropolitical imagination by rupturing the all-encompassing, planetary-scale vision of one future imagined as singular, predictable, and inevitable in which racialized Others are the first and ultimate victims of climate change. In the words of artists Camae Ayewa (a.k.a. Moor Mother) and Rasheedah Phillips from the Philadelphia-based Black Quantum Futurism:

> Black Quantum Futurism (BQF) is a new approach to living and experiencing reality by way of the manipulation of space-time in order to see into possible futures, and/or collapse space-time into a desired future in order to bring about that future's reality. [...] Under a BQF intersectional time orientation, the past and future are not cut off from the present—both dimensions have influence over the whole of our lives, who we are and who we become at any particular point in space-time. [...] Our [media] work focuses on recovery, collection, and preservation of communal memories, histories, and stories.[49]

As a critical methodology, Afrofuturism and Black Quantum Futurism build critiques of techno-utopian and necropolitical imaginaries through situated experiences that are grounded by diverse and collectively shared memories and particular perspectives. This situatedness contests the abstract and distanced gaze of the visionary sage that melds all experiences and visions of the past and future into one. The potential for radical media and movements to reimagine different futures/subjectivities/modes of living is pivotal for opposing apocalyptic authoritarianism.

With radical futurisms in mind, what would a reimagined climate journalism capable of contending with and contesting apocalyptic authoritarianism *actually* look like? Firstly, a reimagined journalism demands a recalibration of its purpose away from a civilizing and liberal democratic nation-building mission. In its place, a reimagined journalism can commit to a plurality of complex and multidimensional subjects with the objective of fostering robust democracies as opposed to a one-size-fits-all liberal democracy. Robust democracies would center change, context, and dynamic decision-making processes for and by many different subjects who may express themselves beyond the rational speech criteria developed and used by traditionally privileged men to fortify their own centrality. As opposed to a utilitarian tool for U.S. capital accumulation and nation-building, journalism could be a terrain for liberatory coalition-building. The ideals of American moderateness and morality and the myth of American exceptionalism could be replaced by the ideals of climate and social justice and meaningful solidarity.

Reimagined climate journalisms for reimagined communities understood as vibrant collectivities thus require the demystification of tales that U.S. journalists currently tell themselves. As this book has shown, the myths of American exceptionalism and Manifest Destiny are used to uphold and maintain historical centers of power. These national myths are also leveraged to legitimize the policing and purging of so-called militant and threatening Others from the nation-state. The expansion of robustly democratic politics through the recognition of many different subjectivities beyond the binary of moderate/militant can work towards dissolving these myths. This dissolution, in turn, can open up the potential for the radical reimagining of viable alternatives to apocalyptic authoritarianism.

Combatting the Fear-of-the-Masses Syndrome

A crucial step for reimagining what climate journalism *could* be[50] is breaking the binary of moderate versus militant. This requires a fundamental reckoning with what can be understood as "the fear-of-the-masses syndrome." This "syndrome" is a manifestation of elite panic and anxiety stirred by the prospect of currently marginalized groups of people collectively taking control and upending existing structures of power. A critical focus on the dynamics of apocalyptic authoritarianism reveals the array of traditionally privileged figures from the right to the center who seek to fortify their historical positions of power by fearmongering about an apocalyptic future if "the masses" are left to their own devices. This book illuminates how these figures elevate themselves to the status of "gods" during an "unprecedented" moment of "total crisis" in miraculous possession of *the* all-encompassing "solution" to save the nation and the whole Earth from total demise. This Earth-saving work can only be achieved, according to visionary sages, if very smart men like them are revered and unimpeded by militant Others.

Indeed, apocalyptic authoritarians seek to secure their legitimacy by blaming progressive social and climate justice activists as imperiling the nation and planet *because* they question and obstruct visionary sages' planetary projects. Racist, ageist, and misogynistic tropes are amplified in climate news stories in ways that paint an image of a "mass" of threatening young female climate justice "warriors" of color already within the nation *and* a "mass" of threatening climate migrants of color from abroad as conduits of chaos. These Others are portrayed as existential threats that need to be eliminated. The binaries of militant versus moderate/American versus anti-American/self versus Other steer journalistic interpretations of climate change and also embolden calls for the suppression of currently and historically marginalized people both within and outside of the U.S. A reimagined climate journalism capable of contending with and combating apocalyptic authoritarianism, therefore, must center radically divergent subjectivities and engage with as opposed to fearmonger about "the masses." A reckoning[51] with climate journalism's current restrictions and oversights is first required before this reimagination can occur. This book ultimately contributes to this reckoning.

From Reckoning to Reimagination

Journalism scholar Adrienne Russell asks: What kind of a public is climate journalism fostering?[52] This book attends to a related but slightly amended set of questions by asking: What kinds of publics are erased, denigrated, criminalized, and/or Othered in an attempt to foster an imagined American community and a "new" or *re*newed American exceptionalism? What would reimagined journalisms for reimagined communities look like? These questions require collective answers. There is no silver-bullet, static, unbending, or "right" way forward. The liberal democratic "gaze"[53] and nostalgia for a post-WWII golden age, however, are not the answers. The search for journalistic relevancy must address as opposed to entrench the exclusions of the past. The default liberal democratic subject position and "civilizing" mission of traditional journalism impede this necessary and challenging reimaginative work.

As the climate justice–aligned journalist Amy Westervelt states, "it's troubling to watch the global dehumanization of climate activists, who are often painted as annoying mosquitoes, spoiled brats, or 'terrorists.'"[54] In place of this Othering and fearmongering about the "unruly masses" and climate justice "warriors," reimagined climate journalisms for reimagined communities would center the lived experiences and knowledges of a diversity of irreducible, intersectional, and interconnected subjects who are building more robustly democratic futures for a world where many worlds fit.

Notes

Introduction

1. Kolbert, 2020, n.p.
2. Whyte, 2020.
3. Callison, 2014; Callison and Young, 2020.
4. Cohn, 2023.
5. Denvir, 2020.
6. Ruether, 2014.
7. Haynes & Morris, 1997; Ruether, 2014; Sampson, 1995.
8. O'Sullivan, 1845.
9. Woodhead, 2004, p. 7.
10. Mathur-Ashton, 2024.
11. Carlson et al., 2021.
12. Ibid.; McChesney & Pickard, 2011.
13. Pickard, 2019.
14. Usher, 2021.
15. Sulzberger, 2023, n.p.
16. The news magazines and newspapers I analyzed include: *The New York Times*, *The Wall Street Journal*, *The Washington Post*, *Newsweek*, *The New York Times Magazine*, *Foreign Affairs*, *Dissent*, *Jacobin*, *The Nation*, *National Review*, *The New American*, *TIME*, *Mother Jones*, *Harper's*, *In These Times*, *The New Republic*, *New York Magazine*, *The New Yorker*, *The New York Review of Books*, *Washington Monthly*, *The American Prospect*, *Foreign Policy*, *The Atlantic*, *Rolling Stone*, *Bloomberg Businessweek*, *Fortune*, and *WIRED*.
17. Callison & Young, 2020.
18. Nixon, 2011.
19. See, for instance, scholarship by Anderson, 2014; Bødker & Morris, 2021; Boykoff, 2011; Callison & Young, 2020; Hackett et al., 2017; Hansen, 2018; Lester, 2010; Painter et al., 2016; Russell, 2023.
20. Covering Climate Now, n.d.
21. Boykoff et al., 2020.
22. McGinn, 2019.
23. Schuessler, 2019.
24. Leiserowitz et al., 2019.
25. United States Congress, 2019.
26. Gustafson et al., 2018.
27. See, for instance, writings by Aronoff et al., 2019; Johnson & Wilkinson, 2020; Prakash & Girgenti, 2020; Sze, 2020.
28. Morris, 2021a.
29. Gustafson et al., 2018.
30. Morris, 2025, 2021a, 2021b.
31. Morris, 2021a.
32. Ibid.
33. Ibid.
34. Gitlin, 2003.
35. Zelizer et al., 2022.
36. Sullivan, 2019, n.p.
37. Herman & Chomsky, 1988.
38. See, for example, Skey, 2022.
39. Anderson, 1991.
40. Ibid.

41. Sulzberger, 2023, n.p.
42. Zelizer et al., 2022, p. 75.
43. Ibid.
44. Kreiss, 2018, p. 94.
45. Ibid.
46. Zelizer et al., 2022, p. 93.
47. Ibid.
48. Mouffe, 2022.
49. Fenton, 2024.
50. Boykoff & Boykoff, 2004.
51. Sulzberger, 2023, n.p.
52. Ibid.
53. Anderson, 1991.
54. Sulzberger, 2023, n.p.
55. See, for instance, critical scholarship by Callison & Young, 2020; Carlson et al., 2021; Usher, 2021; Zelizer, 2017.
56. Sulzberger, 2023, n.p.
57. Ibid.
58. Velji, 2017, p. 675.
59. Ibid.
60. Bhabha, 1994; Kraidy, 2005.
61. Foucault, 1980.
62. Sulzberger, 2023, n.p.
63. Ibid.
64. Ibid.
65. Ibid.
66. Foucault, 1980, p. 162.
67. Ibid.
68. Stuart Hall in *Representation: Cultural Representations and Signifying Practices* (1997) developed the concept of a "regime of representation," which was an adaptation of Michel Foucault's concept of a "régime of truth" and his associated work on power and knowledge, e.g., Foucault, 1980.
69. See, for instance, Hall, 1997, 1980 and Hall et al., 1978.
70. Hall, 1997.
71. Hall, 2016.
72. Adorno & Horkheimer, 1997.
73. Hall, 1973, 1997, 1980, 2016.
74. Foucault, 1980.
75. Ibid.; Wetherell et al., 2001.
76. Foucault, 1980, p. 102.
77. Foucault, 1980.
78. Ibid.
79. Ibid.; Hall, 1973, 1997.
80. E.g., Bhabha, 1994; Escobar, 1995a; Said, 1978; Spivak, 1985, 1988.
81. Escobar, 1995a.
82. Escobar, 2018.
83. Fandos, 2022.
84. E.g., Cohn, 2023.
85. Klein, 2023.
86. Low, 2024.
87. Mann, 2022, n.p.
88. Ibid.
89. Ibid.
90. Mann, 2020.
91. Mouffe, 2022, p. 24.
92. Mouffe, 2022, pp. 24–25.
93. Gitlin, 2003.
94. Ibid., p. 210.

95. Ibid.
96. Hall et al., 1978.
97. For more on this, see the reporting by Amy Westervelt and her collaborators at *Drilled* on "The Real Free Speech Threat." https://drilled.media/investigations/the-real-free-speech-threat.
98. Gordon, 2024.
99. Lakhani et al., 2023.
100. Rufo, 2024.
101. Gayle et al., 2023.
102. See Eagleton, 2022 for an overview of Starmer's "journey to the right." Eagleton underscores the perils of prosecutors rising to power in the Labour Party in the U.K. A similar argument can be made for the Democratic Party in the U.S.
103. Estes, 2019.
104. Gordon, 2024; Lennard, 2023.
105. Dandekar, 2023.
106. Stop Cop City, 2023, n.p.
107. Ibid.
108. Ibid.
109. Gordon, 2024; Lennard, 2023.
110. Dandekar, 2023.
111. Carrington, 2022.
112. Gustafson et al., 2018, 2019.
113. Carman et al., 2022.
114. Sparkman et al., 2022.
115. Táíwò, 2022.
116. Shellenberger, 2020.
117. Ibid.
118. Ibid.
119. Clarke & Chess, 2008.
120. Solnit, 2009.
121. Ibid., p. 152.
122. Ibid., pp. 152–153.
123. Ibid.
124. Ibid.
125. Ibid., p. 152.
126. Žižek, 2017.
127. Latour, 2017, p. 106, emphasis in the original.
128. Ibid.
129. Escobar, 1995a.
130. Hartmann, 2019.
131. Nixon, 2011.
132. Lilley et al., 2012.
133. Barbour et al., 2010.
134. Táíwò, 2022.
135. Foucault, 1980.

Chapter 1

1. Baquet, 2020, n.p.
2. Foucault, 1980.
3. Ibid.
4. Barthes, 1993, p. 122.
5. Mosco, 2004, p. 30.
6. Tuck & Yang, 2012.
7. Davis & Todd, 2017, p. 762.
8. For more on the concept of the "transhistorical," see LaCapra, 1999.
9. Mouffe, 2005; see also Laclau & Mouffe, 2001 for further critical reading on the concept of "hegemony".

10. Many of these were perpetuated via exploitative systems of labor and mineral extraction entrenched via post-WWII "development institutions" as a form of neo-imperial power. See: Escobar, 1995a; Mitchell, 2011; Nixon, 2011.
11. Foner, 2013, n.p.
12. Ibid.
13. Ibid.
14. Escobar, 1995a; Mitchell, 2011.
15. Foner, 2013, n.p.
16. Foner, 2013; Frum, 2017.
17. Gitlin, 2003.
18. Ibid.
19. President Donald Trump's fearmongering of "Antifa" infiltrating the 2020 Black Lives Matter protests and similar fearmongering of "outside agitators" infiltrating the spring 2024 antiwar student protests are contemporary examples of this same discursive strategy.
20. Gitlin, 2003.
21. Ibid., p. 210.
22. Ibid., p. 216.
23. Ibid., p. 231.
24. Ibid., p. 212.
25. Amenta & Caren, 2022; Jackson, 2020.
26. Browne, 2015.
27. This binary still guides contemporary media coverage as seen, for instance, with the clear distinction made in news reports between Black "violent looters" and white "peaceful protesters" during the 2020 Black Lives Matter protests.
28. Estes, 2019.
29. Estes & Dhillon, 2019.
30. Sze, 2020.
31. Callison & Young, 2020.
32. Morris, 2025, 2021a, 2021b.
33. Estes & Dhillon, 2019.
34. Ibid.
35. Ibid.
36. Ibid.; Sze, 2020.
37. Estes & Dhillon, 2019.
38. Gordon, 2024; Sze, 2020.
39. Estes, 2019; Estes & Dhillon, 2019.
40. Aronoff et al., 2019; Prakash & Girgenti, 2020.
41. Sunrise, 2023.
42. Gustafson et al., 2019.
43. Morris, 2021a.
44. Ibid.; Morris, 2021b.
45. Tice, 2019, n.p.
46. Rattner, 2019, n.p.
47. Tice, 2019, n.p.
48. Freedlander, 2020, n.p.
49. Ibid.
50. Ibid.
51. Morris, 2025.
52. Morris, 2021a.
53. Bruni, 2019, n.p.
54. Mouffe, 2022.
55. Morris, 2025.
56. Loudon, 2019, p. 17.
57. Ibid.
58. Morris, 2025.
59. Ibid.
60. Hartmann, 2019.

61. Lilley et al., 2012.
62. Ibid.
63. Morris, 2025.
64. Loudon, 2019, p. 17.
65. Morris, 2025.
66. Ibid.
67. Loudon, 2019, p. 21.
68. Morris, 2025.
69. Morris, 2021a.
70. Rove, 2018, n.p.
71. Strassel, 2019, n.p.
72. Goldmacher, 2019, n.p.
73. Rosenfeld, 2012.
74. Ibid.
75. Foucault, 1980.
76. Gitlin, 2003.
77. Zelizer, 2018, 2016.
78. Gitlin, 2003.
79. Kreiss, 2018.
80. See, for instance, Sulzberger, 2023.
81. Zelizer et al., 2022.
82. Anderson, 1991.
83. "Let's win the war," 2016.
84. "Warming is over," 2020.
85. Sullivan, 2019, n.p.
86. Ibid.
87. Ibid.
88. Ibid.
89. Ibid.
90. "Let's not blow this," 2020.
91. MCarthy, 2017, p. 76.
92. Baker et al., 2020, n.p.
93. Lustgarten, 2020a, n.p.
94. Zelizer, 1998, p. 5.
95. Ibid.
96. Georgieva, 2020, n.p.
97. Tooze, 2019, p. 16.
98. Bloomberg, 2020, p. 12.
99. Worland, 2022, n.p.
100. Kreiss, 2018.
101. Sulzbeger, 2023.
102. See, for instance, Bonneuil & Fressoz, 2017; Escobar, 1995a; Maier, 1977; Nixon, 2011.
103. Maier, 1977.
104. Frieden, 2006.
105. Maier, 1977, p. 607.
106. Grandin, 2019, p. 3.
107. Ibid., pp. 3–4.
108. Nixon, 2011, p. 75.
109. For example, Friedman & Davenport, 2022.
110. For example, Joselow, 2022.
111. Sullivan, 2023, n.p.
112. Deese, 2024, n.p.
113. Morris, 2021a.
114. Shear & Kanno-Youngs, 2022, n.p.
115. Friedman & Davenport, 2022, n.p.
116. Ibid.
117. Zelizer, 1993.
118. Heglar & Westervelt, 2023, n.p.

119. Usher, 2021.
120. Riofrancos, 2023.
121. Tice, 2019, n.p.
122. Foucault, 1980.

Chapter 2

1. Gore, 2008, p. xix.
2. McKibben is attributed with writing the first popular book about global warming for a "general" audience titled *The End of Nature* published in 1989.
3. Cronon, 1996.
4. *The English Standard Version Bible: Containing the Old and New Testaments with Apocrypha*, Genesis 1:28.
5. NASA, 2005.
6. Hartmann, 2019.
7. Kirk, 2007.
8. Dunaway, 2015.
9. Jobs, 2005, n.p.
10. An earlier, composite image taken by the satellite ATS-3 on November 10, 1967 originally appeared on the cover. The ATS-3 image was replaced by the Apollo 17 photos on later versions and copies of the *Whole Earth Catalog*.
11. Kirk, 2007.
12. Cronon, 1996.
13. Kirk, 2007.
14. Turner, 2006.
15. Ibid., p. 98.
16. Ibid.
17. Ibid.
18. Ibid.
19. Jobs, 2005, n.p.
20. Ibid.
21. Cronon, 1996.
22. Hartmann, 2019.
23. Wiener, 2018, n.p.
24. Klein, 2023.
25. Demos, 2017.
26. *The English Standard Version Bible: Containing the Old and New Testaments with Apocrypha*, Genesis 1:28.
27. Turner, 2006.
28. Carruth & Marzec, 2014.
29. Yusoff, 2009.
30. Carruth & Marzec, 2014, p. 205.
31. Morris, 2022.
32. "Who will save the planet?," 2019.
33. Ibid.
34. Dunaway, 2015, p. 273.
35. Ibid.
36. Ibid., p. 272.
37. Singer, 2010, p. 135.
38. "Growth can be green," 2020.
39. "The new green economy," 2015.
40. Yusoff, 2009.
41. Schneider-Mayerson, 2015.
42. Ibid.
43. Ibid.
44. Ibid.
45. Bowles, 2020, n.p.
46. Butler, 2009.
47. Schneider-Mayerson, 2015.

48. Ibid.
49. Pearl, 2018, n.p.
50. Ibid.
51. Ibid.
52. Schneider-Mayerson, 2015.
53. Kluger, 2017, n.p.
54. Ibid.
55. Masco, 2010.
56. Ibid.
57. Ibid., p. 29.
58. Morris, 2022.
59. Masco, 2010.
60. Klein, 2007.
61. Masco, 2010.
62. Ibid.; Bonilla et al., 2019; Klein, 2007.
63. Kluger, 2017, n.p.
64. Zelizer, 2018, 2016.
65. "Breathtaking," 2015.
66. Ibid.
67. "The fire next time," 2020.
68. Ibid.
69. Browne, 2015.
70. "2050: How Earth survived," 2019.
71. Demos, 2017, p. 17.
72. Taylor et al., 2007.
73. "First, it came for the polar bears," 2017.
74. Carruth & Marzec, 2014, p. 206.
75. Ibid.
76. Ibid.
77. "Paradise lost," 2016.
78. Zelizer, 2017, p. 227.
79. Demos, 2017, p. 28.
80. Ibid., p. 65.
81. Barthes, 1993.
82. "Paradise lost," 2016.
83. Demos, 2017, p. 47.
84. Barbour et al., 2010, p. 40.
85. Ibid.
86. Ibid.
87. Ibid., p. 36.
88. Ibid., p. 32.
89. "Maybe the planet isn't doomed," 2015.
90. Ibid.
91. "The doomed earth catalog," 2017.
92. "Make the world great again," 2018.
93. Demos, 2017, p. 28.
94. Ibid.
95. "Future proofing," 2015.
96. Ibid.
97. Ibid.
98. "The sooner than you think," 2019.
99. Frank, 2016.
100. Gore, 2008, p. xviii.

Chapter 3

1. Steverman, 2019, n.p.
2. "Who will save the planet?," 2019.
3. Hartmann, 2019.

4. Van Engen, 2020.
5. Schmitt, 2019, p. 157.
6. Ibid.
7. Van Engen, 2020, n.p.
8. Ibid.
9. The use of "his" here and elsewhere in this book is meant to underscore how the visionary sage figure is constructed via appeals to traditional notions of American masculinity that deepen and entrench patriarchal structures of power in the U.S.
10. McCarthy, 2008, n.p.
11. Turner, 2006.
12. Ibid. p. 261.
13. McCarthy, 2008, n.p.
14. Turner, 2006.
15. Rothstein, 2006, n.p.
16. Daggett, 2018, p. 29.
17. Ibid.
18. Wiener, 2018, n.p.
19. "We have one Earth," 2020.
20. Ibid.
21. Wiener, 2018, n.p.
22. Ibid.
23. Ibid.
24. Ibid.
25. Likewise, the project's desire to bring back wooly mammoths reads like the script from *Jurassic Park*—except for the film's cautionary tale warning of the perils of men's hubris.
26. Daggett, 2018, p. 29.
27. Ibid.
28. See Bezos' website dedicated to the 10,000 Year Clock, here: https://www.10000yearclock.net/learnmore.html.
29. "American power," 2018, n.p.
30. Hultman, 2013, p. 89.
31. Nixon, 2011.
32. Daggett, 2018, p. 25.
33. Hartmann, 2019, p. 16.
34. Kelly, 2020.
35. "Thirty years ago," 2018.
36. "We've known," 2019, p. 49.
37. Ibid.
38. Velji, 2017, p. 675.
39. Morris, 2021b.
40. Ibid.
41. Alter et al., 2019, n.p.
42. Ibid.
43. Ibid.
44. Morris, 2021b.
45. Ibid.
46. Alter, Haynes, & Worland, 2019, n.p.
47. "What are we missing," 2020.
48. Ibid.
49. "Who's a denier," 2017.
50. Ibid.
51. Mouffe, 2005.
52. Maeseele & Raeijmaekers, 2017, p. 5.
53. Ibid.
54. Ibid.
55. Morris, 2021c.
56. Brain, 2016.
57. Schmitt, 2019.

58. Bloomfield, 2019, p. 397.
59. "Make America toxic again," 2018.
60. "Scott Pruitt is having a wonderful time," 2018.
61. "Make America toxic again," 2018.
62. "Horsemen of the trumpocalypse," 2017.
63. "Journey to the dark side," 2017.
64. Ibid.
65. Ibid.
66. Schumer, 2019.
67. Ibid.
68. Schwarze, 2006, p. 239.
69. Ibid., pp. 239–240.
70. Anderson, 2014; Hansen, 2018; Lester, 2010.
71. Hartmann, 2019, p. 17.
72. Ibid.
73. "Biden's moment," 2020.
74. Ibid.
75. Hartmann, 2019, pp. 18–19.
76. "Biden our time," 2021.
77. Ibid.
78. "Sins of emission," 2019.
79. Ibid.
80. Ibid.
81. Loudon, 2019.
82. Klein, 2023.
83. Bloomfield, 2019, p. 396.
84. Steverman, 2019.
85. "The sooner than you think," 2019.
86. Schumer, 2019.
87. "The socialist moment," 2019.
88. Lunt & Livingstone, 2013, p. 91.
89. Mouffe, 2022.
90. Merchant, 1980.
91. Pellow, 2018; Sze, 2020.
92. Kreiss, 2018.

Chapter 4

1. Said, 1978.
2. Ibid.
3. Hall, 2016, 1997.
4. Spivak, 1985, p. 247.
5. Ibid.
6. Escobar, 1995a.
7. Ibid.
8. Ibid.
9. Escobar, 1995b, p. 41.
10. Patel & Moore, 2017.
11. "Growth engines," 2018.
12. Ibid.
13. Escobar, 1995a.
14. "Growth engines," 2018.
15. Rabasa, 1993.
16. Ibid., p. 322.
17. Escobar, 1995a.
18. Rabasa, 1993, p. 324.
19. Genevieve Guenther in *The Language of Climate Politics* (2024) finds a similar blaming of "India and China" across climate discourse. Guenther argues that this blaming effectively moves attention away from the pressing need to transition from fossil fuels to renewable energy

in the U.S. Guenther shows how fossil fuel companies are complicit in the construction of this scapegoating of India and China in order to distract from and delay a green energy transition. *Apocalyptic Authoritarianism* and this chapter's analysis show how this scapegoating runs even deeper than a manufactured discourse created by fossil fuel companies. Indeed, *Apocalyptic Authoritarianism* reveals how the roots of this Othering and enemy formation stem out of a predominant mode of U.S. national identity and the discursive and nondiscursive "techniques and tactics" (Foucault, 1980) that uphold it.

20. Escobar, 2018.
21. Ibid., p. 81.
22. Ibid.
23. Rabasa, 1993, p. 324.
24. Ibid.; Hall, 1997, 1973.
25. Zelizer, 2018, 2016.
26. Foner, 2013, n.p.
27. Escobar, 2018, p. 86.
28. Pietz, 1988.
29. Hall, 2016.
30. "Mapping the miasma," 2018, p. 61.
31. Armstrong, 2007, pp. 64–65.
32. "Cleaner promises," 2018, p. 67.
33. Ibid.
34. Yuen, 2012, p. 30.
35. Ibid.
36. Hartmann, 2019.
37. Anson & Banerjee, 2023.
38. Foucault, 1978.
39. See Hartmann, 2019 for a pointed critique of Paul and Anne Ehrlich's 1968 book titled *The Population Bomb*—a text that popularly reanimated questionable theories of Malthusianism during the Cold War in the U.S.
40. "Growth engines," 2018.
41. "Mapping the miasma," 2018, p. 61.
42. Foucault, 1978, p. 140.
43. Ibid., 139.
44. Ibid.
45. Macey, 2009, p. 187.
46. "First, it came for the polar bears," 2017.
47. Rieder & Kukla, 2017, p. 27.
48. Ibid.
49. Ibid.
50. Ibid.
51. Shiva, 1989.
52. Mbembe, 2019, p. 71.
53. Hartmann, 2019.
54. Escobar, 1995a.
55. This is an often hypocritical twist of logic especially coming from the U.S., where by its own standards of women's healthcare and accessibility to birth control plus the recent (2022) Supreme Court ruling reversing Roe v. Wade, the U.S. falls short of the status of an "advanced" nation.
56. "Growth engines," 2018.
57. "A simple way to advance women," 2018, p. 45.
58. Ibid.
59. Talpade-Mohanty, 1994.
60. Ibid.
61. "A simple way to advance women," 2018, p. 45.
62. Hartmann, 2019, p. 153.
63. Ibid.
64. Ibid.
65. Ibid., p. 163.

66. "The future of farming," 2015.
67. Isaacson, 2015, n.p.
68. Patel, 2007.
69. Isaacson, 2015, n.p.
70. Ibid.
71. "The socialist moment," 2019.
72. "A planet in crisis," 2020.
73. Walt, 2020, p. 74.
74. Ibid.
75. Ibid., p. 79.
76. Isaacson, 2015, n.p.
77. Weiss, 2015, p. 56.
78. "A hotter planet by the numbers," 2019, p. 9.
79. Ibid.
80. Anson & Banerjee, 2023; Forchtner, 2019.
81. "As warming makes," 2020.
82. "First, it came for the polar bears," 2017.
83. Heaton, 2017, pp. 56–57.
84. "Which world are we living in," 2018.
85. Busby, 2018, n.p.
86. Hale, 2014, n.p.
87. Selby et al., 2017, p. 232.
88. Ibid.
89. Lustgarten, 2020b, n.p.
90. Hall et al., 1978.
91. "First, it came for the polar bears," 2017.
92. Heaton, 2017, pp. 46–47.
93. Ransan-Cooper, 2015, p. 110.
94. Ibid.
95. Spivak, 1985.
96. "Which world are we living in," 2018.
97. Ibid.
98. "Growth Engines," 2018.
99. Other scholars are identifying similar trends. Richard Seymour in his book, *Disaster Nationalism* (2024), for example, amends Naomi Klein's (2007) term of "disaster capitalism" by introducing "disaster nationalism" as a more apt lens for identifying opportunistic responses to disasters in the contemporary, post-2016 political landscape.
100. "Needed: A new foreign policy," 2018.
101. Ibid.
102. Foucault, 2003, p. 247.
103. Mbembe, 2019, 2003.
104. Ibid.
105. Ibid.
106. Mbembe, 2019, p. 66.
107. Morris, 2022.
108. Mbembe, 2019, 2003.
109. Mbembe, 2003, pp. 39–40, italics in original.
110. "The drowned and the saved," 2020.
111. Morris, 2022.
112. Zelizer, 2010.
113. Morris, 2022.
114. "The refinery next door," 2020.
115. Ibid.
116. Morris, 2022.
117. "The climate issue," 2015.
118. Weiss, 2015, p. 49.
119. Farbotko & Lazrus, 2012, p. 386.
120. Ibid.

121. "Our sinking planet," 2019.
122. Ibid.
123. Farbotko & Lazrus, 2012, p. 383.
124. Rokovo et al., 2009, n.p.
125. Ibid.
126. Morris, 2022.
127. Mbembe, 2019, 2003.
128. "The guilty and the damned," 2021.
129. Ibid.
130. Wade, 1989.
131. Wallace-Wells, 2021, n.p.
132. Ibid.
133. Ibid.
134. Ibid.
135. Demos, 2017.
136. Wallace-Wells, 2021, n.p.
137. O'Connell, 2018, n.p.
138. Wallace-Wells, 2021, n.p.
139. Morris, 2022.
140. Onís, 2021, pp. 4–5.
141. Foucault, 1980.

Conclusion

1. Williams, 1961.
2. Parker & Taylor, 2023, n.p.
3. Ibid.
4. Taylor, 2002.
5. Ibid.
6. Pellow, 2018.
7. Ibid., p. 7.
8. Ibid., p. 19, emphasis in the original.
9. Sze, 2020, p. 8.
10. Morris, 2024.
11. Ibid.
12. Kreiss, 2018.
13. Heglar & Westervelt, 2023.
14. Ibid., n.p.
15. Sulzberger, 2023, n.p.
16. As discussed in Chapter 2, this reference to American men "as gods" is in the words of Stewart Brand printed in the 1968 introduction of the *Whole Earth Catalog*: "We are as gods and might as well get used to it."
17. Butler & Spivak, 2007, pp. 58–59.
18. Davidson, 2008, n.p.
19. Ibid.
20. Ibid.
21. Ibid.
22. Brown, 2019.
23. Escobar, 1995a; Harvey, 2005; Patel & Moore, 2017.
24. Davidson, 2008, n.p.
25. Harvey, 2005, p. 86.
26. Ibid.
27. Ibid.
28. Sullivan, 2019.
29. Harvey, 2005, p. 86.
30. Ibid.
31. Mouffe, 2022.
32. Brown, 2019.
33. Mouffe, 2022, p. 66.

34. Sunrise Movement, 2023, n.p.
35. Ibid.
36. Ibid.
37. Aronoff et al., 2019, p. xiii.
38. Sze, 2020, p. 44.
39. Anderson, 1991.
40. Zelizer et al., 2022, p. 102.
41. Ibid., pp. 102–103.
42. Sjølyst-Jackson, 2009, p. 178.
43. Escobar, 2018.
44. Gahman, 2014, n.p.
45. Ibid.
46. Charles, 2017, n.p.
47. Demos, 2020, n.p.
48. Ibid.
49. Black Quantum Futurism, n.d., n.p.
50. Zelizer, 2017.
51. Callison & Young, 2020.
52. Russell, 2023.
53. Foucault, 1980, p. 162.
54. Westervelt, 2023b, n.p.

Bibliography

2050: How Earth survived. (2019, September 23). *TIME*. Cover.

A hotter planet by the numbers. (2019, May). *In These Times*, p. 9.

A simple way to advance women. (2018, November 5). *Bloomberg Businessweek*, pp. 45–53.

A planet in crisis. (2020, April). *Fortune*. Cover.

As warming makes parts of the planet less and less livable, an epic climate migration has begun. (2020, July 26). *The New York Times Magazine*. Cover.

Adler-Bell, S. (2019, September 24). Why white supremacists are hooked on green living. *The New Republic*. https://newrepublic.com/article/154971/rise-ecofascism-history-white-nationalism-environmental-preservation-immigration

Adorno, T. W., & Horkheimer, M. (1997). *Dialectic of enlightenment*. Verso Books.

Agamben, G. (1998). *Homo sacer: Sovereign power and bare life*. Stanford University Press.

Alter, C., Haynes, S., & Worland, J. (2019, December 23/30). TIME 2019 person of the year: Greta Thunberg. *TIME*. https://time.com/person-of-the-year-2019-greta-thunberg/

Amenta, E., & Caren, N. (2022). *Rough draft of history: A century of US social movements in the news*. Princeton University Press.

American power: The West Texas energy miracle. (2018, December 3). *National Review*. Cover.

Anderson, A. (2014). *Media, environment and the network society*. Palgrave Macmillan.

Anderson, B. (1991). *Imagined communities: Reflections on the origin and spread of nationalism* (Revised and extended edition). Verso Books.

Anson, A., & Banerjee, A. (2023). Green walls: Everyday ecofascism and the politics of proximity. *Boundary 2, 50*(1), 137–164.

Armstrong, K. (2007). *The great transformation: The beginning of our religious traditions*. Random House.

Aronoff, K., Battistoni, A., Cohen, D. A., Riofrancos, T. (2019). *A planet to win: Why we need a Green New Deal*. Verso Books.

Baker, J. A., Shultz, G. P., & Halstead, T. (2020, April 13). The strategic case for U.S. climate leadership: How Americans can win with a pro-market solution. *Foreign Affairs*.

Barbour, I., Brooks, H., Lakoff, S., & Opie, J. (2010). Energy and the rise of American industrial society. In Nader, L. (Ed.), *Energy reader* (pp. 32–44). Wiley-Blackwell.

Barr, D. L. (Ed.). (2006). *The reality of apocalypse: Rhetoric and politics in the Book of Revelation*. Society of Biblical Literature.

Barthes, R. (1993). *Mythologies*. Vintage Books.

Baquet, D. (2020). A year like no other. *The New York Times.* https://www.nytimes.com/interactive/2020/world/year-in-pictures.html

Benjamin, R. (Ed.). (2019). *Captivating technology: Race, carceral technoscience, and liberatory imagination in everyday life.* Duke University Press.

Berlant, L. (2007). Slow death (sovereignty, obesity, lateral agency). *Critical Inquiry, 33*(4), 754–780.

Bhabha, H. (1994). *The location of culture.* Routledge.

Biden's moment: Why he is the right leader to rebuild America. (2020, November). *Rolling Stone.* Cover.

Biden our time. (2021, Winter). *Jacobin.* Cover.

Black Quantum Futurism. (n.d.). *What is Black Quantum Futurism?* https://www.blackquantumfuturism.com/about

Bloomberg, M. (2020, November 16). Biden's big climate opportunity: The next president can do a lot to fight global warming, even without Congress's help. *Bloomberg Businessweek*, p. 12.

Bloomfield, E. F. (2019). Rhetorical constellations and the inventional/intersectional possibilities of #MeToo. *Journal of Communication Inquiry, 43*(4), 394-414.

Bødker, H., & Morris, H. E. (2021). *Climate change and journalism: Negotiating rifts of time.* Routledge.

Bonilla, Y., & LeBrón, M. (Eds.). (2019). *Aftershocks of disaster: Puerto Rico before and after the storm.* Haymarket Books.

Bonneuil, C., & Fressoz, J. B. (2017). *The shock of the Anthropocene: The Earth, history, and us.* Verso Books.

Bowles, N. (2020, April 24). I used to make fun of Silicon Valley preppers. Then I became one. *The New York Times.* https://www.nytimes.com/2020/04/24/technology/coronavirus-preppers.html

Boykoff, M., Katzung, J., & Nacu-Schmidt, A. (2020). *A review of media coverage of climate change and global warming in 2019.* Media and Climate Change Observatory, University of Colorado Boulder. http://sciencepolicy.colorado.edu/icecaps/research/media_coverage/summaries/special_issue_2019.html

Boykoff, M. T. (2011). *Who speaks for the climate?: Making sense of media reporting on climate change.* Cambridge University Press.

Boykoff, M. T., & Boykoff, J. M. (2004). Balance as bias: Global warming and the US prestige press. *Global Environmental Change, 14*(2), 125–136.

Brain, S. (2016). The appeal of appearing green: Soviet-American ideological competition and Cold War environmental diplomacy. *Cold War History, 16*(4), 443–462.

Breathtaking: You can't fight climate change without China's help. (2015, December 11). *Newsweek.* Cover.

Brown, W. (2019). *In the ruins of neoliberalism: The rise of antidemocratic politics in the west.* Columbia University Press.

Browne, S. (2015). *Dark matters: On the surveillance of Blackness.* Duke University Press.

Bruni, F. (2019, February 26). In defense of the gerontocracy. *The New York Times.* https://www.nytimes.com/2019/02/26/opinion/older-politicians.html

Busby, J. (2018, June 14). Warming world: Why climate change matters more than anything else. *Foreign Affairs*. https://www.foreignaffairs.com/articles/2018-06-14/warming-world

Butler, J. (2009). *Frames of war: When is life grievable?*. Verso Books.

Butler, J., & Spivak, G. C. (2007). *Who sings the nation-state? Language, politics, belonging*. Seagull Books.

Callison, C., & Young, M. L. (2020). *Reckoning: Journalism's limits and possibilities*. Oxford University Press.

Callison, C. (2014). *How climate change comes to matter: The communal life of facts*. Duke University Press.

Carlson, M., Robinson, S., & Lewis, S. C. (2021). *News after Trump: Journalism's crisis of relevance in a changed media culture*. Oxford University Press.

Carman, J., Lu, D., Low, J., Leiserowitz, A., Barendregt-Ludwig, K., Marlon, J., Rosenthal, S., Goldberg, M., Maibach, E., Kotcher, J., Torres, G. (2022). *Exploring support for climate justice policies in the United States*. Yale Program on Climate Change Communication.

Carrington, D. (2022, October 24). Huge UK public support for direct action to protect environment – poll. *The Guardian*. https://www.theguardian.com/environment/2022/oct/24/huge-uk-public-support-for-direct-action-to-protect-environment-poll

Carrington, D. (2019, May 17). Why the Guardian is changing the language it uses about the environment. *The Guardian*. https://www.theguardian.com/environment/2019/may/17/why-the-guardian-is-changing-the-language-it-uses-about-the-environment

Carroll, R. (2013, July 17). Elon Musk's mission to Mars. *The Guardian*. https://www.theguardian.com/technology/2013/jul/17/elon-musk-mission-mars-spacex

Carruth, A., & Marzec, R. P. (2014). Environmental visualization in the Anthropocene: Technologies, aesthetics, ethics. *Public Culture*, 26(2(73)), 205–211.

Carvalho, A. (2010). Media(ted) discourses and climate change: A focus on political subjectivity and (dis)engagement. *WIREs Climate Change*, 1(2), 172–179.

Carvalho, A. (2008). Media(ted) discourse and society. *Journalism Studies*, 9(2), 161–177.

Chait, J. (2021, October 13). The climate justice movement is helping neither the climate nor justice nor is it a movement, actually. *New York Magazine*. https://nymag.com/intelligencer/2022/10/the-climate-justice-movement-is-bad-for-climate-and-justice.html

Charles, J. (2017, February 26). *A world where many worlds fit: Zapatismo and Chavismo in conversation*. International Strategy Center. https://www.goisc.org/englishblog/2017/02/26/a-world-where-many-worlds-fit-zapatismo-and-chavismo-in-conversation

Clarke, L., & Chess, C. (2008). Elites and panic: More to fear than fear itself. *Social Forces*, 87(2), 993–1014.

Cleaner promises. (November 5, 2018). *Bloomberg Businessweek*, p. 67.

Cohn, N. (2023, March 24). What's 'woke' and why it matters. *The New York Times*. https://www.nytimes.com/2023/03/24/upshot/woke-meaning-democrats-republicans.html

Comfort, S. E., & Park, Y. E. (2018). On the field of environmental communication: A systematic review of the peer-reviewed literature. *Environmental Communication, 12*(7), 862–875.

Connell, R. (2007). *Southern theory: The global dynamics of knowledge in social science.* Polity Press.

Covering Climate Now. (n.d.). *About.* https://coveringclimatenow.org/about/

Cronon, W. (Ed.). (1996). *Uncommon ground: Rethinking the human place in nature.* W. W. Norton.

Daggett, C. (2018). Petro-masculinity: Fossil fuels and authoritarian desire. *Millennium: Journal of International Studies, 47*(1), 25–44.

Dahlberg, L. (2014). The Habermasian public sphere and exclusion: An engagement with poststructuralist-influenced critics. *Communication Theory, 24*(1), 21–41.

Dandekar, A. (2023, October 16). Atlanta voters want to stop Cop City and oppose constructing new jails. *Data for Progress.* https://www.dataforprogress.org/blog/2023/10/16/atlanta-voters-want-to-stop-cop-city-and-oppose-constructing-new-jails

Davidson, J. W. (1977). *The logic of millennial thought: Eighteenth-century New England.* Yale University Press.

Davidson, N. (2008). Nationalism and neoliberalism. *Variant,* 32. https://www.variant.org.uk/32texts/davidson32.html

Davis, H., & Todd, Z. (2017). On the importance of date, or decolonizing the Anthropocene. *ACME: An International Journal for Critical Geographies, 16*(4), 761–780.

Deese, B. (2024, August 20). The case for a clean energy Marshall Plan: How the fight against climate change can renew American leadership. *Foreign Affairs.* https://www.foreignaffairs.com/united-states/case-clean-energy-marshall-plan-deese

Demos, T. J. (2020). *T. J. Demos – Beyond the end of the world* [Video]. YouTube. https://www.youtube.com/watch?v=OgPCDYTUOfk

Demos, T. J. (2017). *Against the Anthropocene: Visual culture and environment today.* Sternberg Press.

Denvir, D. (2020). *All-American nativism: How the bipartisan war on immigrants explains politics as we know it.* Verso Books.

Dirks, N. B., Eley, G., & Ortner, S. B. (Eds.). (1994). *Culture/power/history: A reader in contemporary social theory.* Princeton University Press.

Dunaway, F. (2015). *Seeing green: The use and abuse of American environmental images.* The University of Chicago Press.

Eagleton, O. (2022). *The Starmer project: A journey to the right.* Verso Books.

Escobar, A. (2018). *Designs for the pluriverse: Radical interdependence, autonomy, and the making of worlds.* Duke University Press.

Escobar, A. (1995a). *Encountering development: The making and unmaking of the third world.* Princeton University Press.

Escobar, A. (1995b). The making and unmaking of the Third World through development. In M. Rahnema, & V. Bawtree (Eds.). (2007). *The post-development reader* (pp. 85–93). Zed Books.

Estes, N., & Yazzie, M. (2021). *Beyond the end of the world lecture series: Nick Estes and Melanie Yazzie of The Red Nation* [Video]. YouTube. https://youtu.be/uRMsYPgEeBA

Estes, N. (2019). *Our history is the future: Standing Rock versus the Dakota Access Pipeline, and the long tradition of Indigenous resistance*. Verso Books.

Estes, N., & Dhillon, J. (Eds.) (2019). *Standing with Standing Rock: Voices from the #NODAPL movement*. University of Minnesota Press.

Fairclough, N. (1989). *Language and power*. Longman Group UK Limited.

Fandos, N. (2022, November 11). Sean Patrick Maloney on his loss, the media and A.O.C. *The New York Times*. https://www.nytimes.com/2022/11/10/nyregion/sean-patrick-maloney.html

Fanon, F. (2005). *The wretched of the earth*. Grove Press.

Farbotko, C., & Lazrus, H. (2012). The first climate refugees? Contesting global narratives of climate change in Tuvalu. *Global Environmental Change*, 22(2), 382–390.

Farley, A. (2020, January 28). The apocalyptic ideas influencing Pence and Pompeo could also power the left. *Washington Post*. https://www.washingtonpost.com/outlook/2020/01/28/apocalyptic-ideas-influencing-pence-pompeo-could-also-power-left/

Fedele, A. (2013). 2012: The environmental prophecy that could not fail. *Religion and Society*, (4), 167–195.

Fenton, N. (2024). *Democratic delusions: How the media hollows out democracy and what we can do about it*. Polity Press.

Fernández, J. S. (2018). Decolonial pedagogy in community psychology: White students disrupting white innocence via a family portrait assignment. *American Journal of Community Psychology*, 62(3-4), 294–305.

First, it came for the polar bears. (2017, May/June). *Foreign Policy*. Cover.

Foner, E. (2013). American exceptionalism, American freedom. *The Montreal Review*. http://www.themontrealreview.com/2009/American-Exceptionalism-American-Freedom.php

Forchtner, B. (2019). Climate change and the far right. *WIREs Climate Change*, 10(5), 1–11.

Foucault, M. (2003). *Society must be defended*. Picador.

Foucault, M. (2000). Interview with Michel Foucault. In J. D. Faubion (Ed.), *Power: Essential works of Foucault 1954–1984* (Vol. 3) (pp. 239–297). The New Press. (Original interview by D. Trombadori published in 1980).

Foucault, M. (1980). *Power/knowledge: Selected interviews and other writings 1972-1977*. (C. Gordon, Ed.). Vintage Books.

Foucault, M. (1978). *The history of sexuality* (Vol. 1). Pantheon Books.

Foucault, M. (1975). *Discipline and punish*. Vintage Books.

Frank, A. (2016, December 2). Earth, the final frontier. *The New York Times*, A23.

Freedlander, D. (2020, January 6). One year in Washington Alexandria Ocasio-Cortez reshaped her party's agenda, resuscitated Bernie Sanders's campaign, and hardly has a friend in town. *New York Magazine*. https://nymag.com/intelligencer/2020/01/aoc-first-year-in-washington.html

Frieden, J. A. (2006). *Global capitalism: Its fall and rise in the twentieth century*. Norton.

Friedman, L., & Davenport, C. (2022, August 12). As historic climate bill heads to Biden's desk, young activists demand more. *The New York Times.* https://www.nytimes.com/2022/08/12/climate/biden-climate-bill-young-activists.html

Frum, D. (2017, July 3). The souring of American exceptionalism. *The Atlantic.* https://www.theatlantic.com/politics/archive/2017/07/the-sunset-of-american-exceptionalism/532548/

Future proofing the planet. (2015, December). *The New Republic.* Cover.

Gahman, L. (2014). *Zapatismo.* Global Social Theory. https://globalsocialtheory.org/topics/zapatismo/

Gayle, D., Taylor, M., & Niranjan, A. (2023, October 12). Human rights experts warn against European crackdown on climate protesters. *The Guardian.* https://www.theguardian.com/environment/2023/oct/12/human-rights-experts-warn-against-european-crackdown-on-climate-protesters

Georgieva, K. (2020, October 15). *A new Bretton Woods moment.* International Monetary Fund. https://www.imf.org/en/News/Articles/2020/10/15/sp101520-a-new-bretton-woods-moment

Gitlin, T. (2003). *The whole world is watching: Mass media in the making & unmaking of the New Left.* University of California Press.

Goldmacher, S. (2019, January 13). Ocasio-Cortez pushes Democrats to the left, whether they like it or not. *The New York Times.* https://www.nytimes.com/2019/01/13/nyregion/ocasio-cortez-democrats-congress.html

Gordon, C. (2024). Criminalizing care: Environmental justice under political and police repression. *Environmental Communication, 18*(1–2), 138–145.

Gore, A. (2008). Foreword. In McKibben, B. (Ed.), *American Earth: Environmental writing since Thoreau* (pp. xvii–xix). Literary Classics of the United States.

Grandin, G. (2019). *The end of the myth: From the frontier to the border wall in the mind of America.* Metropolitan Books.

Growth can be green. (2020, February 21). *Newsweek.* Cover.

Growth engines: The world as we know it is about to change. (2018, November 5). *Bloomberg Businessweek.* Cover.

Guenther, G. (2024). *The language of climate politics: Fossil-fuel propaganda and how to fight it.* Oxford University Press.

Gustafson, A., Rosenthal, S., Bergquist, P., Ballew, M., Goldberg, M., Kotcher, J., Leiserowitz, A., & Maibach, E. (2019). *Changes in awareness of and support for the Green New Deal: December 2018 to April 2019.* Yale Program on Climate Change Communication.

Gustafson, A., Rosenthal, S., Leiserowitz, A., Maibach, E., Kotcher, J., Ballew, M., & Goldberg, M. (2018). *The Green New Deal has strong bipartisan support.* Yale Program on Climate Change Communication.

Hackett, R. A., Foxwell-Norton, K., Forde, S., & Gunster, S. (Eds.). (2017). *Journalism and climate crisis: Public engagement, media alternatives.* Routledge.

Hagle, C. (2019, April 12). Six weeks of Fox's Alexandria Ocasio-Cortez obsession: "Totalitarian," "ignorant," "scary," and waging a "war on cows." *Media Matters.*

https://www.mediamatters.org/fox-news/six-weeks-foxs-alexandria-ocasio-cortez-obsession-totalitarian-ignorant-scary-and-waging

Hale, M. (2014, April 11). A climate of complexity. *The New York Times.* https://www.nytimes.com/2014/04/12/arts/television/years-of-living-dangerously-celebrity-filled-documentary.html

Hall, S. (2016). *Cultural studies 1983: A theoretical history* (J.D. Slack, & L. Grossberg, Eds.). Duke University Press.

Hall, S. (Ed.) (1997). *Representation: Cultural representations and signifying practices.* SAGE Publications.

Hall, S. (1980). Cultural studies: Two paradigms. *Media, Culture and Society,* (2), 57–72.

Hall, S., Critcher, C., Jefferson, T., Clarke, J., & Roberts, B. (1978). *Policing the crisis: Mugging, the state, and law and order.* MacMillan Press.

Hall, S. (1973). *Encoding and decoding in the television discourse.* Centre for Contemporary Cultural Studies.

Hansen, A. (2018). *Environment, media and communication* (2nd ed.). Routledge.

Hartmann, B. (2019). *The America syndrome: Apocalypse, war, and our call to greatness.* Seven Stories Press.

Harvey, D. (2005). *A brief history of neoliberalism.* Oxford University Press.

Haynes, S. (2019, May 16). Next generation leaders. The teenager on strike for the planet: Greta Thunberg. *TIME.* https://time.com/collection-post/5584902/greta-thunberg-next-generation-leaders/

Haynes, S. W., & Morris, C. (Eds.). (1997). *Manifest destiny and empire: American antebellum expansionism.* Texas A&M University Press.

Heaton, L. (2017, May/June). The Watson files: What if there were a blueprint for climate adaptation that could end Somalia's civil war? An English scientist spent his life developing one—then he vanished without a trace. *Foreign Policy,* pp. 46–57.

Heglar, M. A., & Westervelt, A. (2023, March 21). Hot Take swan song. *Hot Take.* https://www.hottakepod.com/hot-take-swan-song/

Herman, E. S., & Chomsky, N. (1988). *Manufacturing consent: The political economy of the mass media.* Pantheon Books.

Hertsgaard, M. (2021, March 17). How well does the media cover the climate movement? *Columbia Journalism Review.* https://www.cjr.org/covering_climate_now/climate-activists-fridays-for-future.php

Hertsgaard, M. (2020, December 16). Journalists have a moral obligation to declare a climate emergency. *Columbia Journalism Review.* https://www.cjr.org/analysis/un-guterres-paris-agreement-climate-emergency.php

Hertsgaard, M., & Pope, K. (2019, September 16). A new beginning for climate reporting: Could it be that the press, especially the US press, is finally waking up to the climate story?. *The Nation.* https://www.thenation.com/article/archive/climate-change-journalism/

Hertsgaard, M., & Pope, K. (2019, April 22). The media are complacent while the world burns: But there's a brand-new playbook for journalists fighting for a 1.5°C world. *The Nation.* https://www.thenation.com/article/archive/climate-change-media-aoc-gnd-propaganda/

Hultman, M. (2013). The making of an environmental hero: A history of ecomodern masculinity, fuel cells and Arnold Schwarzenegger. *Environmental Humanities*, (2), 79-99.

Horsemen of the trumpocalypse. (2017, September 11). *The Nation*. Cover.

Isaacson, B. (2015, October 22). To feed humankind, we need the farms of the future today. *Newsweek*. https://www.newsweek.com/2015/10/30/feed-humankind-we-need-farms-future-today-385933.html

Jackson, S. J. (2020). On #BlackLivesMatter and journalism. *Sociologica*, *14*(2), 101-108.

Jäger, S., & Maier, F. (2009). Theoretical and methodological aspects of Foucauldian critical discourse analysis and dispositive analysis. In R. Wodak, & M. Meyer (Eds.), *Methods of critical discourse analysis* (2nd ed.). SAGE Publications.

Jobs, S. (2005, June 12). 'You've got to find what you love,' Jobs says. *Stanford Report*. https://news.stanford.edu/stories/2005/06/youve-got-find-love-jobs-says

Johnson, A. E., & Wilkinson, K. K. (2020). *All we can save: Truth, courage, and solutions for the climate crisis*. One World.

Joselow, M. (2022, August 8). The senate finally passed historic climate bill. Now what?. *Washington Post*. https://www.washingtonpost.com/politics/2022/08/08/senate-finally-passed-historic-climate-bill-now-what/

Journey to the dark side. (2017, Winter). *Jacobin*. Cover.

Kelly, C. R. (2020). *Apocalypse man: The death drive and the rhetoric of white masculine victimhood*. The Ohio State University Press.

Kirk, A. G. (2007). *Counterculture green: The Whole Earth Catalog and American environmentalism*. University Press of Kansas.

Klein, N. (2023). *Doppelganger: A trip into the mirror world*. Farrar, Straus and Giroux.

Klein, N. (2007). *The shock doctrine: The rise of disaster capitalism*. Random House.

Kluger, J. (2017, September 14). The angels of Irma. *TIME*. https://time.com/magazine/us/4941004/september-25th-2017-vol-190-no-12-u-s/

Koch, A., Brierley, C., Maslin, M. M., & Lewis, S. L. (2019). Earth system impacts of the European arrival and Great Dying in the Americas after 1492. *Quaternary Science Reviews*, (207), 13-36.

Kolbert, E. (2020, January 5). What will another decade of climate crisis bring?. *The New Yorker*. https://www.newyorker.com/magazine/2020/01/13/what-will-another-decade-of-climate-crisis-bring

Kolodny, A. (1984). *The land before her: Fantasy and experience of the American frontiers, 1630-1860*. The University of North Carolina Press.

Kraidy, M. (2005). *Hybridity, or the cultural logic of globalization*. Temple University Press.

Kreiss, D. (2018). The media are about identity, not information. In P. J. Boczkowski, & Z. Papacharissi (Eds.), *Trump and the media*. MIT Press.

Krips, H. (1990). Power and resistance. *Philosophy of the Social Sciences*, *20*(2), 170-182.

Laakkonen, S., Pál, V., & Tucker, R. (2016). The Cold War and environmental history: Complementary fields. *Cold War History*, *16*(4), 377-394.

LaCapra, D. (1999). Trauma, absence, loss. *Critical Inquiry*, *25*(4), 696-727.

Laclau, E., & Mouffe, C. (2001). *Hegemony and socialist strategy: Towards a radical democratic politics* (2nd ed.). Verso Books.

Lakhani, N., Gayle, D., & Taylor, M. (2023, October 12). How criminalization is being used to silence climate activists across the world. *The Guardian.* https://www.theguardian.com/environment/2023/oct/12/how-criminalisation-is-being-used-to-silence-climate-activists-across-the-world

Latour, B. (2017). *Down to Earth: Politics in the new climatic regime.* Polity Press.

Leahy, T. (2013). Facing the apocalypse: Environmental crisis and religion. *Religion and Society,* (4), 182–187.

Lee, M. F. (1995). *Earth First! Environmental apocalypse.* Syracuse University Press.

Leiserowitz, A., Maibach, E., Rosenthal, S., Kotcher, J., Bergquist, P., Ballew, M., Goldberg, M., & Gustafson, A. (2019). *Climate change in the American mind: April 2019.* Yale Program on Climate Change Communication and George Mason University Center for Climate Change Communication.

Lennard, N. (2023, April 20). Police shot Atlanta Cop City protester 57 times, autopsy finds. *The Intercept.* https://theintercept.com/2023/04/20/atlanta-cop-city-protester-autopsy/?ref=hottakepod.com

Lester, L. (2010). *Media and environment: Conflict, politics and the news.* Polity Press.

Let's not blow this: An opportunity to address the world's biggest challenges. (2020, November 16). *Bloomberg Businessweek.* Cover.

Let's win the war on warming: How we can mobilize to defeat climate change. (September 2016). *The New Republic.* Cover.

Lilley, S., McNally, D., Yuen, E., & Davis, J. (2012). *Catastrophism: The apocalyptic politics of collapse and rebirth.* PM Press.

Loudon, T. (2019, October 7). The Squad. *The New American,* pp. 17-21.

Low, H. (2024, July 25). JSO pair told to expect jail over soup on painting. *BBC.* https://www.bbc.com/news/articles/c51y99yrj49o

Lunt, P., & Livingstone, S. (2013). Media studies' fascination with the concept of the public sphere: Critical reflections and emerging debates. *Media, Culture and Society, 35*(1), 87–96.

Lustgarten, A. (2020a, December 16). How Russia wins the climate crisis. *The New York Times Magazine.* https://www.nytimes.com/interactive/2020/12/16/magazine/russia-climate-migration-crisis.html

Lustgarten, A. (2020b, July 23). As warming makes parts of the planet less and less livable, an epic climate migration has begun. *The New York Times Magazine.* https://www.nytimes.com/interactive/2020/07/23/magazine/climate-migration.html

Macey, D. (2009). Rethinking biopolitics, race and power in the wake of Foucault. *Theory, Culture & Society, 26*(6), 186–205.

Maeseele, P., & Raeijmaekers, D. (2017). Nothing on the news but the establishment blues? Toward a framework of depoliticization and agonistic media pluralism. *Journalism,* 1–18.

Maier, C. S. (1977). The politics of productivity: Foundations of American international economic policy after World War II. *International Organization, 31*(4), 607–633.

Make the world great again. (2018, September). *Fortune.* Cover.

Make America toxic again. (2018, March/April). *Mother Jones*. Cover.

Maldonado-Torres, N. (2017). Frantz Fanon and the decolonial turn in psychology: From modern/colonial methods to the decolonial attitude. *South African Journal of Psychology, 47*(4), 432–441.

Manheim, K. (1997/1928). The problem of generations. In M. A. Hardy (Ed.), *Studying aging and social change: Conceptual and methodological issues* (pp. 22–65). SAGE Publications.

Mann, M. E. (2022, November 15). Throwing soup at art shifted people's views of climate protests—but maybe not in the right way. *TIME*. https://time.com/6233983/van-gogh-art-climate-protest-survey/

Mann, M. E. (2020). From climate scientist to climate communicator: A process of evolution. In C. Henry, J. Rockstrom, & N. Stern (Eds.), *Standing up for a sustainable world* (pp. 433–437). Edward Elgar Publishing.

Mapping the miasma. (2018, November 5). *Bloomberg Businessweek*, p. 61.

Marcuse, H. (1992). Ecology and the critique of modern society. *Capitalism Nature Socialism, 3*(3), 29–38.

Masco, J. (2010). Bad weather: On planetary crisis. *Social Studies of Science, 40*(1), 7–40.

Maskovsky, J., & Bjork-James, S. (Eds.). (2020). *Beyond populism: Angry politics and the twilight of neoliberalism*. West Virginia University Press.

Mathur-Ashton, A. (2024, May 2). Biden to protesters: 'Dissent must never lead to disorder.' *U.S. News & World Report*. https://www.usnews.com/news/national-news/articles/2024-05-02/biden-to-protesters-dissent-must-never-lead-to-disorder

Maybe the planet isn't doomed after all. (2015, September 7). *New York Magazine*. Cover.

Mbembe, A. (2019). *Necropolitics*. Duke University Press.

Mbembe, A. (2003). Necropolitics. *Public Culture, 15*(1), 11–40.

McCarthy, G. (2017, May/June). Lean in to climate change: To maintain an edge against China, American must continue to be an environmental leader. *Foreign Policy*, p. 76.

McCarthy, A. (2008). Book review of Fred Turner, *From counterculture to cyberculture: Stewart Brand, the Whole Earth Network, and the rise of digital utopianism*, The University of Chicago Press, 2006. *Journal of e-Media Studies, 1*(1).

McChesney, R. W., & Pickard, V. W. (2011). *Will the last reporter please turn out the lights: The collapse of journalism and what can be done to fix it*. New Press.

McGinn, M. (2019, September 20). Pop music and the climate apocalypse — how 2019 changed everything. *Grist*. https://grist.org/culture/billie-eilish-lil-nas-x-lana-del-rey-climate-pop/

McKibben, B. (Ed.) (2008). *American Earth: Environmental writing since Thoreau*. Literary Classics of the United States.

McKibben, B. (1989). *The end of nature*. Random House.

Merchant, C. (2005). *Radical ecology: The search for a livable world* (2nd ed.). Taylor & Francis.

Merchant, C. (1980). *The death of nature: Women, ecology and the scientific revolution*. Harper & Row.

Miller, P. (1956). *Errand into the wilderness*. Belknap Press.

Mitchell, T. (2011). *Carbon democracy: Political power in the age of oil*. Verso Books.

Moore, J. W. (2017a). The Capitalocene, part I: On the nature and origins of our ecological crisis. *The Journal of Peasant Studies, 44*(3), 594–630.

Moore, J. W. (2017b). The Capitalocene, part II: Accumulation by appropriation and the centrality of unpaid work/energy. *The Journal of Peasant Studies, 45*(2), 237–279.

Morris, H. E. (2025). Apocalyptic subjectivities: Representations of Alexandria Ocasio-Cortez, "the Squad", and climate justice activists in US media. In E. F. Bloomfield, & J. Castro-Sotomayor (Eds.), *Intersectional change-makers in environmental activism*. Michigan State University Press.

Morris, H. E. (2024). Digital climate newsletters: The new alternative for climate journalism? In H. Dunn, M. Regnedda, L. Robinson, & M. Ruiu (Eds.), *The Palgrave handbook of everyday digital life*. Springer International Publishing.

Morris, H. E. (2022). Purgatory islands and climate death-worlds: Interrogating the journalistic imperative to witness the climate crisis through the lens of war. *Journal of Environmental Media, 3*(1), 85–100.

Morris, H. E. (2021a). Constructing the Millennial "Other" in United States press-coverage of the Green New Deal. *Environmental Communication, 15*(1), 133–143.

Morris, H. E. (2021b). Generational anxieties in United States climate journalism. In H. Bødker, & H. E. Morris (Eds.), *Climate change and journalism: Negotiating rifts of time* (pp. 68–84). Routledge.

Morris, H. E. (2021c). Apocalypse divided: Analyzing power, media, and climate change before and after Trump. *Politique Américaine, 36*(1), 53–75.

Mosco, V. (2004). *The digital sublime*. MIT Press.

Mouffe, C. (2022). *Towards a green democratic revolution: Left populism and the power of affects*. Verso Books.

Mouffe, C. (2005). *On the political*. Verso Books.

Nandy, A. (1983). *The intimate enemy: Loss and recovery of self under colonialism*. Oxford University Press.

NASA (2005, October 13). History of the Blue Marble. https://earthobservatory.nasa.gov/features/BlueMarble/BlueMarble_history.php

Needed: A new foreign policy. Time for a citizen intervention. (2018, July 16/23). *The Nation*. Cover.

Navarro, L. H. (2004, January 16). *Zapatismo today and tomorrow*. Americas Program, Interhemisphere Resource Centre (IRC). https://www.schoolsforchiapas.org/wp-content/uploads/2014/06/Zapatismo-Today-and-Tomorrow-Understanding-the-Rebellion.pdf

Nixon, R. (2011). *Slow violence and the environmentalism of the poor*. Harvard University Press.

O'Connell, M. (2018, February 15). Why Silicon Valley billionaires are prepping for the apocalypse in New Zealand. *The Guardian*. https://www.theguardian.com/news/2018/feb/15/why-silicon-valley-billionaires-are-prepping-for-the-apocalypse-in-new-zealand

O'Leary, S. (1998). *Arguing the apocalypse. A theory of millennial rhetoric*. Oxford University Press.

Onís, C. M. de. (2021). *Energy islands: Metaphors of power, extractivism, and justice in Puerto Rico*. University of California Press.

O'Sullivan, J. L. (1845, December 27). Lead editorial. *The New York Morning News*.

Our sinking planet: Rising seas, fleeing residents, disappearing villages. (2019, June 24). *TIME*. Cover.

Painter, J., Erviti, M. C., Fletcher, R., Howarth, C., Kristiansen, S., León, B., Ouakrat, A., Russell, A., & Schäfer, M. S. (Eds.). (2016). *Something old, something new: Digital media and the coverage of climate change*. Reuters Institute for the Study of Journalism, University of Oxford.

Parker, J., & Taylor, K. Y. (2023). Hammer & Hope: Toward a radical new future. *Hammer & Hope*. https://hammerandhope.org/article/welcome-introduction

Paradise lost: Three artists capture the destruction of Earth's beauty—and the beauty of its destruction. (2016, September 1). *Foreign Policy*. Cover.

Patel, R., & Moore, J. W. (2017). *A history of the world in seven cheap things: A guide to capitalism, nature, and the future of the planet*. University of California Press.

Patel, R. (2007). *Stuffed and starved: The hidden battle for the world food system*. Penguin.

Pearl, M. (2018, October 10). Climate change edgelords are the new climate change deniers. *VICE News*. https://www.vice.com/en/article/pa9vg8/climate-change-edgelords-are-the-new-climate-change-deniers

Peeples, J. A., & DeLuca, K. M. (2006). The truth of the matter: Motherhood, community and environmental justice. *Women's Studies in Communication*, *29*(1), 59–87.

Pellow, D. N. (2018). *What is critical environmental justice?* Polity Press.

Pepermans, Y., & Maeseele, P. (2016). The politicization of climate change: Problem or solution?. *WIREs Climate Change*, *7*(4), 478–485.

Person of the year: Greta Thunberg. (2019, December 23). *TIME*. Cover.

Petras, J. (1994). Cultural imperialism in the late 20th century. *Economic & Political Weekly*, *29*(32), 2070–2073.

Pietz, W. (1988). The "post-colonialism" of Cold War discourse. *Social Text*, *19/20*, 55–75.

Pickard, V. W. (2019). *Democracy without journalism?: Confronting the misinformation society*. Oxford University Press.

Pilcher, J. (1994). Mannheim's sociology of generations: An undervalued legacy. *The British Journal of Sociology*, *45*(3), 481–495.

Prakash, V., & Girgenti, G. (Eds.). (2020). *Winning the Green New Deal: Why we must, how we can*. Simon & Schuster.

Rabasa, J. (1993). Inventing America: Spanish historiography and the formation of Eurocentrism. In B. Ashcroft, G. Griffiths, & H. Tiffin (Eds.), (2006) *Post-colonial studies reader* (2nd ed., pp. 319–324). Routledge.

Rakova, U., Patron, L., & Williams, C. (2009, June 16). How-to guide for environmental refugees. *OurWorld: United Nations University*. https://ourworld.unu.edu/en/how-to-guide-for-environmental-refugees

Ransan-Cooper, H., Farbotko, C., McNamara, K. E., Thornton, F., & Chevalier, E. (2015). Being(s) framed: The means and ends of framing environmental migrants. *Global Environmental Change*, *35*, 106–115.

Rattner, S. (2019, March 20). Yes, we need a Green New Deal. Just not the one Alexandria Ocasio-Cortez is offering. *The New York Times.* https://www.nytimes.com/2019/03/20/opinion/green-new-deal-carbon-taxes.html

Reich, R. B. (2007). *Supercapitalism: The transformation of business, democracy, and everyday life.* Vintage Books.

Ruether, R. R. (2014). *America, amerikkka: Elect nation and imperial violence.* Routledge.

Rieder, T., & Kukla, R. (2017, May/June). Is there a case to be made against baby making? *Foreign Policy,* 26–27.

Riofrancos, T. (2023). The security–sustainability nexus: Lithium onshoring in the Global North. *Global Environmental Politics, 23*(1), 20–41.

Rudiak-Gould, P. (2013). The revelation of climate change. *Religion and Society,* (4), 176–181.

Rufo, Y. (2024, September 27). Activists jailed for throwing soup on Sunflowers. *BBC.* https://bbc.com/news/articles/cly7zy3d3exo

Russell, A. (2023). *The mediated climate: How journalists, big tech, and activists are vying for our future.* Columbia University Press.

Robertson, T. (2016). Cold War landscapes: Towards an environmental history of US development programmes in the 1950s and 1960s. *Cold War History, 16*(4), 417–441.

Rosenfeld, S. (2012). *Subversives: The FBI's war on student radicals and Reagan's rise to power.* Farrar, Straus and Giroux.

Rothstein, E. (2006, September 25). A crunchy-granola path from macramé and LSD to Wikipedia and Google. *The New York Times.* https://www.nytimes.com/2006/09/25/arts/25conn.html

Rove, K. (2018, November 28). Stopping the socialist resurgence. *The Wall Street Journal.* https://www.wsj.com/articles/stopping-the-socialist-resurgence-1543448445

Said, E. (1978). *Orientalism.* Pantheon.

Sampson, R. D. (1995). *'Under the banner of the democratic principle': John Louis O'Sullivan, the Democracy and the Democratic Review.* ProQuest Dissertations & Theses.

Shellenberger, M. (2020). *Apocalypse never: Why environmental alarmism hurts us all.* HarperCollins.

Schmitt, C. R. (2019). Scapegoat ecology: Blame, exoneration, and an emergent genre in environmentalist discourse. *Environmental Communication, 13*(2), 152–164.

Schneider-Mayerson, M. (2015). *Peak oil: Apocalyptic environmentalism and libertarian political culture.* The University of Chicago Press.

Schuessler, J. (2019, November 20). Oxford names 'climate emergency' its 2019 word of the year. *The New York Times.* https://www.nytimes.com/2019/11/20/arts/word-of-the-year-climate-emergency.html

Schumer, A. (2019, April 9). Alexandria Ocasio-Cortez: Go Green New Deal!: The green (lady) lantern of hope. *The Nation.* https://www.thenation.com/article/archive/alexandria-ocasio-cortez-go-green-new-deal/

Schwartz, M. (2017, December 25). Maria's bodies: The hurricane in Puerto Rico has become a man-made disaster, with a death toll threatening to eclipse

Katrina's. *New York Magazine*. https://nymag.com/intelligencer/2017/12/hurricane-maria-man-made-disaster.html

Schwarze, S. (2006). Environmental melodrama. *Quarterly Journal of Speech*, 92(3), 239–261.

Scott Pruitt is having a wonderful time destroying the EPA. (2018, February 16). *Newsweek*. Cover.

Selby, J., Dahi, O. S., Fröhlich, C., & Hulme, M. (2017). Climate change and the Syrian civil war revisited. *Political Geography*, 60, 232–344.

Seymour, R. (2024). *Disaster nationalism: The downfall of liberal civilization*. Verso Books.

Shaw, M. (2019, April 22). The visual power of Alexandria Ocasio-Cortez. *Columbia Journalism Review*. https://www.cjr.org/analysis/alexandria-ocasio-cortez-aoc.php

Shear, M. D., & Kanno-Youngs, Z. (2022, August 12). A victory for Biden, and a bet on America's future. *The New York Times*. https://www.nytimes.com/2022/08/12/us/politics/biden-house-bill.html

Shiva, V. (1997). Economic globalization, ecological feminism, and sustainable development. *Canadian Woman Studies*, 17(2), 22–27.

Shiva, V. (1989). *Staying alive: Women, ecology and development*. Zed Books.

Singer, N. R. (2010). Neoliberal style, the American re-generation, and ecological jeremiad in Thomas Friedman's "code green." *Environmental Communication*, 4(2), 135–151.

Sins of emission: AOC's absurd Green New Deal. (2019, March 11). *National Review*. Cover.

Sjølyst-Jackson, P. (2009). Postcolonial futures. *New Formations*, (66), 173–179.

Skey, M. (2022). Nationalism and media. *Nationalities Papers*, 50(5), 839–849.

Skrimshire, S. (2013). Challenging the skeptics: False prophecy and climate activism. *Religion and Society*, (4), 188–195.

Solnit, R. (2014, April 7). Call climate change what it is: Violence. *The Guardian*. https://www.theguardian.com/commentisfree/2014/apr/07/climate-change-violence-occupy-earth

Solnit, R. (2009). *A paradise built in hell: The extraordinary communities that arise in disaster*. Penguin Books.

Sparkman, G., Geiger, N., & Weber, E. U. (2022). Americans experience a false social reality by underestimating popular climate policy support by nearly half. *Nature Communications*, 13, 4779.

Spivak, G. C. (2009). *Other Asias*. Blackwell.

Spivak, G. C. (1988). Can the subaltern speak?. *Die Philosophin*, 14(27), 42–58.

Spivak, G. C. (1985). The Rani of Sirmur: An essay in reading the archives. *History and Theory*, 24(3), 247–272.

Stapp, A. (2022, September 25). What many progressives misunderstand about fighting climate change. *The Atlantic*. https://www.theatlantic.com/ideas/archive/2022/09/capitalism-clean-energy-technology-permitting/671545/

Steinberg, T. (2010). Can capitalism save the planet?: On the origins of green liberalism. *Radical History Review*, (107), 7–24.

Steverman, B. (2019, January 17). Investing prophet Jeremy Grantham takes aim at climate change: The veteran money manager will devote $1 billion to helping the world escape catastrophe. *Bloomberg Businessweek*. https://www.bloomberg.com/news/articles/2019-01-17/jeremy-grantham-s-1-billion-plan-to-fight-climate-change#xj4y7vzkg

Strassel, K. A. (2019, February 7). The socialist that could: Meet Alexandria Ocasio-Cortez, the secret Republican weapon for 2020. *The Wall Street Journal*. https://www.wsj.com/articles/the-socialist-that-could-11549583738

Stop Cop City. (2023). What is Cop City? *Stop Cop City*. https://stopcop.city/what-is-cop-city/

Sullivan, J. (2023, April 27). *Remarks by national security advisor Jake Sullivan on renewing American economic leadership at the Brookings Institution*. The White House. https://www.whitehouse.gov/briefing-room/speeches-remarks/2023/04/27/remarks-by-national-security-advisor-jake-sullivan-on-renewing-american-econoic-leadership-at-the-brookings-institution/

Sullivan, J. (2019, January/February). What Donald Trump and Dick Cheney got wrong about America. *The Atlantic*. https://www.theatlantic.com/magazine/archive/2019/01/yes-america-can-still-lead-the-world/576427/

Sulzberger, A. G. (2023, May 15). Journalism's essential value. *Columbia Journalism Review*. https://www.cjr.org/special_report/ag-sulzberger-new-york-times-journalisms-essential-value-objectivity-independence.php

Sunrise Movement. (2023). Green New Deal for communities. *Sunrise Movement*. https://www.sunrisemovement.org/campaign/green-new-deal-for-communities/

Superstorm Research Lab. (2013, December). *A tale of two Sandys*. https://superstormresearchlab.org/white-paper/

Sze, J. (2020). *Environmental justice in a moment of danger*. University of California Press.

Táíwò, O. O. (2022). *Elite capture: How the powerful took over identity politics (and everything else)*. Haymarket Books.

Talpade-Mohanty, C. (1994). Under western eyes: Feminist scholarship and colonial discourse. In P. Williams, & L. Chrisman (Eds.), *Colonial discourse and postcolonial theory: A reader* (pp. 196–220). Columbia University Press.

Taylor, B. C., Kinsella, W. J., Depoe, S. P., & Metzler, M. S. (Eds.). (2007). *Nuclear legacies: Communication, controversy, and the U.S. nuclear weapons complex*. Rowman & Littlefield.

Taylor, D. E. (2002). Race, class, gender, and American environmentalism. *Gen. Tech. Rep. PNW-GTR-534*. U.S. Department of Agriculture, Forest Service, and Pacific Northwest Research Station. https://research.fs.usda.gov/treesearch/3259

The climate issue. (2015, January/February). *Foreign Policy*. Cover

The doomed earth catalog. (2017, July 10). *New York Magazine*. Cover.

The drowned and the saved: Why real climate justice is so hard. (2020, October 5/12). *The Nation*. Cover.

The fire next time: How to prevent a climate catastrophe. (2020, May/June). *Foreign Affairs*. Cover.

The future of farming: The nuts and bolts of how we will feed the world. (2015, October 20). *Newsweek*. Cover.

The guilty and the damned. (2021, November 8/21). *New York Magazine*. Cover.

The new green economy: Think we can't stabilize the climate while fostering growth? (2015, November 16). *The Nation*. Cover.

The refinery next door. (2020, August 2). *The New York Times Magazine*. Cover.

The socialist moment. (2019, June). *The New Republic*. Cover.

The sooner than you think issue. (2019, June 10). *Bloomberg Businessweek*. Cover.

Thirty years ago, we could have save the planet. (2018, August 5). *The New York Times Magazine*. Cover.

Tice, P. H. (2019, March 12). On climate, the kids are all wrong. *The Wall Street Journal*. https://www.wsj.com/articles/on-climate-the-kids-are-all-wrong-11552430379

Tooze, A. (2019, Summer). Central banks: A decade after the world bailed out finance, it's time for finance to bail out the world. *Foreign Policy*, p. 16.

Traverso, E. (2017). *Left-wing melancholia: Marxism, history, and memory*. Columbia University Press.

Trumbo, C. (1996). Constructing climate change: Claims and frames in US news coverage of an environmental issue. *Public Understanding of Science*, 5(3), 269–283.

Tuck, E., & Yang, K. W. (2012). Decolonization is not a metaphor. *Decolonization: Indigeneity, Education & Society*, 1(1), 1–40.

Turner, F. (2006). *From counterculture to cyberculture: Stewart Brand, the Whole Earth Network, and the rise of digital utopianism*. The University of Chicago Press.

Turner, F. J. (1893). The significance of the frontier in American history. *Annual Report of the American Historical Association*, 199–227.

United States Congress. (2019, February 7). *H. Res. 109: Recognizing the duty of the Federal Government to create a Green New Deal*. https://www.congress.gov/116/bills/hres109/BILLS-116hres109ih.pdf

Usher, N. (2021). *News for the rich, white, and blue: How place and power distort American journalism*. Columbia University Press.

Van Dijk, T. A. (2008). *Discourse and power*. Palgrave Macmillan.

Van Engen, A. (2020). How America became "a city upon a hill." *Humanities*, 41(1). https://www.neh.gov/article/how-america-became-city-upon-hill

Velji, J.A. (2017). Apocalyptic rhetoric and the construction of authority in medieval Isma'ilism. In S. Günther, & T. Lawson (Eds.), *Roads to paradise: Eschatology and concepts of the hereafter in Islam* (pp. 675–688). Brill.

Vergès, F. (2017, August 30). Racial Capitalocene: Is the Anthropocene racial? *Verso Blog*. https://www.versobooks.com/blogs/3376-racial-capitalocene

Wade, N. (1989, October 8). The sky is melting. *The New York Times*, section 7, p. 9.

Wallace-Wells, D. (2021, November 1). Climate reparations: A trillion tons of carbon hangs in the air, put there by the world's rich, an existential threat to its poor. Can we remove it? *New York Magazine*. https://nymag.com/intelligencer/2021/11/climate-change-reparations.html

Walt, V. (2020, April). Vicious (re)cycle: With the world drowning in plastic, the need for recycling is more acute than ever. But the industry that handles all that waste is on the verge of collapse. *Fortune*, pp. 72–84.

Warming is over! If we pay for it: Only massive R&D can save us now. (January/February 2020). *Mother Jones*. Cover.

We have one Earth—and the technology to save it. Go! (2020, April). *WIRED*. Cover.

We've known for 30 years. (2019, May). *In These Times*, p. 49.

Weiss, K. R. (2015, January/February). Exile by another name. *Foreign Policy*, pp. 48–56.

Westervelt, A. (2023a, August 24). The real free speech threat. *Drilled*. https://drilled.media/investigations/the-real-free-speech-threat

Westervelt, A. [@amywestervelt] (2023b, August 29). "It's troubling to watch the global dehumanization of climate activists, who are often painted as annoying mosquitoes, spoiled brats, or "terrorists"" [Tweet]. Twitter. https://twitter.com/amywestervelt/status/1696539450388750625?s=20

Weston, K. (2012). Political ecologies of the precarious. *Anthropological Quarterly*, 85(2), 429–455.

Wetherell, M., Taylor, S., & Yates, S. J. (Eds.). (2001). *Discourse theory and practice: A reader*. SAGE Publications.

What are we missing? Predicting the next crisis. (2020, November/December). *Foreign Affairs*. Cover.

Which world are we living in? A half dozen choices of grand narrative for an increasingly turbulent era. Take your pick. (2018, July/August). *Foreign Affairs*. Cover.

Who will save the planet? Meet five unlikely saviors. (2019, July 22). *Foreign Policy*. Cover.

Who's a denier now? Climate apocalypticism ignores the science. (2017, May 1). *National Review*. Cover.

Whyte, K. (2020). Against crisis epistemology. In B. Hokowhitu, A. Moreton-Robinson, L. Tuhiwai-Smith, C. Andersen, & S. Larkin (Eds.), *Routledge handbook of critical Indigenous studies* (1st ed., pp. 52–64). Routledge.

Wiener, A. (2018, November 16). The complicated legacy of Stewart Brand's "Whole Earth Catalog." *The New Yorker*. https://www.newyorker.com/news/letter-from-silicon-valley/the-complicated-legacy-of-stewart-brands-whole-earth-catalog

Williams, R. (1961). *The long revolution*. Parthian.

Wodak, R., & Meyer, M. (Eds.). (2009). *Methods of critical discourse analysis* (2nd ed.). SAGE Publications.

Woodhead, L. (2004). *Christianity: A very short introduction*. Oxford University Press.

Worland, J. (2022, October 27). The selfish case for climate justice. *TIME*. https://time.com/6225469/climate-justice-inequity-self-interest/

Worland, J. (2019, June 24). Rising seas, fleeing residents, disappearing villages: Our sinking planet. *TIME*.

Yuen, E. (2012). The politics of failure have failed: The environmental movement and catastrophism. In S. Lilley, D. McNally, E. Yuen, & J. Davis (Eds.), *Catastrophism: The apocalyptic politics of collapse and rebirth* (pp. 15–43). PM Press.

Yusoff, K. (2009). Excess, catastrophe, and climate change. *Environment and Planning D: Society and Space, 27*(6), 1010–1029.

Zelizer, B., Boczkowski, P. J., & Anderson, C. W. (2022). *The journalism manifesto*. Polity Press.

Zelizer, B. (2018). When the wrong kind of authority neutralizes journalism: Cold War enmity, journalism and the US presidential race. *Comunicazioni Sociali*, (1), 9–20.

Zelizer, B. (2017). *What journalism could be*. Polity Press.

Zelizer, B. (2016). Journalism's deep memory: Cold War mindedness and coverage of Islamic State. *International Journal of Communication, 10*, 6060–6089.

Zelizer, B. (2015). Terms of choice: Uncertainty, journalism, and crisis. *Journal of Communication, 65*(5), 888–908.

Zelizer, B. (2010). *About to die: How news images move the public*. Oxford University Press.

Zelizer, B. (1998). *Remembering to forget: Holocaust memory through the camera's eye*. The University of Chicago Press.

Zelizer, B. (1993). Journalists as interpretive communities. *Critical Studies in Mass Communication, 10*(3), 219–237.

Žižek, S. (2017). *The courage of hopelessness: Chronicles of a year of acting dangerously*. Penguin Books.

Index

Figures are indicated by an italic *f* following the page number.

For the benefit of digital users, indexed terms that span two pages (e.g., 52–53) may, on occasion, appear on only one of those pages.

A
accelerationism, 26
Adorno, Theodor, 16
Afrofuturism, 162–163
agriculture, 111, 130–133
Amazon rainforest, 120–121
American Earth (McKibben), 57, 87
American exceptionalism
    about, 26–27, 28–29, 31–32
    Bretton Woods System, reanimation of, and, 49–52, 53
    desire for renewed, 9, 47–49, 51–52, 56, 89, 148, 157–159
    dissolving, 163–164
    moderateness and, 35–36
    reactivation of, 33–35, 49, 158–159
    visionary sage figures and, 88
    See also Manifest Destiny
American Gothic (painting), 114–116, 132–133
American jeremiad, 88–90, 95–96
Anderson, Benedict, 9–10, 12
Anderson, C. W., 10–11, 161
Anthropocene
    adherents of, 69–70
    Anthropocene gaze, 77–81, 82
    Good and Bad visions of, 82–87
Antifa, 98, 169 n.19
apocalyptic authoritarianism
    about, 3–4, 23, 28–30, 151
    climate journalism and, 4–5, 9, 27–28, 55–56
    contesting, 156
    elite panic and, 23–25
    exclusionary modes of, 25–26, 156–157
    fear-of-the-masses syndrome and, 164–165
    vs. robust democracy, 152–154
    See also American exceptionalism; civilizational collapse; dualisms; Global South; Others and Othering; planetary scale; visionary sage figures

apocalyptic environmentalism, 67–70
Aronoff, Kate, 160
Atlanta (GA), Cop City protests (2023), 21–23
Atlantic, The, 47
Avengers, The (film), 106
Ayewa, Camae (a.k.a. Moor Mother), 162–163

B
Barbour, Ian, 82
Barthes, Roland, 32–33
Battistoni, Alyssa, 160
Bezos, Jeff, 92–95
Biden, Joe (Biden administration), 3–4, 47, 89, 108, 110–111
binaries. *See* dualisms
biopower (biopolitics)
    about, 126–128
    climate migration and, 134–139
    lifeboat ethics and, 125–126
    overpopulation and, 127–134
    See also necropower
birth control, 128, 175 n.55
Black Lives Matter protests, 21–22, 38, 169 n.19, n.27
Black Quantum Futurism, 162–163
Bloomberg, Michael, 49–50
Bloomberg Businessweek
    on Bretton Woods System, reanimation of, 49–50
    on climate change as war, 48
    on geoengineering, 84*f*, 84–86
    on Global South as threat, 121–123, 122*f*, 124–127, 138–139
    on racialized women, 129
    on visionary sage figures, 113–114
Bloomfield, Emma Frances, 105–106, 112–113
Blue Marble, The (Earth image), 58–60, 62, 92
Boczkowski, Pablo J., 10–11, 161
Bolsonaro, Jair, 120

Bolton, Herbert, 34
Brand, Stewart, 58–62, 70, 81–82, 84–87, 90–91, 92–94, 177 n.16
Brazil, 120, 132
Bretton Woods System, 26–27, 49–52, 53
Brown, Wendy, 159
Browne, Simone, 75–77
Buck, Holly Jean, 148
Burke, Kenneth, 105–106
Butler, Judith, 157

C
Callison, Candis, 5
capitalism
  disaster capitalism, 72–73, 176 n.99
  green capitalism, 65–66, 72–73, 82–83, 87
  nationalism and, 157–158
Captain Planet and the Planeteers (animated TV show), 105–106, 109–110
carbon capture and removal technology, 149
Carruth, Allison, 63, 78
Carteret Islands, 144–145
Cartesian model, 123–124
cartoon representations, 105–111
Charles, Jeanette, 161–162
Chess, Caron, 24–25
China, 73–75, 124–126, 130–132, 174 n.19
civilizational collapse
  anti-American, progressive Others blamed for, 17, 23–24, 25–26, 41, 97–98, 151–152
  European intelligentsia on, 26
  peak oil movement and, 68
  petro-nationalism and, 27
  preppers and, 68–69
  Winthrop on, 88–89
Clarke, Lee, 24–25
climate change
  Cold War optics and, 31–32, 43–44, 49, 73, 75
  elite panic and, 23–25
  militarized gaze and, 63
  popular culture and, 6
  "total war" discourse, 43–45, 55, 73, 152
  as weapon of mass destruction, 71–73, 75
  See also climate journalism; climate justice activists; environmental justice movement; global climate models (GCMs); technological solutions
climate change edgelords, 70. *See also* techno-libertarianism

climate journalism
  about, 1–2, 4–5, 27–30, 55–56, 152
  2019 significance, 6–8
  2020 significance, 31
  "apocalypse beat," 31
  Covering Climate Now initiative, 6
  disconnect from climate justice movement, 56
  on Green New Deal, 7–8, 37–38, 52–53
  hero/villain binary, 105–111, 112–113
  on Inflation Reduction Act (IRA), 52–55
  "I told you so" trope, 98–100
  Malthusian-influenced, 134–135
  nation-centric, 12–13
  nostalgia for "golden age," 8–9, 43
  Othering and vilification by, 2–3, 7–8, 14–15, 18–20, 22–23, 114–116, 134
  portrait photos in, 113–114
  reimagined, 161, 163–165
  See also American exceptionalism; climate change; dualisms; Global South; journalism, traditional; Others and Othering; planetary scale; visionary sage figures
climate justice activists
  activism portrayed as pointless, 143–144
  American exceptionalism questioned by, 9
  climate justice warrior stereotype, 19–20, 36–37, 55–56, 103
  conflation with Thunberg, 101
  disconnect from journalism, 56
  fearmongering, vilification, and police repression of, 18–19, 21–23, 42–43, 56
  Inflation Reduction Act and, 52–55
  reimagined community by, 159–161
  Sunrise Movement, 7, 39–40, 159–160
  See also environmental justice movement; Green New Deal; Others and Othering; young progressives; young progressive women of color
climate migration (climate refugees), 118, 134–139, 143–145
climate photography, 80
A CoEvolution Book (Brand), 70
Cohen, Daniel Aldana, 160
Cold War
  American exceptionalism and, 26–27, 33–35
  Anthropocene gaze and, 78
  Captain Planet and the Planeteers and, 105–106, 109–110
  China seen through, 74–75

climate change seen through, 31–32, 43–44, 49, 73, 75
criminalization of young progressives and, 42–43
militarized gaze, 62–63
zero-sum game logic and, 124–125
See also Bretton Woods System
Collapsologie, 69–70
communities, reimagined, 159–161, 164–165
Comprehensive Designers, 91–92
consumer choices, individual, 65–66, 67–68
Cop City protests (2023), 21–23
Covering Climate Now initiative, 6
COVID-19 pandemic, 18, 31, 68–69
criminalization, of young progressives, 20–22, 35, 37, 42–43, 55–56
cultural studies, 15–16
culture shift, 127–128

D
Daggett, Cara, 91, 94–95
Dakota Access Pipeline (DAPL), protests against (2016), 21–22, 36, 37–38, 160–161
Davidson, Neil, 157–158
Davis, Heather, 33
death-world. *See* life-world/death-world dualism
Defense Innovation Unit Experimental, 68–69
democracy
journalism and liberal democracy, 11, 15, 43, 165
liberal "rationality," 39–40, 161–162
robust democracies, 152–154, 163–164
Democratic Party, 41–42, 47, 156–157, 168 n.102
Democratic Socialists, 114–116, 159
Demos, T. J., 62, 77, 80, 81–82, 84–86, 162–163
development discourse, 16–17, 119–121, 125–126
development institutions, 169 n.10
disaster capitalism, 72–73, 176 n.99
disaster nationalism, 176 n.99
discursive formations, 32–33
drones, aerial view of, 75–78, 80–81
dualisms
civilized/uncivilized, 118–120
drowned/saved, 140–143, 144–145, 150
good and evil/right and wrong, 3–4, 26–27, 51–52, 97–98, 104–109, 112–113, 124, 152
hero/villain, 105–111, 112–113
life-world/death-world, 140–150, 152–153
moderate/militant, 20–21, 35–36, 43, 52–53, 101, 116, 153, 156, 164–165
need to break free from, 123–124
Dunaway, Finis, 65–66

E
Eagleton, O., 168 n.102
Earth
American Earth, 57–58, 145–147, 161–162
The Blue Marble image, 58–60, 62, 92
burning Earth imagery, 145–147
Google Earth, 62
Whole Earth Catalog, 58–62, 59*f*, 65, 80–81, 82–83, 171 n.10
See also planetary scale
ecofascism, 125–126, 135, 156–157
edgelords, climate change, 70. *See also* techno-libertarianism
Ehrlich, Paul and Anne
The Population Bomb, 130, 175 n.39
elite capture, 26–28
elite panic, 23–25
Enlightenment, 16–17, 123–124
Eno, Brian, 92–94
environmentalism, apocalyptic, 67–70
environmental justice movement, 154–155. *See also* climate justice activists
environmental melodrama, 108–109
Escobar, Arturo, 16–17, 119–120, 123–124
exceptionalism. *See* American exceptionalism
exclusionary modes of governance, 27, 54, 56, 90, 112–116, 151, 156–157
extinction rates, 135

F
fallacies, 103–104
false equivalencies, 39–40, 104–105, 111
family planning, 127–128
Farbotko, Carol, 143–145
fear-of-the-masses syndrome, 164–165. *See also* masses, the
Foner, Eric, 34
Foreign Affairs, 48, 52, 74–75, 104, 135–137, 138–139
Foreign Policy
Anthropocene gaze and, 77–79, 79*f*, 80–81
on climate change as war, 48
on climate migrants, 134–138, 143–144
on family planning, 127–128
on global finance, 49–50
on visionary sage figures, 63–65, 64*f*
Fortune, 83, 133–134

fossil fuel industry, 12, 27, 70, 73, 82, 94–97, 111, 174 n.19
Foucault, Michel, 15–16, 32, 126–128, 139, 167 n.68
Frank, Adam, 86–87
Friedman, Thomas L., 137
frontiersman (pioneer-man), 58–62, 87, 90–91. *See also* rugged individualism
Fuller, Buckminster, 91

G
Gahman, Levi, 161–162
gaze
    Anthropocene gaze, 77–81, 82
    liberal democratic gaze, 15, 165
    militarized gaze, 62–63, 71–78, 109–110
genius complex, 90–92
geoengineering, 84–87, 90, 113–114
Georgieva, Kristalina, 49–50
Gitlin, Todd, 20–21, 35–36
global climate models (GCMs), 57, 63, 67–68, 71, 75, 78, 82
global dominion, 62
globalization, 33–34, 65, 157–158
Global South
    climate migration from, 118, 134–139, 143–145
    Earth on fire imagery and, 145–147
    male violence trope, 137–138
    necropower and life-world/death-world dualism, 139–150, 152–153
    as Other, 118–126
    overpopulation and, 126–128, 130
    U.S. savior discourse, 132–134
good and evil/right and wrong dualism, 3–4, 26–27, 51–52, 97–98, 104–109, 112–113, 124, 152
Google, 60–61
Google Earth, 62
Gore, Al, 57, 75–77, 81–82, 87, 100–101
Grandin, Greg, 50–51
Grantham, Jeremy, 113–114
green capitalism, 65–66, 72–73, 82–83, 87
Green New Deal (GND), 7–8, 18, 22–23, 37–38, 40–41, 52–53, 159–161
gross domestic product (GDP), 119, 121–123, 128
Guenther, Genevieve, 174 n.19
Guterres, António, 144

H
Habermas, Jürgen, 116
Hall, Stuart, 15–16, 118–119, 167 n.68
    Policing the Crisis, 21
Hammer & Hope, 152–155, 161
Hansen, James, 98–100, 149
Harris, Kamala, 21
Hartmann, Betsy, 61–62, 97, 109–110, 125–126, 129–130
Harvey, David, 158
Heglar, Mary Annaïse, 53–54, 155–156
hero/villain binary, 105–111, 112–113
Hillis, Danny, 92–94
Holland, Anna, 18–19, 21
Horkheimer, Max, 16
Hot Take (newsletter and podcast), 53–54, 155–156
House Un-American Activities Committee (later House Committee on Internal Security), 36
Hultman, Martin, 96–97
Hurricane Dorian (2019), 140–143
Hurricane Irma (2017), 71–72
Hurricane Katrina (2005), 72–73

I
imperialism, 118–119. *See also* development discourse
Inconvenient Truth, An (documentary), 57
India, 124–125, 129, 132, 174 n.19
Indigenous Peoples, 33, 120–121, 161–162. *See also* #NoDAPL (Standing Rock) protests
individualism, rugged, 58–63, 65–66, 67–70, 81–82, 86–87, 90–92
Inflation Reduction Act (IRA), 52–55, 89
interstitiality, 13–14, 100, 150
In These Times, 100, 134–135
"I told you so" trope, 98–100

J
Jacobin, 108, 110–111
jeremiad, American, 88–90, 95–96
Jobs, Steve, 60–61, 81–82
journalism, traditional
    American exceptionalism and, 55
    boundary formation and, 20
    Foucault on, 15
    good and evil/right and wrong dualism and, 124
    as "interpretive community," 53–54
    nation-centric, 9–13
    nostalgia for "golden age," 32, 43, 45–47

postwar, 43
reimagined, 161, 163–165
rigidity of, 13–15, 17
universal truth claims and, 33
See also climate journalism
Just Stop Oil, tomato soup protest (London, 2022), 18–21, 22–23

K

Kelly, Casey Ryan
  Apocalypse Man, 98
King, Martin Luther, Jr., 154
Klein, Naomi, 72–73, 176 n.99
Kluger, Jeffrey, 71–72
Kolbert, Elizabeth, 1
Kreiss, Daniel, 10–11
Kukla, Rebecca, 127–128

L

Labour Party (U.K.), 168 n.102
Latour, Bruno, 26–27
Lazrus, Heather, 143–145
liberation movements, postcolonial, 34
libertarianism, 60. *See also* techno-libertarianism
lifeboat ethics, 125–126. *See also* biopower; ecofascism
life-world/death-world dualism
  climate journalism on, 140–144, 150
  Earth on fire imagery and, 145–147
  rejection of and moving beyond, 144–145, 152–153
  Wallace-Wells's article and, 145, 147–150
liminality, 13–14, 16–17
Long Now, 92–94, 96–97
Long Now Foundation, 92–94

M

Macey, David, 126–127
Maeseele, Pieter, 104–105
Maier, Charles S., 50–51
"Make America Great Again" (MAGA), 83, 89–90
Make America Great Again (MAGA) right, 3, 55–56, 151–152
Malcolm X, 154
Maloney, Sean Patrick, 18
Malthus, Thomas, 130
Malthusianism, 129–130, 134–135, 175 n.39
Manifest Destiny
  about, 2–3, 57–58
  Bretton Woods System and, 50–51
  dissolving, 161–162, 164
  perpetual progress and, 81–82
  planetary scale and, 57–58
  reactivation of, 15, 32, 49, 158–159
  visionary sage figures and, 9
  See also American exceptionalism
Mann, Michael, 19–20
Mars colonization, 70, 150
Marzec, Robert P., 63, 78
Masco, Joseph, 72
masculinity
  climate change edgelords, 70
  petro-masculinity, 94–97
  rugged individualism, 58–63, 65–66, 67–70, 81–82, 86–87, 90–92
  10,000 Year Clock project and, 92–95, 173 n.25
  very smart men "as gods," 58–60, 62, 70, 75–77, 82–83, 84–87, 92–94, 149–151, 157, 177 n.16
  visionary sage figures and, 173 n.9
masses, the, 10–11, 12–13, 23–25, 55, 98–100, 109, 153, 164–165
Mbembe, Achille, 128, 139–140, 144–145
McCarthy, Anna, 90–91
McKibben, Bill
  American Earth, 57, 87
  The End of Nature, 145–147, 171 n.2
media. *See* climate journalism; journalism
Media and Climate Change Observatory (University of Colorado Boulder), 6
melodrama, environmental, 108–109
men. *See* masculinity
miasma, 124–127
migration, climate (climate refugees), 118, 134–139, 143–145
militant
  militant Others, 8, 17–19, 20–23, 35–36, 38, 137–138, 151–152, 169 n.19
  moderate/militant binary, 20–21, 35–36, 43, 52–53, 101, 116, 153, 156, 164–165
militarized gaze, 62–63, 71–78, 109–110
Millennials, 37–38
moderateness
  vs. climate justice activists, 19–20
  contesting, 163–164
  moderate/militant binary, 20–21, 35–36, 43, 52–53, 101, 116, 153, 156, 164–165
  U.S. as exceptionally moderate, 35–36
Mosco, Vincent, 32–33
Mother Jones, 44–45, 46f, 106
Mouffe, Chantal, 11, 20, 33–34, 104–105, 159

Muir, John, 154
Musk, Elon, 61–62, 70, 86–87, 102–103
myths, 32–33

N

Nation, The
 biopolitics and, 139
 Covering Climate Now initiative and, 6
 on "Horsemen of the Trumpocalypse," 106–108, 107*f*
 necropolitics and, 140–143, 141*f*, 142*f*
 Ocasio-Cortez, comic book image of, 108, 111, 114
 on perpetual progress, 66
nationalism
 about, 28–29, 56, 156–157
 capitalism and, 157–158
 disaster nationalism, 176 n.99
 white nationalism, 39–40, 55–56, 98
 See also American exceptionalism; Manifest Destiny
National Review, 95–96, 96*f*, 104–105, 111, 112*f*
national security discourse, 71–73
nation-centric journalism, 9–13
Nature Conservancy, 154
necropower (necropolitics)
 about, 139–140
 contesting and moving beyond, 144–145, 152–154
 Earth on fire imagery and, 145–147
 life-world/death-world dualism and, 140–150
 See also biopower
neoliberalism, 65, 158–159
neo-Promethean fantasy, 84–87, 149
New American, The, 40–41, 111
New Communalism, 90–91
New Republic, The, 44–45, 45*f*, 84–86, 85*f*, 114–116, 115*f*, 132–133
news media. *See* climate journalism; journalism
Newsweek, 66, 67*f*, 74, 106, 130–133, 131*f*, 134–135
New York Magazine, 38–39, 82–83, 145, 146*f*, 147–150
New York Times, The, 2, 31, 38, 39–40, 41–42, 52–53, 54–55, 68–69. *See also* Sulzberger, A. G.
New York Times Magazine, The, 48, 98–100, 99*f*, 135, 136*f*, 137, 143

Nixon, Richard (Nixon administration), 20–21, 35
#NoDAPL (Standing Rock) protests (2016), 21–22, 36, 37–38, 160–161

O

Ocasio-Cortez, Alexandria
 cartoon representations, 108, 111, 112*f*
 comparison to Thunberg, 101
 exclusionary and Othering representations, 3, 8, 18, 23–24, 25–26, 36–37, 38–42, 114–116, 115*f*
 Green New Deal and, 7, 37–38
 inspiration for running for office, 37, 160–161
Olufemi, Kwame, 21–22
Omar, Ilhan, 40–41
"One-World World," 16–17, 124, 161–162
Onís, Catalina M. de, 150
O'Sullivan, John Louis, 2–3
Others and Othering
 of Black people, 36, 169 n.27
 elite panic against, 23–25
 environmental justice movement and, 154–155
 fearmongering against and exclusion of, 2–4, 9, 17, 27, 55–56, 114–116, 156–157
 fear-of-the-masses syndrome, 164–165
 generational Othering, 38
 of Global South, 118–126
 liberal democracy against, 11, 16–17
 militant Others, 8, 17–19, 20–23, 35–36, 38, 137–138, 151–152, 169 n.19
 Oriental Other, 118–119
 racialized Others, 30, 117–118. *See also* Global South
 scapegoats, 105–108, 109–110, 112–113, 174 n.19
 of The Squad, 40–42, 111
 of Thunberg, 100–103
 of young progressive women of color, 3, 14–15, 18–20, 36–37, 38–41, 151–152
 See also climate justice activists; Global South; necropower; young progressives; young progressive women of color
overpopulation, 126–128, 130, 134

P

Paez Terán, Manuel Esteban (Tortuguita), 21–22
Papua New Guinea, 144–145
Parker, Jennifer, 152–154

peak oil movement, 68–70
Pearl, Mike, 70
Pellow, David Naguib, 155
Pelosi, Nancy, 37–38
people of color, 30, 117–118, 143, 154. *See also* Global South; young progressive women of color
petro-masculinity, 94–97
petro-nationalism, 27
Phillips, Rasheedah, 162–163
photography
 climate photography, 80
 portrait photos, 113–114
pioneer-man (frontiersman), 58–62, 87, 90–91. *See also* rugged individualism
planetary scale
 about, 29, 58, 87
 Anthropocene gaze, 77–81, 82
 apocalyptic environmentalism and, 67–70
 geoengineering, 84–87, 90, 113–114
 global climate models (GCMs), 57, 63, 67–68, 71, 75, 78, 82
 global dominion, 62
 Good and Bad Anthropocene visions, 82–87
 vs. individual consumer choices, 65–66, 67–68
 Manifest Destiny and, 57–58
 militarized gaze, 62–63, 71–78, 109–110
 neo-Promethean fantasy, 84–87, 149
 "One-World World," 16–17, 124, 161–162
 very smart men "as gods," 58–60, 62, 70, 75–77, 82–83, 84–87, 92–94, 149–151, 157, 177 n.16
 Whole Earth Catalog, 58–62, 59f, 65, 80–81, 82–83, 171 n.10
 See also Earth
Plumer, Brad, 31
Plummer, Phoebe, 18–19, 21
popular culture, 6
population bomb, 130, 134. *See also* overpopulation
postcolonialism, 16–17
power, 15–17
preppers, 68–71
Pressley, Ayanna, 40–41
progress, perpetual, 81–82, 86
progressives. *See* young progressives; young progressive women of color
prophecies
 American jeremiad and, 88–90
 apocalyptic, 97–98
 fallacies and false equivalencies, 104–105

 genius complex and, 90–92
 "I told you so" trope, 98–100
 Thunberg and, 100–103
 See also visionary sage figures
Proud Boys, 39–40
Pruitt, Scott, 72–73, 106–108

Q
QAnon, 89–90

R
Rabasa, José, 121–122, 123–124
racialized Others, 30, 117–118, 143, 154. *See also* Global South; young progressive women of color
Raeijmaekers, Daniëlle, 104–105
Rakova, Ursula, 144–145
Ramey, John, 68–70
Ransan-Cooper, Hedda, 138
Reagan, Ronald, 89–90
refugees, climate (climate migration), 118, 134–139, 143–145
regime of representation, 15, 167 n.68
Republican Party, 18, 41, 89–90
Rich, Nathaniel, 98–100
Rieder, Travis, 127–128
right and wrong/good and evil dualism, 3–4, 26–27, 51–52, 97–98, 104–109, 112–113, 124, 152
Riofrancos, Thea, 160
Rolling Stone, 110
Roosevelt, Teddy, 154
rugged individualism, 58–63, 65–66, 67–70, 81–82, 86–87, 90–92
Russell, Adrienne, 165
Russell, Dick, 100

S
Said, Edward, 118–119
Sanders, Bernie, 108, 114–116, 115f
saved/drowned dualism, 140–143, 144–145, 150
scapegoats, 105–108, 109–110, 112–113, 174 n.19
Shellenberger, Michael, 23–24
Schmitt, Casey, 88–89, 105–106
Schneider-Mayerson, Matthew, 68–70
Schumer, Arlen, 108, 111
Schwarze, Steven, 108–109
Selby, Jan, 137
Seymour, Richard
 Disaster Nationalism, 176 n.99

Shiva, Vandana, 128
Showtime (TV company), 137
Sierra Club, 154
Silicon Valley. *See* preppers; techno-libertarianism
Singer, Norie Ross, 65–66
Sjølyst-Jackson, Peter, 161–162
societal guilt, 105–106
Solnit, Rebecca, 24–25
Spivak, Gayatri Chakravorty, 118–119, 138–139, 161–162
Squad, The, 40–42, 111
Standing Rock (#NoDAPL) protests (2016), 21–22, 36, 37–38, 160–161
Starmer, Keir, 21, 168 n.102
subject/object binary, 16–17
Sullivan, Jake, 9, 47–48, 52, 55
Sulzberger, A. G., 4, 12–13, 14–15, 17, 20
Sunrise Movement, 7, 39–40, 159–160
superhero and supervillain narrative, 105–111, 112–113
sustainable development experts, 120–121
Sze, Julie, 155, 160–161

T
Talpade-Mohanty, Chandra, 129
Taylor, Bryan, 77–78
Taylor, Dorceta, 154
Taylor, Keeanga-Yamahtta, 152–154
techno-libertarianism, 57, 60–62, 81–83, 90–91, 95–97. *See also* edgelords, climate change
technological solutions, 60, 65, 83–87, 91–92, 95–97, 130–133
Teitota, Ioane, 143–144
10,000 Year Clock project, 92–95, 173 n.25
Thoreau, Henry David, 154
Thunberg, Greta, 99f, 100–103, 116
TIME, 19, 50, 71–73, 75–77, 76f, 99f, 100–101, 144
Tlaib, Rashida, 40–41
Todd, Zoe, 33
"total crisis" discourse, 1–2, 3–4, 7–9, 18, 26, 31–32, 41–44
"total war" discourse, 43–45, 55, 73, 152
"toxic tide" trope, 133–134
Trump, Donald (Trump administration)
American exceptionalism and, 45–47
comparison to Ocasio-Cortez, 39–40
Dakota Access Pipeline and, 37
on Green New Deal, 37–38
"Horsemen of the Trumpocalypse," 106–108, 107f
"Make America Great Again," 83, 89–90
reactionary politics and, 17
as supervillain, 106–108, 109–110
on Thunberg, 102–103
"total crisis" and, 1, 74–75
Trump exceptionalism, 109–110
against young progressives, 61–62, 169 n.19
Žižek on, 26
Tuck, Eve, 33
Turner, Fred, 60, 90–91
Turner, Frederick Jackson, 60–61
Tuvalu, 144–145

U
United Kingdom, 18–19, 21, 168 n.102
United States of America
"advanced nation" shortfall, 175 n.55
biopower and, 126
Bretton Woods System, reanimation of, and, 26–27, 49–52, 53
as exceptionally moderate, 35–36
fossil fuel identity, 82
Global South and, 119–121
Green New Deal (GND), 7–8, 18, 22–23, 37–38, 40–41, 52–53, 159–161
Inflation Reduction Act (IRA), 52–55, 89
January 6, 2021 Capitol insurrection, 41, 98
moral goodness and authority, 33–35, 147–150
nostalgia for "golden age," 2, 8–9, 25–26, 45–47, 50–52, 55, 151–152, 156–159
overpopulation as threat to, 126–128, 130
technological savior discourse and, 130–134
very smart American men, 58–60, 62, 63–65, 69–70, 149, 157–158
See also American exceptionalism; Biden, Joe; climate journalism; Cold War; Manifest Destiny; Nixon, Richard; Trump, Donald; visionary sage figures
universal truth claims, 32–34, 112–113, 169 n.10
University of Colorado Boulder, Media and Climate Change Observatory, 6

V
Velji, Jamel, 13–14
villain/hero binary, 105–111, 112–113
visionary sage figures
about, 2, 9, 29–30, 87–88, 116–117
American exceptionalism and, 88

apocalyptic authoritarianism and, 3–4, 25–26, 151, 156–157
authoritative claims of, 147–150
Earth on fire imagery and, 145–147
exclusion of Others, 90, 114–116
fallacies and false equivalences, 103–105
genius complex and, 90–92
vs. Green New Deal, 7–8
hero/villain binary and, 108–109, 112–113
vs. *Hot Take* (newsletter and podcast), 155–156
jeremiad and, 88–90
Long Now and, 92–94, 96–97
masculinity and, 173 n.9
portrait photos of, 113–114
prophetic knowledge and "I told you so" trope, 97–100
QAnon and, 89–90
Thunberg reduced to, 100–103
very smart men "as gods," 58–60, 62, 70, 75–77, 82–83, 84–87, 92–94, 149–151, 157, 177 n.16

W

Wallace-Wells, David, 83, 145, 147–150
Wall Street Journal, The, 38, 41–42
war
 conflation with climate change, 135–137
 "total war" discourse, 43–45, 55, 73, 152
Washington Consensus, new, 52–53
Washington Post, The, 52, 54–55
weapons of mass destruction (WMD), 71–73, 75
Westervelt, Amy, 53–54, 155–156, 165
white nationalism, 39–40, 55–56, 98
Whole Earth Catalog, 58–62, 59*f*, 65, 80–81, 82–83, 171 n.10
Wiener, Anna, 61–62, 91–94

Williams, Raymond, 151
Winthrop, John, 88–89
WIRED, 92, 93*f*
women of color, 128–130. *See also* Global South; young progressive women of color
worlding, 118–120, 134, 138–139, 140–143, 145
World War II, 31–32, 43–44, 47, 49, 55

Y

Yang, K. Wayne, 33
Years of Living Dangerously (documentary), 137
Young, Mary Lynn, 5
young progressives
 criminalization of and police repression, 20–23, 35, 37, 42–43, 55–56
 Musk's hatred of, 61–62
 vilification of, 2–3, 8
 white nationalists against, 55–56
 See also climate justice activists; Green New Deal; Others and Othering
young progressive women of color
 climate justice activism by, 7
 climate justice warrior stereotype and, 19–20
 elite panic and, 24–25
 exclusion of, 114–116
 Othering and vilification of, 3, 14–15, 18–19, 36–37, 38–41, 151–152
 The Squad, 40–42, 111
 See also climate justice activists; Ocasio-Cortez, Alexandria; Others and Othering
Yuen, Eddie, 125–126
Yusoff, Kathryn, 67–68

Z

Zapatistas, 30, 161–163
Zelizer, Barbie, 10–11, 49, 80, 140–143, 161
Žižek, Slavoj, 26–27

www.ingramcontent.com/pod-product-compliance
Ingram Content Group UK Ltd.
Pitfield, Milton Keynes, MK11 3LW, UK
UKHW020906080226
467760UK00014B/96